# THE BALLISTIC BARD

## Postcolonial Fictions

## JUDIE NEWMAN

*Professor of American and Postcolonial Literature*
*University of Newcastle upon Tyne*

ARNOLD

A member of the Hodder Headline Group
LONDON • NEW YORK • SYDNEY • AUCKLAND

First Published in Great Britain in 1995 by
Arnold, a member of the Hodder Headline group
338 Euston Road, London NW1 3BH
175 Fifth Avenue, New York, NY10010

Distributed exclusively in the USA by
St Martin's Press Inc.,
175 Fifth Avenue,
New York, NY 10010

*British Library Cataloguing in Publication Data*
A catalogue entry for this book is available from the British Library

Newman, Judie.
    The ballistic bard: postcolonial fictions / Judie Newman.
        p.   cm.
    Includes bibliographical references and index.
    ISBN 0–340–53914–3. –ISBN 0–340–53915–1
        1. Commonwealth fiction (English)–History and criticism.
    2. English fiction–Great Britain–Colonies–History and criticism.
    3. English fiction–Developing countries–History and criticism.
    4. Commonwealth countries–In literature. 5. Decolonization in
    literature. 6. Colonies in literature. 7. Intertextuality.
    I. Title
    PR9084.N49   1995
    823′.91099171241—dc20                                    95–16018
                                                             CIP

*Library of Congress Cataloging-in-Publication Data*

ISBN 0 340 53915 1 (Pb)
ISBN 0 340 53914 3 (Hb)

1 2 3 4 5  95 96 97 98 99

Composition by Anneset, Weston-super-Mare, Avon
Printed and bound in Great Britain by J W Arrowsmith Ltd, Bristol

For James

# Contents

# *Preface*

'Postcolonial' is such a vexed term that I am tempted to flyspeckle my text with quotation marks to signal its provisionality. On the debit side the term suggests a literature which is still tied to the past by imperial apron-strings. It has to cover a multitude of very different cultures and risks a loss of specificity. Strictly speaking, the former settler colonies (the United States, Canada and Australia) are all 'postcolonial', though they are also First World societies and the colonisers themselves of their indigenous peoples. South Africa declared its independence from the British colonising power some time ago, but in other respects remained classically colonial in its internal and external relations (as witness Namibia). A further complication is the illusory resemblance to 'postmodernism'. Reams of paper have been consumed on the relationship between the two terms, in a debate which oddly mirrors the postcolonial contestation of the relative positions of master narrative and local story. The crucial opposition is between a style (postmodernism) and a sociopolitical identity (postcolonialism). Postmodernism cannot brook a threat to its institutional dominance; it has been constructed as subversive, irreverent and parodic, although its practitioners and adherents are almost entirely male, white and metropolitan. Postmodernism is thus often a means of packaging and commodifying an acceptable form of dissent; the risk is that the use of the term 'postcolonialism' may send the same signals.

There are, however, advantages to the term. It is not as specific as a national identity and therefore allows resemblances between cultures to be perceived. It foregrounds the history of oppression without undue euphemisation. It is politically charged but not prescriptive, unlike 'resistance literature' which rather confines its practitioners to the binarism of opposition. When colonialism ends, writers must have the right to write about trees or love. 'Third World' or 'Fourth World' tends to perpetuate an image of potbellied starvelings (the 'Oxfam baby' victim syndrome). 'Commonwealth' (drily amended to 'common poverty' by Diana Brydon) is antiquated, never includes Britain (the absent yardstick), ignores the differences between old and new Commonwealth, and tends to foster an image of happy families rather than acknowledging the realities of domination. 'Terranglian' has never found a following. 'Postimperial' has more resonance for the colonising than for the colonised power. Pragmatically speaking, 'postcolonialism' allows for the formation of an adjective – as opposed to its alternatives, 'New Literatures in English' or (the Modern Language Association of America heading) 'English Literatures Other Than British and American'. It does not involve constant problems with editors (as opposed to the lower case 'english literature', an ingenious possibility). In short, I have stuck with the term until a better one presents itself.

# Acknowledgements

In writing what follows I have incurred many debts, too many indeed to name individually here. The responsibility for any errors is, of course, entirely mine. I am grateful especially to all the students in my Postcolonial Fiction Seminar at the University of Newcastle upon Tyne, particularly the 1993–4 group who complained so vociferously that postcolonial fiction was depressing. The chapter on *Jasmine* is for them. Among other individuals who helped with queries or made useful suggestions, I take this opportunity of thanking Herman Moisl, Allan Lloyd-Smith, Angus Calder, Gail Ching-Liang Low, Dennis Walder, Shirley Chew, John Thieme, James Knowles, Anita Roy, Liz Gunner, Susheila Nasta, Rowena Bryson, John Saunders, Margaret Jones, Mike Rossington, Victor Ramraj, Patsy Stoneman, Liz Statham, Jo Dodd, David Attwell, Paul Rich, Johan Jacobs, Laura Niesen de Abruña, Claire Lamont, Patrick Williams, Laura Chrisman, Elleke Boehmer, Sarah Mills, Elaine Fido, Elaine Ho, Margaret Lenta, Pauline Ravenscroft, Maya Jaggi, Dorothy Driver, Bruce Babington and especially my editor, Christopher Wheeler, for his patience and understanding in very trying circumstances. I should also like to thank the editors of *Motherlands: Black Women's Writing From Africa, The Caribbean, and Asia* (London, Women's Press, and New Brunswick, Rutgers University Press, 1991); *British Women Writing Fiction* (University of Alabama Press, 1995); *World Literature Written in English; Modern Fiction Studies; Commonwealth; Current Writing; College English;* and the *Journal of the Short Story in English* for the opportunity to try out on their readers preliminary pilot versions of material which is developed in the book. I am also grateful to Professor Wolfgang Zach for organising a splendid conference of the European Association for Commonwealth Language and Literature Studies in Graz in 1993, to all the organisers of the ESSE Conference in Bordeaux in 1993, and to the School of English and the Staff Travel Fund of the University of Newcastle upon Tyne, and the British Academy for funding my attendance at both. I gratefully acknowledge the assistance of the Research Committee of the University of Newcastle upon Tyne for paid research leave. A special debt is due to the staff of the Robinson Library, University of Newcastle upon Tyne, especially the Inter-Library Loans Department and Robert Firth, for invaluable assistance in tracking down materials, and to the staff of the National Library of Scotland in Edinburgh. As usual my grateful thanks go to Alice and Cash Newman, Ivy Revie, Chris Revie and Ian Revie for all their encouragement and support. This book is dedicated to my son James whose arrival in 1992 interrupted it, but gave me a much better reason for writing.

The author and publishers wish to thank the following publishers and agents for permission to quote:

V. S. Naipaul c/o Aitken, Stone and Wylie and Penguin Group for V. S. Naipaul, *Guerrillas* (© 1975; Penguin, 1976); and Nadine Gordimer c/o A. P. Watt Ltd. on behalf of Felix Licensing for Nadine Gordimer, *Something Out There* (© 1984; Cape, 1984); Ruth Prawer Jhabvala and John Murray (Publishers) Ltd. for Ruth Prawer Jhabvala, *Heat and Dust* (© 1975; John Murray, 1975); Anita Desai c/o Rogers, Coleridge and White Ltd., for Anita Desai, *Baumgartner's Bombay* (© 1988, Heinemann, 1988) and her Canadian and American Publishers, Alfred A. Knopf, Bowker, Viking Penguin and Lester and Orpen Dennys; Bharati Mukherjee, *Jasmine* (© 1989; Virago, 1990). Reprinted by permission of Penguin Books Canada Limited.

Every effort has been made to try to trace copyright holders of material reproduced in this book. Any rights not acknowledged here will be acknowledged in subsequent printings if notice is given to the publisher.

# 1

# *Introduction*

## *The ballistic bard: intertextuality and postcolonial fiction*

In *The Siege of Krishnapur* J. G. Farrell sets out to expose the sham of Victorian Imperialist culture as a veneer over exploitation. Besieged by Indian nationalists, in the so-called Indian Mutiny, the British find both their sense of mission and their ideals of universal progress collapsing in the face of the need to defend themselves against the successive onslaughts of sepoys, cholera and starvation. Culture and conquest go visibly hand in hand here, as the artefacts representing the high tide of Victorian civilisation – pianos, statues, books – go to shore up the fragile siege defences. The connection between cultural hegemony and straightforward military domination is dramatised in the conversion of the electroplated heads of British poets into cannonballs. (There is an acute shortage of ammunition.) Predictably Shakespeare proves particularly deadly:

> Without a doubt the most effective missiles in this matter of improvised ammunition had been the heads of his electrometal figures .... And of the heads ... the most effective of all had been Shakespeare's; it had scythed its way through a whole astonished platoon of sepoys advancing in single file through the jungle. The Collector suspected that the Bard's success in this respect might have been a great deal to do with the ballistic advantages stemming from his baldness. The head of Keats, for example, wildly festooned with metal locks ... had flown very erratically indeed, killing only a fat moneylender and a camel standing at some distance from the action.[1]

Quite apart from its comic effects, the description makes a serious literary point. The idea of a 'colonial context' for the rise of English studies, the deployment of literature as a means not just for imparting cultural literacy but also for exercising cultural power is not a new one. Both Terry Eagleton and Chris Baldick have acknowledged the role of Empire in the development of 'Eng. Lit.' as a discipline.[2] But Gauri Viswanathan's recent research has demonstrated much more precisely that the beginnings of English can be traced back to early nineteenth-century colonial India, which saw the establishment of the discipline long before it became a subject in British schools and universities. Viswanathan traces the ways in which the literature of England was put to use to convey an ideal Englishman to the Indians, especially after the 1835 English Education Act officially required natives of India to submit to its study. Teaching English served to get round the prohibitions on large-scale missionary activity. Shakespeare was described as 'full of the commonsense principles which none but Christian men can recognise', and his 'sound Protestant Bible principles' were applauded.[3] 'Eng. Lit.' was also presented as the bearer of universal truths, and as a means to discipline the mind to think objectively. As a result, making the Englishman known to the natives through the products of his mental labour removed him from the plane of ongoing colonial activity – commerce, military operations and administration. Production of thought came to define the true essence of the Englishman. His material reality as subjugator and alien ruler was dissolved in his mental output. Viswanathan thus fully substantiates the Gramscian idea that cultural hegemony can be best established and maintained through the consent of the dominated; that the Bard is no less ballistic, just as detrimental to the forces of Indian nationalism, when he issues forth from the curriculum, rather than from the mouth of a cannon. Farrell, of course, does not suggest that all English literature is equally and homogeneously culpable. As a Romantic poet, Keats is altogether less deadly, appropriately given the Romantic emphasis on the regional and the marginal rather than the 'centre'. None the less Farrell reminds us that the study of postcolonial literature sheds light not merely on the object of study itself but also on the means by which English literature has been – and continues to be – shaped, inviting us to speculate on the relation between postcolonial literature and its predecessors, and highlighting the topic of intertextuality.

As intertextuality is a capacious term, some working definitions seem to be in order. Most readers will be familiar with the term, as coined by Julia Kristeva, as founded upon the proposition that 'every text builds itself as a mosaic of quotations, every text is absorption and transformation of another text'.[4] At its narrowest this has been taken to limit the applicability of the term to parody, mere allusion, source criticism or casual generic resemblances. More commonly, however, the intertext of a given story may be defined as the set of plots, characters, images and conventions which it brings to mind for a given reader. One can, of course, go one step further (following Kristeva's lead) to define a 'text' as a system of signs, whether in literary works, spoken language or symbolic systems, so that intertextuality is defined as the transposition of one or several systems of signs into another. In its furthest expansion, therefore, intertextuality may incorporate all sorts of social phenomena, from nursery rhymes to fairy tales, films, the language of dress, the staging of public events or the practice of sati. We may wish to consider that paradigmatic plots abound, not just in literary culture, but in general culture. The term 'intertextuality' can describe this sense of life as repeating a previously heard story, of life predestined by the notions that shape our consciousness. In this way 'real life' may be structured according to patterns familiar from literary culture – just as literary culture may be structured according to patterns familiar from 'real life'.[5]

For the postcolonial writer, of course, the sense of reality is often a vexed one. In 'Jasmine' (1964) V. S. Naipaul comments that as a native of Trinidad, identity and reality were always elsewhere, accessible only by proxy, through books or films: 'To us, without a mythology, all literatures were foreign. Trinidad was small, remote and unimportant and we knew we could not hope to read in books of the life we saw about us. Books came from afar; they could offer only fantasy.'[6] In response, one of Naipaul's fellow writers adopted the strategy of an assertive 'Caribbean' style. Naipaul read the novel: 'The nationalism was aggressive. Women swayed like coconut trees; their skins were the colour of sapodillas, the inside of their mouth the colour of a cut star-apple, their teeth were as white as coconut kernels, and when they made love they groaned like bamboos in a high wind.'[7] It is, of course, as a result of such comments that Naipaul is often regarded as one of the running dogs of neocolonialism. Here, however, he is perceptive. If the surrender to the so-called universal norms of Eurocentric fiction is one danger, nationalism poses others, from parochialism, inverse racism, or indigenist obscurantism to the tendency towards the representational and documentary.[8] By the logic of its arguments, **all** literature would end up confined to its country of origin. Partha Chatterjee has argued that even the nationalist quest for difference from the British was imbricated in Western rational discourse.[9] A second problem is that anti-colonialism and collective redefinition are not the same thing. Clifford Geertz has argued that to make Italy is not to make Italians: 'Most Tamils, Karens, Brahmins, Malays, Sikhs, Ibos, Muslims, Chinese, Nilotes, Bengalis and Ashantis found it a good deal easier to grasp the idea that they were not Englishmen than that they were Indians, Burmese, Malayans, Ghanaians, Pakistanis, Nigerians or Sudanese.'[10] The 'who are we?' question, in Geertz's analysis, also asks what cultural forms to employ to validate a people's activities. The 'epochalist' approach, using forms implicated in recent history, tends, like a lingua franca, to be internationalising but psychologically forced. The essentialist approach (national ideologies built out of local traditions and symbolic forms) may be psychologically immediate, but socially isolating. A more successful strategy lies in intertextual revisionings.

Postcolonial writers frequently begin from a self-conscious project to revise the ideological assumptions created by Eurocentric domination of their culture, and to undermine and delegitimise the centrality of Western man. Political and literary rewritings therefore go hand in hand, as the postcolonial novelist revises the fictions of influential predecessors in order to deconstruct conventional images of the postcolonial situation. J. M. Coetzee's novel *Foe*, for example, rewrites Defoe's *Robinson Crusoe*, in order to centre upon the wretched existence of the enslaved Friday, rather than upon the master, Crusoe.[11] Significantly, Coetzee also introduces a female narrator (a 'Mrs Crusoe') whose story has been hijacked and appropriated within patriarchal Defoe's master narrative. Postcolonial novelists, therefore, write with an informed awareness that stories condition their readers and influence future events. In order to repossess their own stories, to take control of their own reality, they often employ literary strategies which reposition the novel in relation to its point of origin, or historical position, or which offer revisionings of the 'classics' of the past. Rewritings of *The Tempest* probably hold the record, of which Marina Warner's *Indigo* (1992) is one of the most recent. But *Robinson Crusoe*, *Jane Eyre*, *Heart of Darkness* and *Passage to India* are not far behind. The intertextual strategy, then, as opposed to the representational or nationalistic, produces works which are highly self-conscious – novels about novels, which problematise the relation of fiction to the world. Paradoxically it is this self-consciousness which makes the political point. Whereas the British writer can merge with his or her society, since that society has, in a sense, appropriated reality, the postcolonial writer must avoid any loss of self-awareness. Postcolonial writers are therefore often at their politically sharpest, when they are also at their most 'literary'.

It is as well, however, to anticipate various objections to this intertextual enterprise. The transfer of a European genre to a colonial environment is not without nefarious consequences. The point has been made that in *Out of Africa* Isak Dinesen creates a fictional Africa which is simply the counterpart of the eighteenth-century European feudal world of her Gothic tales.[12] Setting out into the African forest, she writes: 'You ride out into the depths of an old tapestry, in places faded and darkened with age, but marvellously rich in green shades.'[13] It seems unlikely, however, that the Kikuyu shared her view of a leopard as a 'tapestry animal'. Salman Rushdie has argued against the assumption that postcolonial writers 'write back' to the centre, rather than to each other. There is a danger, here, in perpetuating a 'centre versus margin' form of binary thinking. Arun Mukherjee comments that 'This kind of theorizing leaves us only one modality, one discursive position. We are forever forced to interrogate European discourses . . . . [On the contrary] our cultural productions are created in response to our own needs, and we have many more needs than constantly to "parody the imperialists".'[14] As Mukherjee notes, Indian literatures may be in dialogic relation with other social discourses circulating in Indian society, rather than with those at the 'centre'. Discussions of postcolonial fiction need to remember that postcolonial societies may have their own internal centres and peripheries, dominants and marginals, that the postcolonial subject is not a unitary subject, and that there are nationalisms within nationalism.

The Jamaican novelist, John Hearne, has also questioned why so many postcolonial writers feel the need to write back against texts like *Jane Eyre*, producing, in the example of Jean Rhys's *Wide Sargasso Sea*, a novel which depends on a book from elsewhere, rather than from a basic assumed life. Hearne, however, recognises the potential strength of the strategy: 'Is this not a superb and audacious metaphor for so much of West Indian life? Are we not still in so many of our responses, creatures of books, and inventions fashioned by others who use us as mere producers or figments of their imagination.'[15] In this sense the central experience of life in colonial and postcolonial cultures has been and continues to be 'written' by the terms of colonial discourse. By its inscription of a complex network of textuality upon colonial subjects, colonial discourse has 'preconstituted' social existence in the marginalised territories of Empire.

As a result of this awareness V. S. Naipaul, telling a tale of horrible murder in the Caribbean in *Guerrillas*, deliberately sets out to argue that life imitates art, in the postcolonial subject's awareness that reality is defined elsewhere, and that postcolonial existence is scripted by Western paradigms. *Guerrillas* opens in thoroughly Eurocentric fashion, intertextually: 'After lunch, Jane and Roche left their house on the Ridge to drive to Thrushcross Grange.'[16] As readers we are therefore immediately invited to consider whether we are dealing with 'real' people or with characters in a novel – Jane Eyre and Rochester – and as the pair descend from the 'Heights' of the Ridge to the Grange, whether they are moving across a physical reality – an unnamed Caribbean island – or from one text to another – from *Jane Eyre* to *Wuthering Heights*. Naipaul highlights here the tendency of the West to textualise the colonial, to transform the Other into a set of codes and discourses which can be recuperated into its own system of recognition. In this particular novel Jane supplies the sadomasochistic victim to the occupants of the Grange, now a revolutionary commune. At the close (after rape, sodomy, mutilation and murder) the men write Jane out of the story, denying that she ever set foot on the island. As a transplanted Eyre (heir), therefore, this particular Jane's return to the Caribbean to exorcise her colonial guilts leads to the total annulment of her story. It is a revenge on the part of the silenced colonial which, disquietingly, positions him in the role of villain.

Intertextual rewritings may also give the impression that non-metropolitan culture can **only** rework, has no creativity of its own, and is fundamentally dependent for its materials on the centre. Jean Rhys's *Wide Sargasso Sea*, a retelling of the story of *Jane Eyre* to supply the untold story of the first Mrs Rochester, for example, chooses not to tell the story of Tia, the heroine's black friend, and only partly tells the story of Christophine, her black nurse. For all its revisionings, the tale remains apparently that of the white slaveowner's daughter. Rhys nevertheless adroitly counters the charge of parasitism on an 'original' by historically positioning her novel before *Jane Eyre*. *Wide Sargasso Sea* is a 'post-dated prequel'[17] not a sequel, and therefore enjoins future readers to envisage Victorian Britain as parasitic on its colonies, just as Brontë's heroine depends on both a colonial inheritance and the warning example of her predecessor, in the negotiation of her own independence. A reader-centred model of reading practice therefore substitutes for a paradigm based on literary history. It supplies as much a geography of English literature as a history. Readers do not 'begin at the beginning', reading from origins, and a reading of *Wide Sargasso Sea* first, and as a frame for *Jane Eyre*, is not only possible, but even highly desirable.

As a result, intertextuality is achronological and anachronistic, inviting us to consider (in David Lodge's phrase) the influence of T. S. Eliot on Shakespeare. In consequence, however, it may be objected that it plays fast and loose with material history, textualising events in order to revise their meanings in a cavalier fashion, opening the doors once more to mythic readings of the 'madwoman in the attic' variety. In *The Rape of Shavi*, Buchi Emecheta's interweaving of a Biafran war allegory with a fable in the manner of George Bernard Shaw risks neo-Tarzanism in its Shavian temporal and geographical dislocation. Underlying both the objection of parasitism and that of ahistoricism lies the difficulty implicit in any counter-discourse – the danger of reinscribing the norms of the dominant discourse within its own apparent contestation, as 'the contesters discover that the authority they sought to undermine is reinforced by the very fact of its having been chosen, as dominant discourse, for opposition'.[18] Rewritings, counter-texts, run the risk of slippage from oppositional to surreptitiously collusive positions. The problem confronting the reader of *Wide Sargasso Sea* or *Guerrillas* is that of revision as redemonisation – victims turned into villains. Naipaul's murderers are at least based on fact, as detailed in 'Michael X and the Black Power Killings in Trinidad'. In producing the untold story of the first Mrs Rochester, Rhys, however, deliberately exacerbates the Gothic mode of her predecessor, supplying omens, zombies, obeah and poisonous potions as part of the process of reclaiming the first wife for West Indian culture. The description of her may therefore transform her from Jane Eyre's 'foul German spectre – the Vampyre', but does it merely substitute the zombie in her place?

The trajectory described by Moses, the hero of a trilogy of novels by Sam Selvon, is an example of a revision which boomerangs back on itself, as Selvon's parody effectively scores an own goal. Selvon's first novel, *The Lonely Londoners*, has been rightly understood as a benchmark for the

West Indian novel in Britain, a novel which concentrates upon the immigrant experience – at least in its masculine particulars. Selvon's characters are emphatically male and in hot pursuit of the opposite sex, a fault ascribed, in part at least, to white culture. White women are seen as brutalising blacks: 'the cruder you are the more the girls like you . . . they want you to live up to the films and stories they hear about black people living primitive in the jungles'.[19] Faced with the coercive force of pre-existent stories, Moses finds it difficult to fight back with his own constructions. Indeed he ends the novel wondering whether **he** could ever write a book himself, to impose his own pattern on events. In *Moses Ascending* that book is written, though in a very different register. *The Lonely Londoners* uses the 'nation language' to the full, exploiting West Indian English, dialect and Creole speech patterns. In *Moses Ascending* Selvon deliberately chooses to allow his hero to write his 'Memoirs' in an archaic form of English, heavily influenced by Shakespeare, in order to satirise his hero's cultural pretensions. Moses's identification with Englishness extends to such utterances as 'Egad . . . let us away.'[20] On the one hand his bookishness provides a thoroughgoing satire on Eurocentric norms. Totally acculturated, Moses has become a slum landlord, renting out rooms to other immigrants, on whom he looks down from his 'penthouse' – a double image of both his ascension from – not with – his class, and his withdrawal to an ivory tower of art. He is contrasted with a new generation of black Britons who set up a Black Power party in his basement. Selvon sets out to turn the tables on Moses by parodying a cultural and literary myth. As landlord, Moses has a white 'Man Friday' (p. 4), Bob, who hails from the 'Black Country' of the industrial Midlands and fulfils all the stereotypical expectations of the 'savage'. He is illiterate ('but being as he's white we say he is suffering from dsylexia', p. 128), sex-mad, and at one point 'runs amok' (p. 55). Bob's slavery is none the less short-lived. Eventually Crusoe swaps places with Friday. Demoted to the basement, Moses is left to the realisation that 'some black power militants might choose to misconstrue my Memoirs for their own purposes, and put the following moral to defame me, to wit: that after the ballad and the episode it is the white man who ends up Upstairs and the black man who ends up Downstairs' (p. 139). Indeed for all Selvon's fun at the expense of the posturings of the Black Power activists, the novel comes close to supporting their view. Moses' fate reveals the double bind besetting the immigrant, condemned to 'savage' identity in 'jungle stories', or swallowed whole by Anglocentric norms. It is perhaps small wonder that in *Moses Migrating*, the final volume of the trilogy, Moses goes back to Trinidad, where he wins a prize in the carnival as Britannia.

Like Selvon, Hanif Kureishi employs the metaphor of relocation, though in *The Buddha of Suburbia* relocation from the suburbs to the city centre (rather than from tenant to landlord) becomes emblematic of cultural arrival. As Alamgir Hashmi has noted, the hero, Karim Amir, is centrally in the tradition of the provincial young man of British social realism, with specific links to the H. G. Wells of *Kipps* and *The History of Mr Polly*.[21] At one point Karim (Bromley-bred) stands for a moment in Bromley High Street 'next to the plaque that said "H. G. Wells was born here" '.[22] Karim's experiences of British society, mired in class violence, and of his own mental impoverishment in its education system, call forth from him the cry, 'Fuck you, Charles Dickens, nothing's changed' (p. 63). Unlike Selvon's migrants, Karim finds little solidarity between white and black working class. It is the 1970s, the era of 'Paki bashing' and widespread, growing racism. 'Jungle' stereotypes persist. Kureishi's satire exploits the ironic disjunction between the various ways in which the hero is consti-tuted as exotic Other by his white compatriots, and his resistant multi-cultural identity. Karim sets off for an audition, having rehearsed a Sam Shepard speech, only to discover himself starring, blacked up and in a loincloth, as Mowgli in *The Jungle Book*. The director forces 'Indian' iden-tity upon him, together with a Bengali accent, ironically informing him that he has been cast 'for authenticity and not for experience' (p. 147). His friend Terry, a revolutionary Trotskyite (aka Kaa the deaf snake in *The Jungle Book*) stands passively by. Unable to understand Punjabi or Urdu, or to make conversation about Satyajit Ray or Rabindranath Tagore, Karim none the less outwits the director by highlighting the dis-tance between role and reality, sending up the accent and lapsing into Cockney ('Leave it out, Bagheera') to the audience's delight. Society mobilises to incorporate him once again and he is promptly offered a part in *Le Bourgeois Gentilhomme*.

The performative emphasis persists in the novel, in which Karim's occu-pation as an actor permits a distribution of emblematic texts between word and performance, highlighting problems of ideological emphasis and fore-grounding both the bankruptcy of Britain's traditional self-images and the limited nature of the social roles available to blacks. Rejecting the role of bourgeois gentleman, Karim moves into alternative theatre, specifically a play evolved by a group of actors on the theme of class. Eleanor, his lover, assumes the role of an Englishwoman of the Raj, reflecting Karim's aware-ness that Eleanor sees herself as possessing the master narrative. In their personal relationship he edits his own life story and keeps silent about his background: 'it was her stories that had primacy, her stories that connected to an entire established world. It was as if I felt my past wasn't important enough' (p. 178). Sure enough, when Karim draws directly on his own experience to create an Indian character for the play, he is promptly accused by a black actor of peddling self-hate and trading in facile caricatures of Asians (an accusation also levelled at Kureishi's screenplays for the films *My Beautiful Laundrette* and *Sammy and Rosie Get Laid* which established him as the chronicler of contemporary immigrant London). The exchange of views is telling: 'We have to protect our culture at this time, Karim. Don't you agree?' 'No. Truth has a higher value' (p. 181). Forced none the less to suppress his own experience, Karim settles for the character of a newly arrived immigrant, sex-mad and heavily accented. It is wildly successful and becomes the key to the play. The other actors, given the heavy political analyses, are marginalised, and complain that Karim seems to be 'in a different play to the others, a farce, perhaps' (p. 221). On the one hand, Kureishi's satire is squarely aimed at the pretensions of radical chic. The alternative theatre scene involves plays three hours long, bursting with anarchic and defiant images, and posited on the assumption that England is in the last throes of class struggle: 'the science-fiction fantasies of Oxford-educated boys who never left the house. The middle class loved it' (p. 207). Tellingly, however, Karim's ability to convert agit-prop back into farce, to re-frame the dramatic situation, defining his role anew and establishing it as central, suggests some of the ways in which functioning intertextually fosters resistance. 'Cast' by society, scripted into a fake role as exotic Other, his experience discounted in favour of the totalising narratives of the dominant, Karim is still able to wrench the focus around to himself and to construct his own role. Tellingly he subverts, not by straightforward contestation or refusal, but by parodic proliferation. As a result, slippage is a risk which he has to run. Both Terry and Karim end up in television drama, radical Terry as a policeman, Karim as the rebellious son of an Indian shopkeeper in a soap opera, a role which brings him fame and fortune, and a direct (if commodified) place in working-class culture. Karim has made a place for himself, but at some cost to idealism and morality. He is none the less still 'in play'. The compromised nature of the denouement is essential to Kureishi's message. In a moving autobiographical essay, 'The Rainbow Sign', Kureishi writes that he knows Indians and Pakistanis, born and brought up in Britain, who consider their identity in terms of a diaspora; they are in exile, awaiting return to a better place, full of 'belonging'.[23] For Kureishi, however, the lure of the return to the original homeland is a sentimental illusion. He opts instead for a reality of pragmatic struggle, even if it involves conflict, self-hatred and a continual battle against British racism.

As Karim's varied roleplay suggests, one solution to the problem of collusive slippage is to focus less on single specific models, adopting instead a broader heteroglossic strategy. Rather than repropagating an influence by contesting it, such fiction lays the emphasis on re-reading, creative adaptation from at least two traditions, in order to create what Les Murray, the Australian poet, has called a 'convergent culture'. Not all cultural revision is a one-way process, as Shashi Tharoor's *The Great Indian Novel* demonstrates. Encyclopaedically intertextual, the novel rewrites history through both British and Indian intertexts. On the one hand Tharoor offers hilarious parodies of Forster, Scott, Rushdie and Kipling. Chapter titles include 'The Duel with the Crown', 'Midnight's Parents' and 'The Bungle Book'. Forster's Ronnie Heaslop steps out of the pages of *A Passage to India* to learn that books mean trouble: 'Basic truth about the colonies, Heaslop. Any time there's trouble you can put it down to books . . . . If ever the Empire comes to ruin, Heaslop, mark my words, the British publisher will be to blame'. [24] The speaker, Sir Richard (whose brother David is interested in animals), bears a more than family resemblance to the Attenborough of the film version of Forster's novel. Forster himself turns up, tutoring young boys, Paul Scott is a lieutenant governor, and Kipling is assassinated. The structural interest of the novel, however, resides in the way the story of modern India is framed and retold through the *Mahabharata*, the great Sanskrit epic which describes the struggle between the descendants of the great king Bharata for possession of the Ganges valley. In Sanskrit 'Maha' means great, 'Bharata' (if we set aside complicatory historical and geographical factors) is India, hence the novel's title. The *Mahabharata* is presented as composed by Vyasa (here, Ved Vyas) and dictated to the elephant god, Ganesh (here his clerk, Ganapathi, who appears dragging an enormous trunk behind him). Dritarashtra becomes Nehru, and Duryodhani Indira Gandhi, with the final great battle, Kurukshetra, taking the shape of the struggle for democracy during the Emergency of 1975–7, when Indira Gandhi suspended civil liberties. The novel's epigraph quotes P. Lal describing the tale of Vyasa:

> a tale told and retold,
> > that people will never cease telling;
> a source of wisdom
> > in the sky, the earth, and the lower world;
> a tale the twice-born know.

For some readers such a retelling as Tharoor's may none the less amount to violation of an authenticity which should not be parodied. Diana Brydon objects that 'When directed against the Western canon, postmodernist techniques of intertextuality, parody and literary borrowing may appear radical and even potentially revolutionary. When directed against native myths and stories, these same techniques would seem to repeat the imperialist history of plunder and theft'.[25] Tharoor, however, recognises that intertextuality is its own *pharmakon* – both the disease and its cure. In desacralising the epic he lambasts both familiar colonial targets **and** the mythic approach to India's past. For Tharoor there are no master narratives masquerading as eternal verities. At the close Ved Vyas validates the removal of canonical status by announcing that he has told his story from an entirely mistaken perspective, and immediately sets about a retelling, ending his tale (some 400 pages) with its opening sentence: 'They tell me

India is an underdeveloped country' (p. 418). Tharoor's awareness that 'stories never end, they just continue somewhere else' (p. 418) forms an appropriate point of entry into the present study.

# Notes

1　J. G. Farrell, *The Siege of Krishnapur* (London, Penguin, 1973), p. 335.
2　Terry Eagleton, *Literary Theory: An Introduction* (Oxford, Blackwell, 1983); Chris Baldick, *The Social Mission of English Criticism, 1848–1932* (Oxford, Clarendon, 1983).
3　Gauri Viswanathan, 'Currying Favor: The Politics of British Educational and Cultural Policy in India, 1813–1854', *Social Text* 19/20 (1988), p. 96. See also Gauri Viswanathan, *Masks of Conquest: Literary Study and British Rule in India* (New York, Columbia University Press, 1989). For a critique of Viswanathan as overly preoccupied with the British point of view of her subject and insufficiently aware of the reception of English literature by Indians, see Harish Trivedi, *Colonial Transactions. English Literature and India* (Calcutta, Papyrus, 1993), pp. 204–5.
4　Julia Kristeva, *Semiotike, recherches pour une semanalyse* (Paris, Seuil, 1969), p. 146 (my translation).
5　For two clear theoretical accounts see Laurent Jenny, 'The Strategy of Form', in Tzvetan Todorov, ed., *French Literary Theory Today* (Cambridge University Press, 1982), pp. 34–64; and Jeanine Parisier Plottel and Hanna Charney, eds., 'Intertextuality: New Perspectives in Criticism', *New York Literary Forum*, 2 (1978). For an excellent demonstration of ways of working with intertextuality see John Hannay, *The Intertextuality of Fate* (Columbia, University of Missouri Press, 1986) and Susan Stewart, *Nonsense: Aspects of Intertextuality In Folklore and Literature* (Baltimore, Johns Hopkins University Press, 1979) p. 26.
6　V. S. Naipaul, 'Jasmine' in *The Overcrowded Barracoon* (London, Penguin, 1976), p. 24.
7　Naipaul, 'Jasmine', p. 24.
8　See Aijaz Ahmad, *In Theory: Classes, Nations, Literatures* (London, Verso, 1992).
9　Partha Chatterjee, *Nationalist Thought and the Colonial World: A Derivative Discourse?* (London, Zed, 1986).
10　Clifford Geertz, *The Interpretation of Cultures* (London, Hutchinson, 1975), pp. 239–40.
11　J. M. Coetzee, *Foe* (London, Secker and Warburg, 1986).
12　See Eric O. Johannesson, *The World of Isak Dinesen* ( Seattle, University of Washington Press, 1961), p. 129.
13　Isak Dinesen (Karen Blixen), *Out of Africa* (New York, Random House, 1938), p. 65.
14　Arun P. Mukherjee, 'Whose Postcolonialism and Whose Postmodernism?', *World Literature Written in English* 30, 2 (1990), pp. 1–9.
15　John Hearne, 'The Wide Sargasso Sea: A West Indian Reflection', *Cornhill Magazine* 180 (1974), p. 325.

16 V. S. Naipaul, *Guerrillas* (London, Penguin, 1976), p. 9.

17 The phrase is Susan Gubar's, quoted in Elizabeth Abel, Marianne Hirsch and Elizabeth Langland, eds., *The Voyage In* (Hanover and London, University Press of New England, 1983), p. 335.

18 Richard Terdiman, *Discourse/Counter-discourse. The Theory and Practice of Symbolic Resistance in Nineteenth Century France* (Ithaca, Cornell University Press, 1985), p. 65.

19 Sam Selvon, *The Lonely Londoners* (London, Longman, 1956), p. 108.

20 Sam Selvon, *Moses Ascending* (London, Heinemann, 1984), p. 96. Subsequent page references follow quotations in parentheses.

21 Alamgir Hashmi, 'Hanif Kureishi and the Tradition of the Novel', *Commonwealth Novel in English* 6 (1993), pp. 50–60.

22 Hanif Kureishi, *The Buddha of Suburbia* (London, Faber, 1990), p. 64. Subsequent page references follow quotations in parentheses.

23 Hanif Kureishi, *My Beautiful Laundrette and The Rainbow Sign* (London, Faber, 1986).

24 Shashi Tharoor, *The Great Indian Novel* (London, Penguin, 1990), p. 38. Subsequent page references follow quotations in parentheses.

25 Diana Brydon, 'The White Inuit Speaks: Contamination as Literary Strategy', in Ian Adam and Helen Tiffin, eds., *Past the Last Post: Theorizing Post-Colonialism and Post-Modernism* (New York, Harvester, 1991), pp. 195–6. Brydon's discussion of cultural purity versus 'contamination' chimes with my own view of the relation between intertextuality and pollution anxiety. See Judie Newman, 'Intertextuality, Power and Danger: *Waiting for the Barbarians* as a Dirty Story', *Commonwealth*, Special Issue No. SP3 (1992), pp. 67–77, and Chapter 6 below.

# 2

## I walked with a zombie

### Jean Rhys, Wide Sargasso Sea

In his review of *Wide Sargasso Sea*, John Hearne described the novel as the account of a marginal community, run over and then abandoned by history in a country which had never been a polity, only a plantation. In consequence, despite her identity as white creole, Hearne applauded Rhys, along with Wilson Harris, as belonging absolutely to the West Indies, as

> Guerrillas, not outsiders. Independent of official supply lines; but perhaps more committed in the gut to the desperate campaign we are waging for identity than many who wear the issued uniforms, and who receive battle orders from the certified commanders in chief: whether these commanders be foreign readers; our own established politicians and administrators; the complacent, newly cultivated West Indian middle-class . . . or the self-appointed priests of mass culture.[1]

In this ringing denunciation, almost the only group to go unmentioned are women. Yet the need to question acculturated models is particularly acute for women writers whose double marginalisation brings into sharp focus the question: whose story is it? Adrienne Rich has emphasised the general need for women to lay claim to their own stories and to revise or 're-vision' those of the past:

> Re-vision – the act of looking back, of seeing with fresh eyes, of entering an old text from a new critical direction – is for women more than a chapter in cultural history: it is an act of survival. Until we can understand the assumptions in which we are drenched we cannot know ourselves.[2]

Jean Rhys's *Wide Sargasso Sea*, a retelling of the story of *Jane Eyre* in order to supply the untold, silenced story of the first Mrs Rochester, therefore comes appropriately from both a female and a postcolonial pen. Few readers are unacquainted with the story of Jane Eyre, the orphan who finds true love with Mr Rochester, only to discover at the altar itself that he already has a wife – 'Bertha Antoinetta Mason' – a madwoman incarcerated in his attic. Charlotte Brontë depicts Rochester as a victim of his father and elder brother (the system of patriarchy operating on a younger son) who marry him off to Bertha for her dowry in the full knowledge that madness runs in her family. For Jean Rhys the vital point was that Bertha was West Indian, a white Creole from Jamaica. Rhys had this to say of Bertha:

> The mad first wife in *Jane Eyre* has always interested me. I was convinced Charlotte Brontë must have had something against the West Indies and I was angry about it. Otherwise why did she take a West Indian for that horrible lunatic, for that really dreadful creature?[3]

Certainly Charlotte Brontë's portrayal of Bertha is designed to obliterate all sympathy for her. Bertha is described in the novel in terms which appeal to both racial and sexual prejudices. Her hereditary madness, which is supposedly accelerated by sexual excess, clearly reflects Victorian syphilophobia. (The nineteenth century had shifted the point of origin of syphilis to Africa.)[4] Brontë's Bertha has 'a discoloured face', 'a savage face' with 'fearful blackened inflation' of the features: 'the lips were swelled and dark'.[5] Successively described as a demon, a witch, a vampire, a beast, a hyena, and even an Indian Messalina, Bertha unites in one person all the available pejorative stereotypes. Even worse, according to Rochester, she turns out to be five years older than him. In addition, Brontë's Rochester describes Jamaica as 'hell' (p. 370), its sounds and scenery those of the 'bottomless pit' (p. 370). On one 'fiery West Indian night' (p. 370) Rochester even contemplates suicide, only to be saved by 'A wind fresh from Europe' (p. 370). When this 'pure air' recalls him to England, he does not, of course, return empty-handed. Penny Boumelha has observed that in *Jane Eyre* all the money comes from colonial exploitation.[6] Jane Eyre herself gains her financial independence as a result of a legacy from an uncle in Madeira who is connected to the same firm which Mr Mason, Bertha's brother, represents in Jamaica. Jane shares out this loot, appropriately, between the church (her cousin Mary's husband), the military (her cousin Diana's husband) and the forces of cultural imperialism, in the shape of her cousin, St John, who plans to 'labour for his race' (p. 548) as a missionary in India. With Bertha dead in a fire at Thornfield Hall, Jane and Rochester settle down to a happy married life on the proceeds of the Empire.

When Jean Rhys sets out to vindicate the 'madwoman' she emphasises her role as 'the legacy of imperialism concealed in the heart of every English gentleman's castle'.[7] Rechristening Bertha 'Antoinette', Rhys arranges the story in three parts, the first narrated by Antoinette, describing her childhood in Jamaica, the second largely narrated by Rochester describing his honeymoon in Dominica, and the third narrated partly by Antoinette's jailer, Grace Poole, partly by Antoinette herself. The narrative method emphasises the fact that Antoinette loses control of her own story, once married to Rochester: 'Entry into the patriarchal order entails the silencing of women.'[8] Rochester's now becomes the master narrative, and Antoinette is subject to the tales and inventions of others. It is only at the very end that she regains her voice and her ability to speak for herself. In Part One, which provides Antoinette with a history, Rhys cleverly reverses Brontë's tactics.[9] Brontë makes Bertha and Jane opposites, the one an obstacle to the other's happiness, a dark subconscious *alter ego* of passion and anger. She makes it a war between women. Rhys, however, gives Antoinette a similar background to Jane Eyre: orphanhood, poverty, social humiliation, repressive religious schooling, lack of love. The only real difference between the two women is their cultural position, the one on the margins of Empire, the other at its centre. Throughout the novel, Antoinette's personal history is firmly politicised. As the hated offspring of a slaveowner in post-emancipation Jamaica, she is automatically detested by blacks and also by more prosperous whites, emancipation having reduced the family fortunes. Antoinette is also rejected by her mother, whose energies are focused on a younger brother. Imagistically Rhys emphasises the weakness of the mother–daughter bond as not only fatal to Antoinette's individual sense of self (a view which modern psychoanalysis confirms) but also as symbolic of the lack of sustenance and definition offered by the 'mother country' to its dependencies. *Wide Sargasso Sea*, a text which may be described as born from *Jane Eyre*, is deliberately situated before most of the events of *Jane Eyre* take place, in order to reconstitute itself as the 'mother text' or point of origin of the English novel.[10] Rhys therefore links reproduction and textual production[11] so that *Wide Sargasso Sea*, a 'postdated prequel'[12] to *Jane Eyre*, becomes its necessary precursor. By commandeering *Jane Eyre* as **her** sequel, therefore, Rhys enjoins future readers to envisage Victorian Britain as dependent upon her colonies, just as Brontë's heroine depends upon a colonial inheritance to gain her own independence.

Antoinette's history also becomes representative of West Indian history in broader terms. In a society founded upon the buying and selling of human beings, Antoinette's marriage to Rochester is also envisaged as an economic transaction. Acquired for profit, given a more 'English' name, transported overseas, economically enslaved and then quite literally a captive with a keeper, treated as an animal and a degenerate, Antoinette experiences some, at least, of the evils of slavery in her own person.[13] It is not surprising that she reacts, much as her father's ex-slaves did, by setting a torch to the Great House.

Rhys's Rochester – never named in the novel – is also a creature of his culture and history, his motivation reflecting both his engrained racial prejudice and the attitudes of his time to purity in women.[14] In Part Two, on his honeymoon in Dominica, in a house which originally belonged to Antoinette's mother, Rochester clearly resents the female-identified world around him. He is dependent on Antoinette, here. Like Caliban in *The Tempest* she acquaints the newcomer with the flora and fauna of the island and interprets its customs to him. Like Prospero, Rochester's reaction is to resent her independent knowledge, accuse her of sexual guilt and to enslave her. Initially Rochester and Antoinette had enjoyed a honeymoon to their mutual satisfaction. Rochester, however, espouses proto-Victorian views on the proper forms of female sexuality.[15] For him only a prostitute – or a madwoman – could take pleasure in sex. He comments that Antoinette would 'moan and cry and give herself as no sane woman would'.[16] Once he learns that Antoinette's mother was insane he jumps at the chance to redefine his wife in conventional terms. Antoinette's failure to 'lie back and think of England' is well nigh fatal to her. After one last night of love, Rochester covers his wife's face with a sheet, as though she were dead, and retreats to the arms of her maid, a woman whom he can possess and dominate sexually without any complications – a paid woman.[17] Henceforward Antoinette is essentially silenced. Rochester takes over her voice, and renames her (from Antoinette to Bertha, and even to Marionette). He finds himself drawing her as a stick-woman: 'a child's scribble, a dot for a head, a larger one for the body, a triangle for a skirt, slanting lines for arms and feet' (p. 134). As most readers would agree, Antoinette's identity has been erased by the politics of imperialism and of patriarchy.[18] Only the skirt, the sexual marker, identifies her as a woman. Dehumanised, depersonalised, renamed, she is now a helpless puppet, a character under Rochester's control.

Or so it seems. If the story ended here, it would be difficult to quarrel with those critics who have argued that Rhys's novel is deterministic, that Antoinette cannot escape the fate which Brontë has prepared for her. In this connection the third part of the novel bears close examination, and will be fully comprehensible only in the light of an image which pervades *Wide Sargasso Sea* – that of the zombie. In *Wide Sargasso Sea* Rhys deliberately exacerbates the Gothic mode of her predecessor, supplying omens, premonitory dreams, references to zombies, obeah and poisonous potions, as part of the process of reclaiming the first wife for West Indian culture. Obeah, also known as voodoo, is the black religion of Jamaica, Dominica and other West Indian islands, a survival and development of West African religious beliefs, brought over by slaves. West African religion particularly venerates ancestors, who are believed to maintain a presence and an influence over their kinspeople's lives for many years after their deaths: they return as spirits, or living dead, to revisit their families. In the Caribbean context, the phrase 'living dead' has a rather different ring. Most of Rhys's readers will be familiar with the figure of the zombie from such horror films as *Night of the Living Dead, I Walked With A Zombie, White Zombie* and so forth. A zombie may be defined as 'a body without character, without will',[19] generally as the result of sorcery, involving the raising of the dead. In *Wide Sargasso Sea* there can be little doubt that zombification occurs. Several different commentators have called attention to the number of references to obeah in the novel, to Rhys's own background knowledge (via her black nurse), and to a key incident in the plot: the use of a love-potion by Antoinette, bought from Christophine, the obeah woman, in an attempt to reclaim Rochester's affections.[20]

Now, why does Rhys introduce this material? If her aim is to revise Brontë's Bertha – described by Jane Eyre as the 'foul German spectre – the Vampyre' (p. 341) – it is not much of an advance merely to substitute a zombie in her place. (Most readers would be just as unhappy meeting a zombie in the dark as a vampire.) And if the aim is to refuse to provide the stereotypical image of the West Indies as tropical hell, the same objection arises. The popular image of voodoo, from horror film to James Bond, tends to involve sensational acts of cannibalism, human sacrifice and sexual orgies, a trend which was encouraged by the media during the American occupation of Haiti in order to legitimise the latter. So why employ this particular image? The answer, arguably, lies in the unique way in which the zombie, a figure with a special autobiographical significance for Rhys, unites issues of economic and sexual exploitation with questions of Eurocentric literary domination and resistance, problematising the nature of the 'real'.

In the classic folklore accounts, a zombie is created by the giving of a drug of some kind, which creates the appearance of death.[21] A common method is to sprinkle 'zombie poison' across the threshold where it is absorbed through the feet of the victim. The drug supposedly lowers the metabolic rate so that the victim seems dead, is cold, but can be restored to some sort of life by an antidote. The sorcerer digs up the body, administers a second potion (drugged rum is often cited) and gives the zombie a new name. From this point on, the zombie is the slave of the sorcerer, lacking all memory, willpower or thought, but capable of working night and day in the fields. The image suggests an obvious connection with the history of slavery. Frances Huxley, the anthropologist, speculates that 'the folklore surrounding [zombies] is partly a reminiscence of plantation days when the Negroes learned to endure forced labour . . . by acting stupid and not allowing their resentment to show'.[22] In the myths the zombie can be recognised by staring eyes, lack of expression and a hoarse voice. Zombies will go on working forever, as long as they do not taste salt. One grain of salt, however, will restore the memory, and the zombie returns to the grave to 'die' all over again. Tales of zombies are particularly prevalent in Martinique, known as 'le pays des revenants' – the country of those who come back. Both Christophine and Antoinette's mother come from Martinique; Rhys originally entitled her novel 'Le Revenant'.

The zombie has a long pedigree in colonial fiction. The first West Indian novel was *Le Zombi du Grand Pérou* by Pierre Corneille Blessebois (1697).[23] Rhys, however, draws her zombie from a rather less prestigious source. Jane Eyre has walked with a zombie before. When the zombie enters Western discourse it is largely through the medium of popular film, which tends to focus on themes of economic or sexual exploitation. Zombies labour for masters in a sugar mill for example *(White Zombie)* or a mine *(Plague of the Zombies)*. In *King of the Zombies* and *Revenge of the Zombies*, zombies are enlisted to aid the Nazi cause, reflecting the idea that people may be turned by war into mindless killers.[24] And in some films – *White Zombie, The Voodoo Men* and *Voodoo Women* – the exploitation is implicitly sexual.

More specifically interesting, in the context of *Wide Sargasso Sea,* is *I Walked With A Zombie* (1943) described by its producer, Val Lewton, as 'Jane Eyre in the tropics'.[25] In the film a white first wife (Jessica Holland) is supposedly turned into a zombie by her husband's mother, infuriated by her daughter-in-law's adultery with her brother-in-law. The plot: unchaste first wife, noble suffering husband and even more selfless Canadian nurse (the modern version of the governess who will become the second wife) is straightforwardly stolen from *Jane Eyre*. Two features of the film, however, are suggestive. First the director (Jacques Tourneur) goes to some lengths to emphasise the history of slavery as a curse both upon the fictional island of Saint Sebastian and the Holland family, who were entirely responsible for introducing it to the island. The economic exploitation continues in the film's present: menacing drums in the background turn out to be the rural factory hooter, summoning workers to the family sugar mill. Second, the introduction of a mother figure responsible for zombification has interesting connections with Rhys's own vexed relations with her mother, Antoinette's with her mother, and the relationship between mother- and daughter- texts. As her biography demonstrates (see below), Jean Rhys felt herself 'zombified' by the mother country. Internal evidence strongly suggests that Rhys had seen *I Walked with a Zombie*. Quite minor incidents in the film are echoed in *Wide Sargasso Sea*. Holland, the Rochester figure, feels partly responsible for his wife's apparent madness, because when her adultery was discovered, he refused to allow her to leave him, insisting that he would keep her by force. Rochester similarly refuses to countenance separation from Antoinette. The islanders sing calypsos about the family scandal. Rochester fears featuring in **his** islanders' songs (p. 134). The islanders suspect that Jessica is a zombie and attempt to take her by force. It is suggested that, for her safety, she should be removed to Saint Thomas. In *Wide Sargasso Sea* Antoinette's brother, Pierre, lies in a similar trance to Jessica's and is at similar risk. His mother insists that the family depart on the grounds, otherwise unmotivated, that 'It is not safe for Pierre' (p. 29). When the blacks fire the house they begin with Pierre's bed. Though he dies shortly afterwards, Antoinette comments that 'He died before that' (p. 39). In the film there is a tower with stone steps, up which Jessica climbs by night in her trance. Antoinette repeatedly dreams of climbing stone steps. Most importantly, the initiator of the obeah curse is white (the mother-in-law) acting to prevent the break-up of her family. Things go badly wrong, however, with Jessica eventually stabbed by her lover who then kills himself. The nurse also resorts to obeah, on one occasion taking her patient to visit the voodoo priest, though without success. In *Wide Sargasso Sea* Rhys places particular emphasis on the fact that white people meddling with obeah is dangerous. Christophine argues that 'that is not for béké. Bad, bad trouble come when béké meddle with that' (p. 93).

Just how much Antoinette does meddle with obeah becomes obvious in one crucial scene. On their last night of love, Rochester questions Antoinette about her mother. The dialogue is worth quoting in full.

'Is your mother alive?'
'No, she is dead, she died.'
'When?'
'Not long ago.'
'Then why did you tell me that she died when you were a child?'
'Because they told me to say so and because it is true. She did die when I was a child. There are always two deaths, the real one and the one people know about' (pp. 105–6).

When Rochester enters Antoinette's room he notices 'the white powder strewn on the floor' (p. 112) ostensibly against cockroaches. As he drinks from the glass she offers him, he tells her to forget the past: 'We are letting ghosts trouble us.' Antoinette replies, 'Christophine knows about ghosts too, but that is not what she calls them' (p. 113). Rochester's voice alters, and he succumbs to her charms. When he awakens it is as an almost-dead man. 'I woke in the dark after dreaming that I was buried alive, and when I was awake the feeling of suffocation persisted. Something was lying across my mouth; hair...I was cold too, deathly cold' (p. 113). He is also almost incapable of thought or action: 'I thought, I have been poisoned. But it was a dull thought, like a child spelling out the letters of a word which he cannot read, and which if he could would have no meaning or context' (p. 113). Rochester appears to have narrowly escaped zombification. The scene apparently incriminates Antoinette and makes Rochester, however imperfect, a victim of female witchcraft.

Antoinette, however, sees things rather differently. Earlier Rochester has insisted on calling her 'Bertha': 'On this of all nights, you must be Bertha' (p. 112). When next he sees her she has indeed become 'Bertha': 'Her long

hair hung uncombed and dull into her eyes which were inflamed and staring' (p. 120). Her voice is hoarse. For Antoinette, Rochester is guilty of
obeah: 'Bertha is not my name. You are trying to make me into someone
else, calling me by another name. I know, that's obeah too' (p. 121).
Rochester has already scripted Antoinette into the role of sex-mad
Caribbean lunatic – his puppet, a character under his control. Such is his
cultural conditioning that when he receives the letter denouncing her, he
feels no surprise. It is as if he had been expecting it. It is rather as if he
already knew the plot which Antoinette's life must now imitate. As a typical nineteenth-century Englishman, Rochester's view of his wife is entirely
the product of paradigmatic plots promulgated by his culture, which
expects anywhere outside England to be a place of evil and madness. In
addition, Rochester's voodoo is also sexual. When Brontë's Jane Eyre is
serenaded by Rochester, inviting her to die with him, her response is both
characteristically forthright and obtuse: 'I had no intention of dying with
him – he might depend on that' *(Jane Eyre, p. 327)*. Antoinette, however,
is in a state of complete erotic surrender. She whispers to Rochester: 'If I
could die. Now, when I'm happy. Would you do that? You wouldn't have
to kill me. Say die and I will die' *(Wide Sargasso Sea, p. 77)*. Rochester's
response is decidedly less romantic. 'Die, then, die. I watched her die many
times. In my way, not in hers' (p. 77). Rochester understands death as the
French understand the phrase *la petite mort*: as sexual orgasm. Unlike Jane
Eyre, Antoinette is sexually bewitched. Rhys makes the point, forcefully,
that it is sexuality which enslaves the woman and destroys her independence. Antoinette has become Rochester's sexual zombie before she
attempts to turn the tables on him. There is, then, a form of double zombification at work here, in which both Rochester and Antoinette feature as
victim and aggressor, possessor and possessed. The image underlines the
dual dependence of coloniser and colonised – and it also has implications
for questions of literary domination and independence.

In literary terms, Jean Rhys may also be said to have suffered a double death. In the 1940s she had disappeared from view and was presumed
dead. Francis Wyndham even referred to her publicly as 'the late Jean
Rhys'.[26] In 1948 she saw an advertisement in the *New Statesman*, placed
by Selma Vaz Dias who had adapted Rhys's *Good Morning Midnight* for
radio and needed to find Rhys to obtain permission to perform it. The
BBC had told her that Rhys was dead. Rhys commented that it made her
feel like a ghost: 'I feel rather tactless being still alive.'[27] Even worse, when
she did make contact with the BBC one of her neighbours claimed that
Rhys was 'an imposter impersonating a dead writer called Jean Rhys'.[28]
When Selma met her she expressed surprise that Rhys was so quiet and
well behaved. She had expected a raving and not too clean maniac with
straws in gruesome, unwashed hair.[29] (This was an unsurprising reaction,
given that Rhys was continually arrested for being drunk and disorderly.

She had appeared in court eight times in two years.) To cut a long story short, England had already 'zombified' Jean Rhys, who came back from the dead only when 'dug up' by another writer who wanted to use her work. What better revenge then, on Rhys's part, than to dig up Charlotte Brontë, to make **her** novel serve Rhys's purposes?

Rhys's work frequently displays her unease with the power of the book. In 'Temps Perdi' a character reflects:

> Now I am almost as wary of books as I am of people. They are also-capable of hurting you, pushing you into the limbo of the forgotten. They can tell lies – and vulgar trivial lies – and when they are so many saying the same thing, they can shout you down and make you doubt, not only your memory, but your senses.[30]

Helen Tiffin has argued persuasively that Eurocentic writing may be seen as a kind of obeah, as magically powerful, creating the sense in the Caribbean reader of being deadened, enslaved to other people's words, one's reality removed by Eurocentric definitions.[31] Rhys clearly undercuts the power of Western books in *Wide Sargasso Sea*: the books in Rochester's dressing room are being steadily eaten away by the West Indian climate. Yet while undercutting the power of Eurocentric fiction, Rhys was also, of course, writing a novel herself, taking over another woman's book – in a sense writing with Brontë's ghost at her elbow, a ghost powerless to intervene, but susceptible to economic exploitation. Rhys's unease is tangible. In her letters she progressively denies the connection to her literary ancestor; she claims that Brontë's story was based on reality; that there were many Antoinettes; and even that the tale came from a different novel. One letter, of 5 October 1957, is typical:

> this fiction was founded on fact or rather several facts. At that date and earlier, very wealthy planters <u>did</u> exist, their daughters <u>had</u> very large dowries, there <u>was</u> no married woman's property act. So a young man who was not too scrupulous could do very well for himself and very easily. He would marry the girl, grab her money, bring her to England – a faraway place – and in a year she would be an invalid or mad. I could see <u>how</u> easily all this could happen. It <u>did</u> happen and more than once . . . . There have been one or two novels about this. One was called *The Little Girl From Dominica*.[32]

Rhys was clearly uneasily aware that, in outgunning Charlotte Brontë, she risked becoming a slaver in her turn. It is a problem which recurs when dealing with intertextuality: its relation to intellectual property is a vexed one. Where does parody, intertextuality or play-giarism end, and the reader exclaim, 'It's a steal'? That Rhys was aware of this danger of exploiting Brontë is suggested in her repeated attempts to distance herself from *Jane Eyre*, both in her letters and within the novel itself. When she introduced the figure of the zombie into her text, she knew that what she was doing was to make issues of creative control central to her novel. If the figure of the zombie highlights issues of economic and sexual possession, it is no less relevant to the need to possess one's own imaginative reality.

Within the text of *Wide Sargasso Sea*, the connection to *Jane Eyre* is purposefully oblique. 'Antoinette Cosway' does not immediately suggest 'Bertha Mason'; Rochester is never so named. Only the name Mason provides a clue, until the appearance of Grace Poole in Part Three. In addition, the time is out of joint. *Jane Eyre* is set in the early nineteenth century: Jane is given a newly published copy of *Marmion* (1808) near the end of the novel.[33] *Wide Sargasso Sea*, however, begins with Emancipation in 1833. The one date in the novel, 1839, is sewn on to a sampler by Antoinette in her seventeenth year. Of course, for Rhys's purposes the time scheme has to be 'wrong'. In terms of events, the action of *Jane Eyre* follows that of *Wide Sargasso Sea*, just as Jane follows Bertha. But in terms of influence, *Jane Eyre* precedes *Wide Sargasso Sea* and 'haunts' it for many readers, so the dates place *Wide Sargasso Sea* after the 1808 of *Jane Eyre*. The change also allows the novel to begin at the moment when slavery has ostensibly ended. In the West Indies, however, a period of 'apprenticeship' was envisaged, during which slaves were only gradually given full freedom. They were neither quite free nor quite enslaved, rather like the zombie's position between life and death.

Rhys's oblique handling of the relationship to her literary ancestor, therefore, creates a productive sense of liminality in the reading experience, redefining Gothic and problematising notions of possession in the process. Even the most informed reader is independent of Charlotte Brontë at first. But slowly, in the process of reading, we become haunted by another text – *Jane Eyre* – a kind of ghost inside the words, an echo, at times indistinct, at others very definite. As the two novels battle for dominant text status, for a position as master narrative, it is not going too far to argue that intertextuality becomes a form of zombification.[34] The reader has a sense of illegitimately crossing the boundaries between texts, an uneasy awareness of something already familiar returning to consciousness: a process which fulfils Freud's classic definition of the uncanny.[35] *Wide Sargasso Sea* becomes a vast echo chamber, a text criss-crossed by repetitions, hauntings, mirrorings, plot-parallels and reenactments, as Antoinette reenacts her mother's fate, as Rochester acts out the role which his culture has prepared for him, and as both move towards the action of *Jane Eyre*.

One scene in particular focuses on these issues of possession, narrative control and domination: Rochester's interview with Christophine (pp. 126–7). When Christophine speaks to Rochester he does not immediately respond. Instead the text gives the reader a response in parentheses, reproduced in italics. The first two utterances are clearly Rochester's own thoughts. Then suddenly, 'every word she said was echoed, echoed loudly in my head'. The final parenthetical utterance, however, is not Rochester's: 'I lay awake all night long after they were asleep, and as soon as it was light I got up and dressed and saddled Preston. And I came to you. O Christophine. O Pheena, Pheena, help me' (p. 127). The voice is that of Antoinette, on one of only two occasions in Part Two where it interrupts Rochester's narrative; the other occasion is her visit to Christophine to seek the love-potion, an episode which could not logically be narrated by Rochester. What is happening here? Is Rochester becoming subordinate to Christophine, and to Antoinette, his mind able only to echo their words. Mary Lou Emery reads the scene persuasively in these terms.[36] On the other hand, the echoes are not quite identical to their source (as in the larger literary echoing which it models). In some cases they express Rochester's inner determination to abandon Antoinette:

'So that you can leave her alone.'
*(Leave her alone)*
'Not telling her why.'
*(Why?)*
'No more love, eh?'
*(No more love)*

During their last night of love, Rochester had attempted to force Antoinette to cry and to speak, but she had resisted. Now Rochester thinks/echoes '(*Force her to cry and to speak)*' and her voice is heard. Has he finally succeeded in controlling her voice? When the voice speaks, however, it speaks to Pheena. The scene deliberately confronts the central questions raised by the novel. Is Antoinette merely an echo? Or is she independent? Can she speak for herself? Or only when enclosed, bracketed, by Brontë? Is the patriarchal Englishman calling the shots? Or is he simply echoing the dominant culture? Is the story coming to the reader from the male or the female, the imperialist or the imperialised? Rochester wins the duel with Christophine by threatening her with the 'letter of the Law': police action. He reads her a letter from the local police chief, making the point that one word from him will be enough to gaol her. His words can become realities, deeds. At the close of the interview, however, the reader sees the same possibility in Christophine's hands. Rochester, exasperated, cries out, 'I would give my eyes never to have seen this abominable place' (p. 132). Christophine laughs, 'And that's the first word of truth you speak.' The reader may remember that *Jane Eyre* sees Rochester blinded at its close. In allowing Christophine to pronounce the curse on Rochester, Rhys reverses the current of determinism.[37] What she does is to make the action of *Jane Eyre* the result of a West Indian obeah woman's curse. It is poetic justice for Rochester. He had insisted on the reality of

England, and of English words. Now his words are echoed in the curse and made into a reality: he does give his eyes.

The scene also raises questions which can be extended to the novel itself. Who zombifies whom? Is Rhys dependent on Brontë? Or Brontë on the Empire? Does Rhys exploit Brontë? Or can the current of economic exploitation flow only towards England? Rochester believes that Antoinette has attempted to bewitch him by illicit means. Yet he has transformed her into a nameless automaton, entirely under his control. How actual is zombification? Is it merely a suggestive image, to be read in metaphoric terms? Western readers tend to recoil from any other reading: after all, unlike European ghosts, zombies are not 'real' to the Eurocentric reader, though they may be to African or Caribbean readers. Who controls the reality of the story, the imperial master narrative or the West Indian folk myth? Which woman is 'real' and which a ghost? If the reader has read *Jane Eyre* there is a ghost haunting *Wide Sargasso Sea*. If we read *Wide Sargasso Sea* first, it will 'possess' and control any subsequent reading of *Jane Eyre*.

It is in the light of these concerns that the final part of the novel makes sense. The ending of *Wide Sargasso Sea*, the burning of Thornfield Hall, has aroused considerable critical debate. For some readers, the idea that Antoinette is tied to a destiny created by Charlotte Brontë makes the whole novel an exercise in cultural determinism. Antoinette may have been revised from malevolent vampire to innocent victim, but she is a passive victim just the same. It is worth noting, however, that Rhys ends her novel before Antoinette's death. As readers, we may choose to 'finish her off' in Brontë's terms – or not. We know that her death lies just beyond the ending, but we are at liberty to ignore that knowledge; our imaginations are not the slaves of Charlotte Brontë. After all, Rhys was perfectly free to rewrite *Jane Eyre* in any way she pleased, as a more recent rewriting suggests. Robbie Kidd's *The Quiet Stranger* (1991) centres on black revolutionary women, with Jane Eyre as a witch and adventuress.[38]

In her dreams Antoinette sees herself fleeing to the battlements, and looking down to see **not** the stones of the yard, but the pool at Coulibri, her childhood home, which was burned by ex-slaves. In the pool she sees not her own reflection but the face of her black friend Tia, beckoning: 'I called "Tia" and jumped and woke' (p. 155). On the simplest level, therefore, Antoinette's final action aligns her with a female and West Indian world and with a revolt against slavery. The 'suicidal' quality of the ending, potentially masochistic in European terms, is quite altered from the perspective of West Indian culture. In the first place the ending represents an awakening from a state of zombiehood. When last seen in Dominica, Antoinette had become 'only a ghost. A ghost in the grey twilight' (p. 148). Now, however, the text moves back to Antoinette's voice. The italics of quotation are reserved for Grace Poole. Antoinette's memory is also returning, thanks to illicit swigs of Grace Poole's alcohol, after which she feels that 'I could remember more, and think again. I was not so cold' (p. 147). The process of recall is assisted by a visit from Richard Mason, whom she bites. In blood and fire Antoinette finds the antidote to her benumbed state. Up to this point **she** has been identified as the ghost of Thornfield. In her dream, however, the ghost is a separate entity.

> It seemed to me that someone was following me. Someone was chasing me, laughing. Sometimes I looked to the right or to the left but I never looked behind me for I did not want to see that ghost of a woman whom they say haunts this place (p. 153).

It is almost as if Jane Eyre were speaking, not the madwoman. Finally Antoinette encounters the 'ghost': 'It was then that I saw her – the ghost. The woman with streaming hair. She was surrounded by a gilt frame, but I knew her' (p. 154). The reader has two possibilities here. Either the frame is that of a mirror and the ghost is Antoinette, now so lacking in substance as to be unreal, ghostly. Or it may be the frame of a picture. In Brontë's novel, Jane Eyre paints a picture of a woman with streaming hair (*Jane Eyre*, p. 147). In short, is this a mirror echoing Antoinette, or is it an independent, though familiar, work of art? The same duplicity reigns over the ending as a whole. It is a dream but a dream of a familiar book. It gives the reader precisely the feeling experienced by the victim of colonialism of real life being enclosed inside somebody else's fiction. At the close, however, it is *Jane Eyre* which has become the dream, from which Rhys's heroine can wake up and move forward into the future. The ending also revises the 'hellish' overtones of the West Indies. When Antoinette stands on the battlements she experiences a flood of memories as she looks at the sky: 'It was red and all my life was in it. I saw the grandfather clock and Aunt Cora's patchwork, all colours. I saw the orchids and the stephanotis and the tree of life in flames' (p. 155). The final reference is to pre-Columbian myth.[39] The Arawak people, predecessors of the Caribs in Dominica, have a myth of the tree of the world, which reaches to heaven across the ages, a tree of life, bearing food and sustenance. In time of war, when the Arawaks took refuge in its branches, the tree was fired by the Caribs. The fire drove the Arawaks up and up into space, until they burned and were converted into sparks which flew up into heaven to become the stars. At the end of the novel Antoinette tells us that 'The wind caught my hair and it streamed out like wings. It might bear me up, I thought' (p. 155). Imagistically then, Antoinette's dream-death is both a retaliation and a reentry into a lost paradise, a lost West Indian point of origin. In Christian myth fire and hellfire go together. Antoinette, however, takes flight into the heaven of a different culture.

# Notes

1 John Hearne, 'The Wide Sargasso Sea: A West Indian Reflection', *Cornhill Magazine* 180 (1974), p. 323.
2 Adrienne Rich, *On Lies, Secrets and Silence* (New York, W. W. Norton, 1979), p. 35.
3 Quoted by Hannah Carter, 'Fated to be Sad', *The Guardian*, 8 August 1968, p. 5.
4 Joyce Carol Oates, 'Romance and Anti-Romance: From Brontë's *Jane Eyre* to Rhys's *Wide Sargasso Sea*', *Virginia Quarterly Review* 61, 1 (1985), pp. 44–58.
5 Charlotte Brontë, *Jane Eyre* (Oxford University Press, 1963), p. 340. Subsequent references follow citations in parentheses.
6 Penny Boumelha, 'Jane Eyre, Jamaica and the Gentleman's House', *Southern Review*, 21, 2 (July 1988), pp.111–22.
7 Boumelha, 'Jane Eyre, Jamaica and the Gentleman's House', p. 112.
8 Mona Fayad, 'Unquiet Ghosts: The Struggle for Representation in Rhys's *Wide Sargasso Sea*', *Modern Fiction Studies* 34, 3 (1988), pp. 437–52.
9 Elizabeth R. Baer, 'The Sisterhood of Jane Eyre and Antoinette Cosway', in Elizabeth Abel, Marianne Hirsch and Elizabeth Langland, eds., *The Voyage In: Fictions of Female Development* (Hanover and London, University Press of New England, 1983), pp. 131–49.
10 Ronnie Scharfman, 'Mirrors and Mothering in Simone Schwarz-Bart's *Pluie et Vent sur Telumée Miracle* and Jean Rhys's *Wide Sargasso Sea*', *Yale French Studies* 62 (1981), pp. 88–106.
11 Scharfman, 'Mirrors and Mothering'.
12 Baer, 'The Sisterhood of Jane Eyre and Antoinette Cosway', p. 132.
13 Helen Tiffin, 'Mirror and Mask: Colonial Motifs in the Novels of Jean Rhys', *World Literature Written in English*, 17, 1 (1978), pp. 328–41.
14 Arnold E. Davidson, *Jean Rhys* (New York, Frederick Ungar, 1985).
15 Davidson, *Jean Rhys*.
16 Jean Rhys, *Wide Sargasso Sea* (London, Penguin, 1968), p. 136. First published by André Deutsch, 1966. Subsequent references follow citations in parentheses.
17 Davidson, *Jean Rhys*.
18 As these bristling footnotes indicate, there has been a wealth of work on Rhys in the last ten years, with a distinct emphasis on feminist and postcolonial readings. See, for example, Molly Hite, *The Other Side of the Story* (Ithaca, Cornell University Press, 1989); Deborah Kelly Kloepfer, *The Unspeakable Mother: Forbidden Discourse in Jean Rhys and H. D.* (Ithaca, Cornell University Press, 1989); Nancy R. Harrison, *Jean Rhys and the Novel as Woman's Text* (Chapel Hill, University of North Carolina, 1988); Lee Erwin, 'Like A Looking Glass – History and Narrative in *Wide Sargasso Sea*', *Novel* (1989), pp. 143–57; Judith Kegan Gardner, *Rhys, Stead, Lessing and the Politics of Empathy* ( Bloomington, Indiana University Press, 1989); Paula Le Gallez, *The Rhys Woman* (London, Macmillan, 1990); Gayatri Chakravorty Spivak, 'Three Women's Texts and a Critique of Imperialism', *Critical Inquiry* 12 (1985), pp. 243–61.
19 Wade Davis, *The Ethnobiology of the Haitian Zombie* (Chapel Hill, University of North Carolina Press, 1988), p. 31.
20 Among those who have commented on the role of obeah in the works of Jean Rhys, Thomas Loe, 'Patterns of the Zombie in Jean Rhys's *Wide Sargasso Sea*',

*World Literature Written in English* 31, 1 (1991) , pp. 34–42, concentrates on the zombie as a significant allusive base and central metaphor energising and unifying the text, and relates it to West Indian belief systems and social control mechanisms. See also Anthony E. Luengo, '*Wide Sargasso Sea* and the Gothic Mode', *World Literature Written in English* 15, 1 (1976), pp. 229–45; Elaine Campbell, 'Reflections of Obeah in Jean Rhys's Fiction', *Kunapipi* IV, 2 (1982), pp. 42–50; Françoise Defromont, 'Mémoires Hantées: De *Jane Eyre* à *Wide Sargasso Sea*', *Cahiers Victoriens et Edouardiens* 27 (1988), pp. 149–57; Mona Fayad, 'The Struggle for Representation in Rhys's *Wide Sargasso Sea*', *Modern Fiction Studies* 34, 3 (Autumn 1988), pp. 437–52. Perhaps because of the concern with establishing Rhys's authenticity as a West Indian writer, the influence of film, and of Rhys's own experience of being presumed dead, do not form part of their arguments.

21 See Wade Davis, *The Ethnobiology of the Haitian Zombie*, and C. H. Dewisme, *Les Zombis ou le secret des Morts-Vivants* (Paris, Grasset, 1957).

22 Quoted in Gene Wright, *Horror-Shows: The A- To Z- of Horror in Film, TV, Radio and Theatre* (London, David and Charles, 1986), p. 227.

23 Pierre Corneille Blessebois, *Le Zombi du Grand Pérou* (Paris, Editions Civilisations Nouvelles, 1970). See Jack Corzani, 'West Indian Mythology and its Literary Illustrations', *Research in African Literatures* 25 (1994), pp. 131–9.

24 See Ellen Draper, 'Zombie Women When the Gaze is Male', *Wide Angle* 10, 3 (1988), pp. 52–62 (discussing early zombie films as exploring the camera's domination of women); Alan Frank, *The Horror Film Handbook* (London, Batsford, 1982); Barry Keith Grant, ed., *Planks of Reason: Essays on the Horror Film* (London and Metuchen, Scarecrow Press, 1984); Peter Haining, ed., *Stories of the Walking Dead* (London, Severn House, 1986).

25 Leslie Halliwell, *The Dead That Walk* (London, Paladin, 1988).

26 Carole Angier, *Jean Rhys* (London, Penguin, 1992), p. 471.

27 Angier, *Jean Rhys*, p. 449.

28 Angier, *Jean Rhys*, p. 450.

29 Angier, *Jean Rhys*, p. 451.

30 'Temps Perdi', in Jean Rhys, *Tales of the Wide Caribbean* (London, Heinemann, 1985), p. 145.

31 Helen Tiffin, 'Transformative Imageries', in Anna Rutherford, ed., *From Commonwealth to Post-Colonial* (Sydney, Dangaroo Press, 1992), p. 434.

32 Letter of 5 October 1957 to Selma Vaz Dias. This letter is cited with the permission of Francis Wyndham, executor of the Jean Rhys estate, and the McFarlin Library, University of Tulsa, which owns the letter. It is quoted by David Leon Higdon, *Shadows of the Past in Contemporary British Fiction* (London, Macmillan, 1984), pp. 104–5. Higdon notes that the letter is difficult to transcribe. Nobody has been able to identify *The Little Girl From Dominica*.

33 Veronica Gregg, 'Ideology and Autobiography in the Jean Rhys Oeuvre', in Rutherford, *From Commonwealth to Post-Colonial*, p. 415. Peter Hulme argues that Jean Rhys adapts the chronology to fit her own family history (the Lockharts). See Peter Hulme 'The Locked Heart: the Creole Family Romance of *Wide Sargasso Sea*', in Francis Barker, Peter Hulme and Margaret Iverson, eds., *Colonial Discourse/Postcolonial Theory* (Manchester University Press, 1994), pp. 72–88.

34 Coral Ann Howells, *Jean Rhys* (London, Harvester, 1992), p. 114, discusses the relationship between *Jane Eyre* and *Wide Sargasso Sea* as a Gothic one.

35 Freud defines the uncanny as that class of the frightening which leads back to what is known of old and long familiar. 'The Uncanny', in James Strachey,

ed., *The Standard Edition of the Complete Psychological Works of Sigmund Freud* (London, Hogarth Press, 1955) XVII.

36 Mary Lou Emery, *Jean Rhys at 'World's End': Novels of Colonial and Sexual Exile* (Austin, University of Texas Press, 1990), Chapter Three.

37 Todd K. Bender, 'Jean Rhys and the Genius of Impressionism', *Studies in the Literary Imagination* 11, 2 (1978), pp. 43–55.

38 Robbie Kidd, *The Quiet Stranger* (Edinburgh, Mainstream, 1991).

39 Wilson Harris, 'Carnival of Psyche: Jean Rhys's *Wide Sargasso Sea*', *Kunapipi* II, 2 (1980), pp. 142–50.

# 3

## Retrofitting the Raj

### Ruth Prawer Jhabvala, Heat and Dust

In August 1987 when Ralph Lauren opened a new Polo emporium on Rodeo Drive in Los Angeles, second in size only to his Madison Avenue flagship, the *Los Angeles Times* reported intense speculation in the design community: 'How would Polo's aristocratic appeal be translated into a fantasy with which Rodeo Drive shoppers would identify?'[1] Perhaps unsurprisingly, given the enduring rage for the Raj, Lauren chose a 'British Colonial' design concept on the basis of its appeal to nostalgia. As his franchise-holder responded: 'Why the colonies? I think the atmosphere lends itself to the design of Ralph's clothes. I think people today like tradition in a world where relationships seem to be more casual and shallow.'[2] Like so many latter-day white hunters, the design team promptly embarked on an antique-hunting safari, shipping back some 3,000 props to be 'retrofitted'[3] – converted into merchandise-display features. The new store exemplifies two disturbing features of the recent treatment of Empire: its commodification as a marketable entity, based on nostalgia for a past never-never land (as in the success of the films of *Passage to India, Out of Africa* and *The Far Pavilions)* and its identification with homogenised, patriarchal values. (The Polo store set out to evoke the atmosphere of 'a British men's club in . . . the colonies of the British West Indies, India and Africa'.)[4] In her successful film partnership with Ismail Merchant and James Ivory, Ruth Prawer Jhabvala might well appear to be implicated in the retrofitting process, particularly in relation to *Heat and Dust*, her most successful novel to date, which was subsequently lushly filmed with all the trappings of its setting in the 1920s in an Indian princely state.

It would, however, be surprising, to say the least, if Jhabvala acceded to the rewriting of the history of Empire in any way which obscured its horrors. In fact, her fiction reveals a keen sensitivity to a past traumatic history. As a German-Jewish Holocaust survivor who reached Britain in 1939 (minus forty family members who perished), moved to a newly partitioned India on her marriage (1951) and thence to America (1975), she has tended in her writing to emphasise themes of loss, disinheritance, exile, alienation and the fragmentation of identity in the flux of history. Jhabvala has described her childhood in terms which suggest an experience of such profound trauma that it remains almost entirely blocked from consciousness. She has spoken of it publicly only once:

> I don't feel like talking much about 1933 and after. Everyone knows what happened to German Jews first and other European Jews after. Our family was no exception .... I have slurred over the years 1933 to 1939, from when I was six to twelve. They should have been my most formative years; maybe they were, I don't know .... I've never written about those years. To tell you the truth, until today I've never even mentioned them. Never spoken about them to anyone.[5]

Jhabvala's response to a literally unspeakable history supports recent theorisations of the phenomenon of trauma as denying our usual modes of access to it. Cathy Caruth has argued that:

> Trauma . . . does not simply serve as record of the past but precisely registers the force of an experience that is not yet fully owned.

> The trauma is the confrontation with an event that, in its unexpectedness or horror, cannot be placed within the schemes of prior knowledge.[6]

It is just such a paradoxical relation between the pervasiveness – and yet the absence – of the past which characterises much of Jhabvala's work. In her early writing the past is everywhere evident. As a student at London University her MA thesis took as its subject 'The Short-Story in England, 1700–1750', and her work has consistently reflected the influence of eighteenth-century writing. Essentially comedies of manners, these early Indian-centred works enclose dramas of courtship and marriage, Austen-fashion, within carefully balanced narrative structures, with the opposition of tradition to modernity a constant theme.[7] Despite the Austenian sense of enclosure, a historical dimension is indicated. *To Whom She Will* draws its title from the Vedic epic, the *Panchatantra,* and concerns itself with Punjabi survivors of partition, and with the ambivalent response to Westernisation in independent India (a theme also prominent in *The Nature of Passion*). *Esmond in India* introduces the topic of the European eroticisation of the relationship to India, in the shape of the eponymous hero and his disenchantment with both India and his Indian wife. In a parallel treatment, *The Householder* examines a young man's slow habituation to the role of 'householder', the second stage of the orthodox Hindu four-stage life pattern. With *Get Ready for Battle*, the pendulum swings once more towards a harsher and more combative satire, exposing the widening gap between rich and poor, and the corruption of Indian society. The last of Jhabvala's novels to focus on the extended Indian family, it is also the last to draw its title from an Indian literary source (the *Mahabharata*).

From this point onwards, Jhabvala's titles have an ironically 'colonial' ring, with the focus shifting to Europeans in India, and to a reversed process of cultural domination, in which Indians (particularly questionable gurus) prey upon Westerners. Themes of cultural confrontation, initiated in *A Backward Place*, move to centre stage. At the same time, after the balanced Augustan defensive structures of the first phase, the nightmares bred of the sleep of reason begin to take hold. Laurie Sucher, one of Jhabvala's most percipient critics, has identified a strong Gothic strain running through the later works (see Chapter 5).[8] Jhabvala's techniques of understatement and telling omission combine in narratives which fragment and embed themselves in intricate webs of deception. Frequently a barrier of some sort exists between teller and tale. In *A New Dominion*, rational 'objective' Raymond is ironised as a neo-Forsterian spokesman, out of touch with both contemporary India and his own blocked emotions. The grand sweep of the novel, indicated in its tripartite structure (Delhi, Benares, Maupur), contrasts with the fragmented narrative, emanating from a variety of viewpoints, each providing a short scene or episode with a *faux naif* heading. These vignettes present Europeans as trapped within Augustan illusions of reason and objectivity, while below the cool surface story lies a buried melodrama (memorably in the example of Lee, who invites herself to stay with an Indian family and cheerfully settles down to eat, unaware that the commotion all around her concerns the rush to cremate the victim of a 'dowry death' in order to destroy the evidence of poisoning).

Jhabvala establishes a similar counterpoint of reason and passion in *Heat and Dust*, which reworks Forster's *The Hill of Devi* in the light of postcolonial hindsight.[9] The stories of Olivia and her Nawab (in 1923) and of the narrator who retraces her steps fifty years later, are spliced (in Jhabvala's filmic metaphor) in order to juxtapose imperial and independent Indias, past and present, and to assess their relative merits. Scenic intercutting is accompanied by interpolated narratives, forming a veritable anthology of different Western textualisations of India – as horror story, epic or romance. Sharp scene-cutting against a sweeping historical backcloth is also a feature of *In Search of Love and Beauty*, in which the guru reappears amidst a group of German-Jewish refugees in New York, whose friendships are charted over three generations from the 1930s on. An Augustan mock-epic quality (with characters playfully based on Greek deities) contrasts with the awareness that surface comedy conceals a deeper tragedy.

The experiences of India, Europe and America combine in *Three*

*Continents*, a deeply disquieting tale which offers a subtle dramatisation of the psychopathology of power and the vulnerability of the rational. Here, the corrupt Sixth World Movement, with its militaristic drills, parades, lobotomised fealty to a leader and air of insane righteousness, clearly looks back to the Third Reich. Myth is once more mystification. Crishi, the charismatic villain, is modelled less on Krishna than on a contemporary Asian mass-murderer, and finds an exceptionally naive victim in an American heiress, whom he despoils of both honour and fortune. Both *In Search of Love and Beauty* and *Three Continents* received a mixed reception, with reviewers commenting on Jhabvala's chilly authorial detachment, the elements of masochism, and the conjunction of phallic anti-heroes with passive, drifting heroines. Her most recent novel, *Poet and Dancer*, returns again to a group of German refugees in New York, and concentrates upon the Sapphic relationship between two of their children, Lara, a failed dancer, and Angel, a would-be poet. The narrator, a writer, has been approached to write Angel's life story by her mother, who is desperate to fill 'this silence, this blank, where her daughter had once been' (p. 6).[10] Lara, the victim of a damaged childhood, has carried Angel with her into a joint suicide pact. Earlier Angel had underscored a favourite quotation in a medieval text: 'And this, truly is what a perfect lover must always do, utterly and entirely despoiling himself of himself for the sake of the thing he loves, and that not only for a time, but everlastingly' (p. 6). The example of Lara and Angel suggests that where creative expression is baulked, Jhabvala's heroines become self-punishing, self-silencing, surrendering to autodestructive urges. Trauma, exile and the long reach of the past come together in the reproduction of violence.

Where Western reviewers tended to concentrate upon the psychology of Jhabvala's protagonists, in India the ambivalence of her vision of India has ensured that she has rarely received the serious critical attention which she deserves. When the Booker Prize was awarded to *Heat and Dust* in 1975, reaction in India was immediately hostile. For many Indians the novel represented an attempt to ridicule India, abetted by the stamp of British approval offered by the prize. Whereas British reviewers tended to see the intercultural encounter in the novel as of secondary interest,

> Indian reviewers dwelt on the India of *Heat and Dust*, on the character of the Indian Nawab or Prince who has an affair with the wife of a British Civil Servant stationed in his town, and on the explicit and implicit commentary on Indian mores as well as the Indian setting. For them, there could be no separation between these and the quality of the novel, its authenticity, its literary substance.[11]

In general, the Indian literary reaction was based upon mimetic, representational criteria, which it refused to sunder from the formal merits of the novel. In 1988 Upamanyu Chatterjee satirised the nature of the reaction in *English, August: An Indian Story.*[12] In the novel, Menon, the subdivisional magistrate of Rameri, offers the hero a copy of *Heat and Dust,* borrowed from the Collectorate library under the mistaken impression that 'it was about an Assistant Collector's life in the British days. But it's not really about that' (p. 39). None the less, Menon has annotated the volume in red ballpoint, in order to correct what he sees as historical misrepresentations – examples, though he does not know the term, of 'retrofitting'. 'Not necessary these days to wear solar topee. Relic of the Raj' (p. 39) is one such emendation. Later in the novel, in an artful allusion to Jhabvala's modern narrator's researches into the events of 1923, an Englishman, John Avery, visits the town in order to view the memorial to his grandfather, a former Collector and district magistrate, who came to a sticky end following an attack by a tiger, also in 1923. John's girlfriend actually appears in a solar topee, to the hero's amusement. 'Just in case the heat and dust get too much?' he queries (p. 196). Like the narrator of *Heat and Dust,* John Avery has read his grandfather's letters and has been struck by their apparent timelessness:

> there is no sense of a living place. In fact all that detail somehow further deadens it. There was apparently a big clock in the dining room, and most of his letters would begin, "It has just struck four and Baldev has brought in my tea," "It is now seven thirty and Natwar, the one who can never get my boots right, is at the door asking about dinner." Everything is static, as though Richard Avery would always remain here in Madna . . . . As though nothing would ever change (p. 212).

John recognises in the static repetitions of the letters the potential for creating, and recreating, a frozen, ahistorical image of India, as if the Gorgon breath of the Raj had petrified everything in its path. Chatterjee's hero, Agastya Sen, has already had to face the same problem. On arrival in Madna he is greeted with the ringing declaration that 'This is India, bhai, an independent country, and not the Raj' (p. 23) only to be immediately offered videos of *A Passage to India* and *The Jewel in the Crown.*

Is Jhabvala then, as Chatterjee's characters suggest, complicit in the retrofitting of the Raj? Or is her historical material overtly **designed** to historicise, to abolish the image of India as timeless Orient and to restore a vital awareness of the traumas of the past? Two novels offer particularly acute examples of test cases; *Three Continents* (see Chapter 5) and *Heat and Dust,* each of which engages with one of the major colonial scare stories of India, 'thuggee' and 'suttee', respectively.

*Heat and Dust* [13] presents two stories: that of Olivia and her Nawab, set more or less contemporaneously with *Passage to India* in 1923; and that of the narrator who retraces Olivia's steps fifty years later and to some extent reenacts her story. Olivia's story has been silenced, declared a 'forbidden topic' (p. 2) by her own generation, and is rediscovered by the narrator through letters, which extend into *belles lettres* – literature, as the narrator repeats Olivia's story in her own words.

Behind these two stories there lurks a third. Richard Cronin has demonstrated the presence of a specific set of revisionings in *Heat and Dust* which act to repoliticise E. M. Forster's liberal humanist creed of the primacy of personal relations over divisive political ideologies.[14] As Cronin points out, Forster visited India in 1921, to spend six months as private secretary to the Maharajah of Dewas. He was particularly keen to experience the hot season (the heat and dust) since he intended the three sections of *Passage to India* (Mosque, Caves, Temple) to represent the three Indian seasons (cold weather, hot weather, rains). The central section, an account of a period of emotional and sexual confusion, was therefore designed to coincide with the heat. Forster later published an account of his days in the princely state in *The Hill of Devi* (1953). Harry, in *Heat and Dust*, is a thinly disguised Forster – an English homosexual who loathes the British in India and idealises the Indian princely state as the antithesis of the imperial world, a place where personal relationships are all, and friendship transcends politics. In the 1983 edition of *The Hill of Devi*, however, it was revealed that Forster had edited the letters which form the basis of his account, in order to conceal his own 'untold story', a sexual relationship with a boy, whose services were procured and paid for by the Maharajah, and who then boasted publicly of going to bed with Forster. Cronin is surely right to suggest that the Maharajah tempted his secretary into an open display of homosexual behaviour in order both to control Forster and to humiliate the British.

Jhabvala sets up a precisely parallel situation in Khatm, where Harry is similarly prized by the Nawab as 'a very improper Englishman' (p. 43):

> a living exemplar of all the possibilities of Englishness that the British in India would rather deny existed. His patronage of Harry is a delicate racial affront. Racial hatred is the motive of much of his behaviour.[15]

Jhabvala's new twist on the old tale is to introduce Olivia as a second victim of the Nawab's revenge. While Harry is aware of the Nawab's darker side (displayed annually in a murderous religious riot), Olivia remains in a state of naivety which rebounds upon her. Where the British administrators use the term 'our friend' as an ironic title for the Nawab, Olivia takes it at face value. She rejects the possibility that the Nawab orchestrates the riot, in highly Forsterian terms: 'she felt it was **she** who knew the Nawab, not they. To them he was just a person they had to deal with officially, an Indian ruler, but to her he was – yes, a friend' (p. 70). Despite mounting evidence of the Nawab's dacoities, extortion and political machinations, Olivia persists in reading the situation in personal terms: 'People can still be friends, can't they, even if it is India' (p. 103). The setting for her response is doubly ironic – Harry's room, hung with Indian miniatures depicting erotic pleasures. Outside lies the town, 'a miserable stretch of broken roofs, and beyond that the barren land: but why look that far?' (p. 103). Quite overtly, Jhabvala frames Olivia's creed of friendship in such a way as to emphasise the riches of the princes, the poverty of their subjects and her own almost wilful blindness. Olivia is happy to remain in an eroticised miniature world which excludes wider political perspectives. Importantly the miniatures have already been presented to the reader by the modern narrator, on a visit to Karim and Kitty, the Nawab's heirs, in London, where they feature as an emblem of the ways in which art can serve to replicate an illusory image. The narrator notes that the miniatures portray the palace at Khatm quite differently from its run-down modern appearance, perhaps because of 'the stylisation of the artist' (p. 99), perhaps because 'Everything was jewelled.' The human beings portrayed, however, seem quite unchanged. 'The princes looked like Karim, the princesses like Kitty' (p. 99). Although Karim and Kitty descend from the subjects of the paintings, the grammar establishes the resemblance in atemporal terms, almost as if ancestors could 'take after' descendants.

This anachronistic suggestion is extended in the denouement of Olivia's story. Eventually her affair with the Nawab culminates in a messy abortion, discovery and flight. Ironically Olivia is seduced in Baba Firdaus Grove, where once a year on Husband's Wedding Day the shrine is sacred to Hindus who seek cures for childlessness there, thus occasioning Hindu–Moslem riots. Olivia's refusal to believe that the Nawab has anything to do with the communal killings, a precondition of her seduction, ultimately leads her to the house of the abortionist, which looks out upon a similar scene of destruction brought about on a husband's wedding day. As a noisy wedding procession was in process, at the very moment when the bridegroom rode by, a house had collapsed, showering masonry and people in all directions. Just as the abortionist's assistant who witnessed the scene 'had not realised what was happening though it was happening before her eyes' (p. 166), so Olivia's blindness to the Nawab's activities has brought her full circle.

To the British, Olivia has simply been destroyed by a scheming Indian: 'No one ever doubted that the Nawab had used Olivia as a means of revenge' (p. 170). The seduction scene itself appears to substantiate the Nawab's duplicity. Immediately beforehand, the Nawab glorifies friendship as a transcendent virtue: our friends on earth are those we sat close to in Paradise. Within the grove, however, a band of dacoits are waiting, also 'friends', with whom the Nawab collaborates in extortion. He comments that 'I suppose you think they are bad men. You must have heard many stories' (p. 133) and counters with a story of his own, that of Amanullah Khan, his ancestor, who lived for booty just like the dacoits. For the Nawab,

Amanullah Khan is an object of envy, ostensibly because he was able to fight his enemies openly, via direct challenge rather than plots and intrigue. He descr:ʹ.s how Amanullah Khan, under pretence of friendship, entertained his enemy to a feast, only to trap him in his tent and stab him to death. It is hardly a heroic image of direct and open challenge, and a distinctly odd prelude to seduction. The suspicion lingers that the Nawab seduces Olivia partly to shut her mouth, to prevent her carrying tales to the British. Rather than emphasising passion or love, the seduction is set in a context which suggests that the Nawab is operating in pursuit of revenge, under cover of affection. Olivia's story therefore revises the personal, liberal views of Forster, to insist on the political consequences of imperial domination, and to make the point that a relation of dominance cannot be converted into an image of friendship or love. It must be destructive. In India, Olivia learns to her cost that the personal is the political.

The Nawab's story ends with a description of Khan's tent, on which the bloodstains are still fresh 'as if it had happened yesterday' (p. 137). The image points to the inherent awkwardness of intertextual revisioning. Repoliticisation may amount to demonisation; the overhaul of Forsterian liberalism may turn the clock back, to horror stories of Indian barbarism, rather than forward, to confront the full implications of imperialism. Olivia is last seen through the eyes of Harry, as she arrives, pale, dishevelled and in native dress, at the Nawab's palace:

> she reminded him of a print he had seen called *Mrs Secombe in Flight from the Mutineers*. Mrs Secombe was also in native dress and in a state of great agitation, with her hair awry and smears of dirt on her face: naturally, since she was flying for her life from the mutineers at Sikrora to the safety of the British Residency at Lucknow. Olivia was also in flight – but, as Harry pointed out, in the opposite direction (p. 172).

Superficially, therefore, the novel appears to reinforce the notion that revisionary retellings court anachronism. The counter-discourse, aimed at revising apolitical liberalism, has merely crossed over into an earlier demonic discourse of India, the 'Mutiny' horror story.[16] Mrs Saunders offers an action replay of this stereotypical image of India as sexuality linked to destruction. She is discovered in a room furnished with scenes from the Mutiny, fully dressed despite illness, since she considers that the sight of her gaunt chest may inflame the servants' passions: '"You hear a lot of stories," Mrs Saunders said.' (p. 119). Neither Olivia nor the reader is treated to the full horror story of what happened to the Somerset lady in Muzzafarbad when her servant was ironing her underwear. The story is too predictable to need an ending. Mrs Saunders simply completes it with the phrase, 'they've got only one thought in their heads and that's to you-know-what with a white woman' (p. 119). All the British display a similar tendency to textualise India: Olivia is regaled at various points by 'interminable anecdotes about things that had happened in Kabul or Multan' (p. 15), by Dr Saunders' stock of racist tales (p. 120), by Major Minnies' account of 'a devilish clever Hindu moneylender in Patna' (p. 16), and by a veritable anthology of anecdotes about suttee.

In *Heat and Dust*, as the setting Satipur (the place of sati) indicates, a central thematic element is sati (Western 'suttee').[17] Two key scenes are particularly important: the discussion of a recent case of sati in 1923, and in the 1970s the death of an elderly widow at the sati memorial stones. In introducing the topic of sati, Jhabvala could hardly expose herself more completely to the accusation of retrofitting. David Rubin, for one, has read Jhabvala as repropagating a demonic view of India, in the footsteps of earlier writers: 'Jhabvala, far from being the "Indian" novelist she is generally held to be, in fact continues the traditions of the colonial British novelists of the half-century preceding Indian independence.'[18] In the earlier period, as Patrick Brantlinger has amply demonstrated, nineteenth-century Utilitarian and Evangelical attacks on Hinduism tended to emphasise sati as an example of the Hindu 'abominations' from which the kindly imperialists were bent on saving the Indian masses.[19] Southey's 'The Curse of Kehama' (1810), for example, includes a tirade against sati. India was seen as locked into patterns of immemorial violence, as a kind of horror story without a history. Oddly, however, not every British writer took quite such a critical view. In 'The Death of Oenone', Tennyson allows Oenone to fling herself upon her husband's pyre, in an act which is seen as expiating her past misdeeds.

> The morning light of happy marriage broke
> Thro' all the clouded years of widowhood,
> And muffling up her comely head, and crying
> 'Husband!' she leapt upon the funeral pile,
> And mixt herself with him and past in fire.[20]

The West was, of course, always ready to appropriate an Indian practice to the Western discourse of romantic love, especially when it allowed the body of woman to be simultaneously transcended, and killed off. Romantic and sentimental codes cross-fertilised here, in the ideas that a romantic lover could have no existence without the beloved, and that the wife should sacrifice herself for her husband. L. E. L. (Letitia Elizabeth Landon) actually appears to endorse the process in 'A Suttee' which ends:

> The red pile blazes – let the bride ascend,
> And lay her head upon her husband's heart,
> Now in a perfect unison to blend.[21]

Clearly sati could serve patriarchal norms as much among imperialists as imperialised.

Indeed sati has become a key concern in modern debates about the relation between feminism and postcolonialism, the construction of the female subject, and the weight to be given to the past as legitimating practice.[22] In *Heat and Dust* all the different discourses on sati circulate, in one key scene, set at a dinner party in 1923. Discussions of sati have tended to focus upon the degree of female autonomy involved, with apologists portraying the sati as unusual, heroic and voluntaristic. Reformers, on the other hand, advance evidence of coercion (drugs, physical violence, family pressure, pyres designed to tip the widow into the flames or to collapse upon her). In Jhabvala's novel the discussion initially moves between the two poles of the sati as victim or as heroine, both of which preclude the possibility of complex female subjectivity.[23] The 1923 sati is presented as involuntary:

> A grain merchant had died and his widow had been forced by her relatives to burn herself with him on his funeral pyre. Although Douglas [Olivia's husband] had rushed to the scene the moment information had reached him, he had arrived too late to save the woman (p. 55).

This description conforms entirely to the stereotypical British view of sati, memorably characterised by Gayatri Chakravorty Spivak as white men saving brown women from brown men: 'Imperialism's image as the establisher of the good society is marked by the espousal of the woman as object of protection from her own kind.'[24] The 'women's issue' gave the British a justification for their own interference in India, though in most other respects they were hardly motivated by liberatory intentions. As a result sati quickly became a focus for Indian resistance. In the novel, Douglas's action leads to unrest, as the arrested relatives are immediately turned into martyrs (p. 57). Olivia, however, sympathises with the Indian view: 'It's part of their religion, isn't it? I thought one wasn't supposed to meddle with that' (p. 58). The comment lays bare the problem facing the modern postcolonial feminist, unwilling to condone practices which exemplify the male abuse of women, yet also chary of appearing to criticise another culture from her own Eurocentric position. (Female circumcision is a contemporary case in point.) Sati was vigorously defended in India as sanctioned by the Vedic scriptures and by immemorial tradition. The extreme British imperial position is represented in the novel by the outburst from Dr Saunders in response to Olivia: 'It's savagery . . . plain savagery and barbarism' (p. 59).

In the argument which follows, Olivia has no real desire to recommend widow-burning but is motivated by her antipathy to the condescension and smug self-certainty of her fellows. At the dinnertable the British exchange a whole series of anecdotes about sati, which are 'drawn not so much from personal experience as from a rich store-house of memories that went back several generations' (pp. 57–8). The tales are recounted in a fashion designed to conceal any ideological content, as if the stories 'spoke for themselves'. They are presented

> with no moral comment whatsoever . . . they even had that little smile of tolerance, of affection, even enjoyment that Olivia was beginning to know well: like good parents they all loved India whatever mischief she might be up to (p. 58).

As that final feminisation implies, an apparent narratorial objectivity conceals a paternalistic project designed to maintain India in a state of infantilised dependence. It also refers out to that hegemonic discourse which Edward Said has characterised as 'Orientalism', in which the West is envisaged as male, the East as passively female, waiting to be rescued from ignorance and fertilised with the seeds of civilisation by Western culture-bearers.[25] Major Minnies restates this particular ideological position, which depends upon the assumption that it is natural for man to dominate woman, later in the novel, when he describes India as requiring the exercise of 'a virile, measured, European feeling' (p. 171). Major Minnies 'loved India so much, knew her so well, chose to spend the end of his days here! But she always remained for him an opponent' (p. 171).

The feminisation of India goes to the heart of the colonial enterprise. The British treat India itself as a sati. On the one hand reformers generally portray the widow as weak, pitiful, frightened and deluded, as fundamentally non-agentive. On the other, as 'The Death of Oenone' reveals, the power of woman as sexual destroyer was implicitly recognised in the practice of sati which clearly responds to a vision of woman as a danger once no longer under male control. The East was thus **either** a foolish woman who needed to be saved from herself **or** a sexual temptress who should be controlled and resisted at all costs. Appropriately, as the discussion develops, it is Major Minnies who provides a less vulnerable image of the sati, as strong-willed and voluntaristic, with a story of a sati in 1829, as originally told by W. H. Sleeman in 1844. Although both Sleeman and the woman's relatives had attempted to dissuade her, she had persisted over several days in her intention to burn herself, declaring that if prevented she would simply starve herself to death. 'She wasn't a fanatic . . . There was something noble there,' says the Major (p. 60). Olivia's response to sati is similarly romantic. While flashing ardent glances at Douglas, she declares her own desire to accompany the beloved in death. (Olivia is conveniently unaware of the number of satis, victims of arranged child marriages, who saw their husbands for the first time on their mutual pyre.)

Up to this point Jhabvala appears to be keeping the arguments for and against sati evenly balanced. Importantly, however, one issue has been omitted from the public discourse: trauma. Rajeswari Sunder Rajan has commented that the rejection of the colonial discourse of sati as a women's issue, to embrace instead an earlier reading of it as an index of conjugal love and female heroism can be fraught with dangerously regressive tendencies.[26] Rajan thus displaces the traditional construction of the sati in terms of one who chooses or is forced to die, first on to questions of the embodied subject (the subject of pain) and then on to the representation of the widow who chooses to live. In an enormously important thesis, Rajan therefore shifts the issue from sati-as-death to sati-as-burning. Defenders of sati deny the woman's pain since sati depends upon the idea of the triumph of spirit over flesh. (Apologists do not argue that the sati embraces pain but that she knows no pain.) Even Sleeman (in a passage carefully not included by Jhabvala in her account) describes the widow as 'consumed without uttering a shriek or betraying one sign of agony'.[27] Indeed, the woman's body is curiously absent from all the debates on sati. Lata Mani comments that 'Even Rammohun, commonly regarded as the first modern champion of women's rights, did not base his support for abolition on the ground that sati was cruel to women.'[28] And yet the pain is apparently recognised in the custom. Thompson notes that because it is considered a bad omen to hear the groans of the sati, the crowd usually yell, sound horns and beat drums.[29]

In anticipation of Rajan's thesis, Jhabvala restores the experience of trauma to history. Douglas has not described the 1923 sati to Olivia,

> wanting to spare her the details (which were indeed very painful –
> he was to hear that woman's screams to the end of his days) (p. 58).

By maintaining the image of the female body in pain, in the foreground of her novel, Jhabvala also constitutes sati as typical, bolstering a whole complex of other practices which victimise women – female infanticide, child marriage and dowry deaths ('kerosene satis'). The modern narrator describes the case of Ritu, an unhappy young wife, whose precarious mental condition deteriorates as the heat of the hot season increases. The narrator comments that 'I can't get used to these screams' (p. 81). The other witness to her mental torment, Chid, a would-be Hindu sadhu, simply increases the volume of his chanting to block them out. Later 'the screams broke out again, but in an entirely different way. Now they were blood-curdling as of an animal in intense physical pain' (p. 81). In an attempt at exorcism by fire, Ritu is being burned by red-hot irons, to drive out evil spirits. The incident constitutes a crypto-sati, with its elements of pain by burning, female victimisation by marriage customs, and the wilful disregard of a religious bystander. Olivia's own bodily suffering is also brought into sharp focus. Although not, of course, a sati, her choice of 'burning' on the plains during the heat and dust of the hot season, in order to remain with the man she loves, is described as an ordeal by fire (p. 90). But the reference is to some degree ironic. Only a faithful wife can become a sati. By this point in the novel Olivia has already transferred her affections to the Nawab.

In the modern plot of the novel the narrator is inclined to view sati as a thing of the past. She notes that all the sati stones look age-old (p. 55), even the 1923 shrine. The death of Leelavati, a widow who had been driven out of her father-in-law's house and had spent her life as a destitute beggar, takes place at the stones and is described in terms which appear to validate the widow-who-survives. Although the description of her death is not sparing of physical details, her attendant comments that 'Leelavati had done well and had been rewarded with a good, a blessed end' (p. 115). Rajan has made the point that historicisation combats the notion of an age-old, platonic sati. Sati may be seen as the result of local practices, and as evolving historically rather than being enjoined by ancient scriptures.[30] Indeed, in 1817 the chief pundit of the Supreme Court argued that a woman burning herself was an unworthy act and a life of abstinence and chastity was preferable. Similarly Lata Mani has argued that the discourse on sati was not a discourse in which preexisting traditions were challenged by an emergent modern consciousness, but one in which both 'tradition' and 'modernity' were contemporaneously produced. The sati was thus emptied of historical resonance, becoming the site on which tradition was debated and reformulated: 'neither subject nor object but ground – such is the status of women in the discourse on sati'.[31]

Importantly, in *Heat and Dust,* the modern narrator spends much of her time with a group of vigorous widows, who range freely about the town, gossiping, joking and clearly having the time of their lives. None the less, a warning note is struck at the sati stones, at which one of the widows makes reverent offerings to those who, in her view, have honoured ancient custom and made the highest sacrifice. 'She even seemed regretful – this merry widow! – that it had been discontinued' (p. 55). Discussing sati in 1978, Stein noted that 'an occasional illegal sati is still reported in the newspapers, and satis of the past are still family and village saints; the places where they burned are considered sacred ground. Otherwise only the thousands of stone memorials and the stony survival of Hindu widowhood remain.'[32] In fact, however, sati is exceptionally, and lamentably, contemporaneous. In 1981 Kumkum Sangari and Sudesh Vaid reported a case of sati (August 1980) and warned that for socioeconomic reasons sati was being actively revived in some areas: 'Unless counter-measures are immediately undertaken at various levels, the incidence of sati in these regions is likely to continue and may even occur with greater frequency.'[33] Writing in 1993, Rajan reveals that there has indeed been a particular increase in sati in the last ten years and describes the case of Roop Kanwar, married only seven months, who died voluntarily on 4 September 1987 on her husband's pyre in Deorala village, two hours journey from

Jaipur, the capital of Rajasthan. Although there were hundreds of witnesses, although sati is, of course, illegal, there was no reaction from the state government until women's groups intervened. Even then, 300,000 people attended the *chunari mahotsav,* the festival marking the thirtieth day after the sati. There were huge pro-sati rallies in Jaipur, and the village of Deorala has developed into a prosperous pilgrim centre. Nobody has yet been convicted of an offence in connection with Roop Kanwar's death, despite the passing of *The Commission of Sati* (Prevention Act, 1987). Almost as disturbing as the act itself is the recent glorification of sati through temples and annual fairs. Rajan points out that all over Rajasthan businessmen have built temples to past satis. In this particular case, the past is being commodified not by Western but by Indian financial interests, as 'the enactment of modern sati derives its features from popular cinema and political meetings rather than hallowed ritual'.[34] One representation of Roop Kanwar's death took the form of a photo-montage, using photographs taken at her wedding. As if actually immolating herself, she smiles out at the camera, apparently oblivious to pain, sitting beside her husband's body in the midst of the flames. Roop Kanwar has, in short, been comprehensively retrofitted, to provide a fantasy for Indians to buy into, a fantasy which excises the pain of woman from the apparently 'historical' record. It is to Jhabvala's credit that nobody who has read *Heat and Dust* could accept such a photograph as genuine. In Jhabvala's writing the point is made that we should never lose sight of trauma – whether it results from European or Indian agency – however difficult or painful it may be to articulate it. Indeed it is precisely this difficulty of conscious articulation which provides a site of resistance to the forces of commodification.

How then is Jhabvala to avoid the alternative dangers of retrofitting, or of repropagating an original demonic discourse? Can she keep the trauma of history alive without commodifying it in a fiction which may itself (as Chatterjee's novel suggested) become coercive? If Olivia's abortion represents the sterility and destructivenmess of imperial rule, under which no love can come to fruition, Jhabvala is careful not to suggest the opposing popular fiction of India as destructive sexual force. Such fictions are recognised as having material consequences. Harry (unwittingly explaining his own fear of being poisoned by the palace food) passes on the tale of a chorus girl, mistress of a former Nawab, who flees the palace after his death, in terror that the Begum will poison her. She is under the spell of 'some tale she had heard' (p. 151) involving poisoned wedding clothes sent to an unwanted bride, the fatal garments having supposedly been prepared by an old woman still resident in Khatm. So afraid is she of a repetition of these past events that she flees in her nightclothes. The imagistic link to Olivia, who flees in the opposite direction in native dress, reinforces the suggestion that fictions may function to coercive effect. No threat was necessary on the Begum's part; the mere existence of the story was enough to put the girl to flight.

Jhabvala's solution is to frame Olivia's story within the tale of her successor in such a way as to lay bare the structure of revisionary processes by focusing upon the role of the reader. Within its double plot structure, the novel moves forward through a succession of interpolated stories, tales and fictions, in a procedure which invites comparison with Wilson Harris's project for a fiction that seeks, through complex rehearsal and repetition, continually to consume its own biases.[35] Most readers have tended to privilege Olivia's story over the narrator's,[36] an emphasis fostered by the narrator: 'India always changes people, and I have been no exception. But this is not my story, it is Olivia's as far as I can follow it' (p. 2). Unfortunately this very nearly turns out to be true. The narrator is in grave danger of being swamped by Olivia's story. In the opening pages of the novel, India is glossed as horror story by an English missionary, veteran of famines, a Hindu–Moslem riot and a smallpox epidemic, who declares that 'Wherever you look it's the same story' (p. 4). 'Paper-white, vaporous', the missionary resembles a ghost, but a 'ghost with backbone' (p. 6), comparable to Olivia, now potentially 'ghosting' the narrator's story.

The narrator is unnamed, but as Douglas Rivers is her paternal grandfather, may be assumed to be 'Miss Rivers'. The lack of a name suggests a weakened identity, and invites comparison with that other unnamed narrator in women's fiction, the heroine of Daphne du Maurier's *Rebecca*, also a plain Englishwoman, transplanted in exotic circumstances, and overshadowed by a more glamorous, artistic predecessor, whose life ended in erotic disaster. *Rebecca* takes its plot from *Jane Eyre*, who narrowly avoided becoming Jane Rivers in a passionless marriage to a missionary, St John Rivers, who was bound for India. In contrast to Olivia, the narrator seems extremely uncertain of her sexual identity. Flat-chested, and so tall that she has to wear men's sandals with her trousers, she is pursued in the streets by urchins, shouting 'hijra' (transvestite). Indeed she is drawn to the spectacle of the hijras dancing (p. 10), enacting a sad parody of womanly gestures and dress. For the narrator, therefore, Olivia offers an idealised 'feminine' *alter ego*: 'She was everything I'm not' (p. 7). Her own lack of sexual confidence appears to explain her extreme passivity to Chid, an English would-be holy man, to whose sexual demands she accedes despite feeling neither respect for his Tantric beliefs, nor any attraction to his body. She admits: 'I have never had such a feeling of being used' (p. 65). Much as the Nawab used Olivia, so Chid uses the narrator, in an explicit image of impersonal sexual exploitation, stripped of its gloss.

The narrator, however, does not seem to have learned from the past. Like the other British she approaches India through framing fictions: 'All those memoirs and letters I've read, all those prints I've seen' (p. 2). She appears to have no other purpose but to follow in Olivia's footsteps, proceeding directly to Satipur, and seeking a repetition of Olivia's amours, substituting the arms of Inder Lal for those of the Nawab. Critics have tended to suggest that Miss Rivers is an unreliable narrator, piecing Olivia's story together from the letters, Harry's memories, and other sources, and inevitably having to fill in the gaps of the story with her own imaginings. But rather than Miss Rivers rewriting Olivia's story to her own ends (as Jhabvala revises Forster's), it is arguable that it is Olivia who very nearly succeeds in scripting the narrator's life for her. The narrator is, at least initially, passive to the discourses which 'write' her.

She is, for example, much more eager to protect Olivia's letters from Chid's pawing than to safeguard her own body. (She locks up the letters, when Chid covers them with dirty fingermarks.) Later Chid himself sends the narrator letters, which she keeps together with Olivia's. The contrast between the sets is instructive. Chid's letters are 'absolutely impersonal' (p. 94), beginning not with a personal salutation but with 'Jai Shiva Shankar!' Their philosophical content makes them eminently suitable for public consumption; the narrator reads them aloud to Inder Lal. Since Chid's spiritual quest has involved a complete renunciation of personal relations, including his name, his own history and all personal attributes, his letters form a living example of the total revision of the Forsterian creed. They do not, however, avoid continuing the demonic image of India; their few factual sentences always report being 'cheated and robbed' (p. 94). In contrast, Olivia's letters are 'intensely personal' (p. 94), written on her own elegant stationery, unlike Chid's 'impersonal post office forms' (p. 94). Unsurprisingly, perhaps, Olivia's letters, fifty years old, look 'as if they had been written yesterday' (p. 95), whereas Chid's appear to have been travelling long distances, absorbing smells and stains along the way. The two sets of letters visibly contrast the hothouse anachronism of the personal with a larger, time-stained vision of India, and draw attention to the danger of the narrator's apparent closeness to Olivia. She is in fact more vulnerable to a past script than to present reality. Her personal life is so empty that it is easily filled with an engrossing, emotional tale like Olivia's. Making a wish at a shrine, the narrator describes herself as 'too lacking in essentials for me to fill up the gaps with any one request' (p. 127).

A variety of echoes, repetitions and parallels suggest that the narrator's story hovers between two possibilities – the reassertion of a past story, as Olivia influences the narrator, or its revision in the present.[37] If Chid is as exploitative as the Nawab, he shares with Harry stomach illness, disillusionment and eventual flight. Inder Lal, the narrator's lover, has, like the Nawab, a wife with mental problems, a dominating mother and a public life marked by plots and treachery, though in his case in the petty sphere of office politics. In the Nawab's palace, oblivious to his surroundings, he complains that in his office 'There is a lot of intrigue and jealousy' (p. 13). Like the Nawab, it is implied, he impregnates his white mistress. Other incidental repetitions include that of the hill-journey (to Simla by the memsahibs, further north on a pilgrimage by Ritu).These juxtapositions invite the reader to compare past and present, and to assess their relative merits. In addition, the comparative method establishes the lack of any fixed yardstick or norm, colonial or independent, by which to measure events. Which figure gains in each comparison? Does the parallel between the Nawab and Inder Lal raise Inder Lal to princely status? Or does it cut the Nawab down to size? Is the Begum a sinister and powerful matriarch? Or merely a meddlesome mother ? Is the Nawab's wife a mysterious madwoman, hidden from view like the first Mrs Rochester? Or is she simply the victim of an unfortunate marriage, as Inder Lal's young wife Ritu so obviously is? And who is more humane, the Nawab in the 1920s, who simply separates from his wife, or the modern Inder Lal who allows Ritu to be burned with red-hot irons? By splicing her two stories, Jhabavala highlights the role of the reader's imagination, as capable of magnifying or diminishing the characters, and compelled to make careful judgments between them.

The juxtapositions also exert a proleptic suggestion upon readers who themselves undergo the process of scripting and revising, wondering whether the narrator will follow Olivia's example, and anticipating what will happen in the one plot from the parallel events of the other. In some respects, therefore, the reader becomes a shadow to the narrator. As narrator, Miss Rivers tells the story, using her diary, letters and personal research. Yet, as the reader of Olivia's letters who then projects herself into the scene, she is extremely close to **the** reader, and exemplifies the perils and rewards of imaginative reading. Similarly, since Olivia wrote the letters, she is to some extent telling her own story. Yet throughout the novel it is only the narrator who knows the whole story. The reader is almost as ignorant as Olivia, and advances towards knowledge at much the same pace, hand in hand with Olivia. The roles, therefore, of reader and narrator criss-cross in order to keep posing the question: Whose story is it? Who is in control – an independent narrator or a colonial one ? In broader terms, to what extent is any reader controlled by a story? How much do any readers actually create that story for themselves?

As readers, for example, we first learn that the narrator made love in the grove with Inder Lal, then in the ensuing scene that Olivia consummated her affair with the Nawab in the same place. In the time of reading, the narrator's seduction precedes Olivia's; in the time of history, of course, it follows. Does the narrator follow Olivia's example, deliberately setting out to imitate her? Or, in intertextual anachronism, does Olivia follow the narrator's – since, after all, it is the narrator who imagines the seduction scene for the reader, inventing some or all of its particulars from her own preceding experience. This proleptic technique also forces the reader to read one story through another, in a continual process of revision. We learn, for example, that the narrator is pregnant. She speculates as to whether Maji's ancestors (midwives) 'attended Olivia' (p. 138). The obvious supposition is that Olivia also became pregnant and had a baby – not, as we later learn, an abortion. In addition, Jhabvala continually makes the reader 'read into' events by a technique of careful unspecificity. We are told that the narrator had 'thoughts other than usual' (p. 67), or that Olivia had mixed feelings in the Nawab's car (p. 42), or that the emotions on the Nawab's face were 'plainly expressed' (p. 122). But we are left to imagine just what these thoughts, feelings and emotions actually were. As readers we therefore have to make similar interpretive and imaginative leaps as those of the narrator *vis-à-vis* Olivia's story, and have to beware of allowing preexistent plots and models to condition our response.

Some expectations are none the less fulfilled. The cheerful Hindu widows tell the narrator the story of a woman, cured of childlessness in the grove, whose husband, under the spell of another woman, subsequently drove her from his home. Although the narrator laughs at the suggestion that she should find a husband, she admits to feeling 'absorbed' (p. 67) by the widows and their stories, and later **does** find a husband – Ritu's – by whom she conceives in the grove, once Ritu has been sent off on a pilgrimage. In a particularly exact repetition, Mrs Saunders' gloomy bungalow is similarly musty in 1973, and her horror stories of Indians as sex-mad robbers are repeated almost verbatim on her verandah by an English tourist, who recites a litany of disasters from sexual molestation in Fatehpur Sikri to pickpockets in Goa, with rascally thieves *passim*, and ringworm and dysentery to boot.

Nor is the narrator merely an exceptional case – one neurotic Englishwoman mesmerised by the past. Her position is generalised by the examples of other characters who are scripted by past stories. Douglas Rivers, now essentially a bureaucrat, yearns for the days of heroic activity in India. He is compared to 'a boy who read adventure stories and had dedicated himself to live up to their code of courage and honour' (p. 40). He particularly enjoys mooning over the 'dead heroes' (p. 107) of the Mutiny in the Christian graveyard. By dint of frequent re-readings, the inscribed epitaphs become increasingly familiar and even (realistically, the effect of the rainy season) fresher, so that 'the lettering stood out clearer' (p. 153), as clear as Olivia's letters fifty years later. Ironically Olivia's own favourite epitaph memorialises Lt Edwards as 'a kind and indulgent Father but most conspicuous in the endearing character of Husband' (p. 105). Douglas, however, is so busy imitating past heroes that he neglects Olivia and loses the opportunity to feature as a character in Lt Edwards' mould. The Nawab's exploits with the dacoits, the source of his eventual ruin, are also pale imitations of the tales he has heard of Amanullah Khan, in which he tends to take refuge whenever he is feeling frustrated. Throughout the novel, therefore, Jhabvala elicits a self-conscious awareness of the potentially destructive power of past 'letters', and the urgent need to foster resistant readings.

The slate, however, cannot be wiped altogether clean. When Chid annuls his personal story, he is eventually destroyed, both mentally and physically. The narrator herself drifts towards anonymity and passivity, but learns her lesson at the emblematic location of the suttee stones. One incident makes the point that the recovery of the silenced stories of women, for all its difficulties, is (to refer back to Adrienne Rich) not merely part of cultural history but imperative for women's survival, and for the establishment of identity. The narrator has discovered Leelavati, dying on a mound of refuse. After some token efforts to arrange medical treatment, she simply gives up and later speaks of the aged widow to Maji 'with the same indifference as everyone else' (p. 113). Maji, however, reacts with force: ' "Leelavati? Her time has come?" Leelavati! The beggar woman had a name! Suddenly the whole thing became urgent again' (p. 113). When Maji finds Leelavati, by the suttee stones, she at once settles down to tell the narrator the story of Leelavati's life. With a name and a story (unlike, as yet, the narrator) Leelavati is humanised once more, and her death in the arms of Maji – the midwife – becomes meaningful, even joyful. The process is shown as a re-mothering: 'Suddenly the old woman smiled, her toothless mouth opened with the same bliss of recognition as a baby's' (p. 114). Anonymous extinction is transformed by story into an image of rebirth, pointing the way towards the narrator's subsequent decision, abetted by Maji, to avoid a reenactment of Olivia's abortion, and therefore to make a decisive break with the past.[38]

Although at the close of the novel the narrator follows Olivia's path to the hills, she names her destination only as 'X'. No other reader will be able to follow in **her** footsteps, as she followed in Olivia's. She also confronts the profound dissimilarity between herself and Olivia, recognising herself as an interloper, when she introduces for the first time an account of the real reader for whom Olivia's letters were intended – their first recipient, Olivia's sister, Marcia. Marcia had insisted that she and Olivia were alike: 'She claimed she could understand Olivia completely' (p. 179). Though Harry is merely sceptical, the Nawab rejects the resemblance without a moment's hesitation: 'The idea seemed to strike him as simultaneously ludicrous and horrifying' (p. 179). Miss Rivers is now forced to recognise that she cannot project herself into Olivia, any more than Marcia could. She acknowledges that the letters from 'X', which are 'short and quite unrevealing' (p. 178), no longer provide a script for her, and that Olivia is beyond the reach of her imagination: 'I still cannot imagine what she thought about all those years, or how she became' (p. 180). Whereas

Harry had written Olivia off in a stereotypical image (Mrs Secombe), the narrator allows the full mystery of her later years to persist.

She tells one more story, as originally narrated by the Nawab, of the final words of a hanged dacoit. At the last moment the dacoit had turned to the hangman to ask 'Are you a . . . ?' (p. 178) but did not live to finish his phrase. The Nawab completes it for him ('chamar', an enquiry about caste), but the narrator refuses to do the same for Olivia. Her life is not rounded off in an exemplary story after all. Though no longer silenced, her story is left with its gaps and omissions, as the narrator takes possession of her own story and moves towards an as yet invisible and unscripted future. At the close, the narrator decides to go beyond Olivia and to give birth to her child further up the mountain in an ashram where swamis study 'those ancient writings that had their birth up in the highest heights of these mountains I cannot yet see' (p. 181). The final image, therefore, is not of the narrator as a predictable reincarnation of Olivia, her fate self-predestined, but of the conjunction of an old, indigenous story with a new beginning. Around her the landscape dissolves in the rains, the air so drenched in moisture that 'the birds seem to swim about in it and the trees wave like seaweed' (p. 180). In 'X' the end of the narrator's imitation of the past and her complete immersion in the present is signalled in a non-representational landscape, in which earth, air and water flow into each other. In *Heat and Dust*, therefore, Jhabvala refuses to establish a hierarchy of discourses, as between plot and subplot, 'frame' and 'tale', which might definitively establish the 'truth' of events. Rather than espousing a mimetic, representational aesthetic, in which a narrator **can** be reliable or unreliable, *Heat and Dust* insists upon the reader as productive of textual meaning, and therefore simultaneously refuses to constitute itself as hegemonic.

# Notes

1  Susan Price, 'Images of Empire', *Los Angeles Times Magazine*, 30 August 1987, p. 30. I am grateful to Laura E. Donaldson for drawing this item to my attention in *Decolonizing Feminisms: Race, Gender, and Empire Building* ( London, Routledge, 1992).
2  Price, 'Images of Empire', p. 30.
3  'Images of Empire', p. 32.
4  'Images of Empire', p. 30.
5  Ruth Prawer Jhabvala, 'Disinheritance', *Blackwoods*, April 1979, p. 6.
6  Cathy Caruth, 'Introduction', *American Imago* 48, 4 (Winter 1991), pp. 417 and 419.
7  For a comprehensive overview see Yasmine Gooneratne, *Silence, Exile and*

*Cunning: The Fiction of Ruth Prawer Jhabvala* (New Delhi, Orient Longman, 1983).

8 Laurie Sucher, *The Fiction of Ruth Prawer Jhabvala: The Politics of Passion* (London, Macmillan, 1989).

9 See Shirley Chew, 'Fictions of Princely States and Empire', *Ariel* 17 (1986), pp. 103–17; Richard Cronin, '*The Hill of Devi* and *Heat and Dust*', *Essays in Criticism* 36 (1986), pp. 142–59; Judie Newman, 'The Untold Story and the Retold Story', in Susheila Nasta, ed., *Motherlands: Black Women's Writing From Africa, the Caribbean and South Asia* (London, Women's Press and New Brunswick: Rutgers University Press, 1991), pp. 24–42.

10 Page references which follow quotations in parentheses are to the following edition of the novel: Ruth Prawer Jhabvala, *Poet and Dancer* (London, John Murray, 1993).

11 Nissim Ezekiel, 'Cross Cultural Encounter in Literature', *The Indian P.E.N.*, (November–December 1977), p. 5. Quoted in Ramlal Agarwal, 'A Critical Study of *Heat and Dust*', *Studies in Indian Fiction in English* (1986), p. 53.

12 Page references which follow quotations in parentheses are to the following edition of the novel: Upamanyu Chatterjee, *English, August: An Indian Story* (London, Faber, 1988).

13 Page references which follow quotations in parentheses are to the following edition of the novel: Ruth Prawer Jhabvala, *Heat and Dust* (London, John Murray, 1975).

14 Richard Cronin, '*The Hill of Devi* and *Heat and Dust*,' *Essays in Criticism*, 36 (1986), pp. 142–59.

15 Cronin, '*The Hill of Devi* and *Heat and Dust*', p. 157.

16 For a discussion of the enduring life of 'Mutiny' stories see Patrick Brantlinger, *Rule of Darkness: British Literature and Imperialism, 1830–1914* (Ithaca, Cornell University Press, 1988), Chapter 7.

17 The term 'sati' is used for both the widow and the practice.

18 David Rubin, *After the Raj: British Novels of India Since 1947* (Hanover and London, University Press of New England, 1986), p. 70.

19 Brantlinger, *Rule of Darkness*, p. 86.

20 T. Herbert Warren, ed., *Tennyson: Poems and Plays* (Oxford University Press, 1971), p. 816.

21 Letitia Elizabeth Landon, *The Poetical Works Of Letitia Elizabeth Landon (L.E.L.)*, ed. W. Bell Scott (London, George Routledge and Sons, 1874), p. 524.

22 See Mary Daly, *Gyn/Ecology* (London, Women's Press, 1979); V. C. Joshi, ed., *Rammohun Roy and the Process of Modernization in India* (Delhi, Vikas, 1975); Madhu Kishwa and Ruth Vanita, 'The burning of Roop Kanwar', *Race and Class* 30, 1 (1988), pp. 59–67; Joanna Liddle and Rama Joshi, *Daughters of Independence: Gender, Caste and Class in India* (London, Zed, 1986); Lata Mani, 'The Production of an Official Discourse of Sati in Early Nineteenth Century Bengal,' in Francis Barker *et al.*, eds., *Europe and its Others*. Proceedings of the Essex Conference on the Sociology of Literature July 1984 (Colchester, University of Essex Press, 1985), pp. 107–28; Lata Mani, 'Contentious Traditions: The Debate on Sati in Colonial India', in Kumkum Sangari and Sudesh Vaid, eds., *Recasting Women: Essays in Indian Colonial History* (New Brunswick, N.J., Rutgers University Press and New Delhi, Kali for Women, 1989), pp. 88–126; Vina Mazumdar, 'Comment on Suttee', *Signs* 4, 2 (Winter 1978), pp. 269–73; Rajeswari Sunder Rajan, *Real and Imagined Women: Gender, Culture and Postcolonialism* (London, Routledge, 1993); Kumkum Sangari, 'There is No Such Thing as a Voluntary Sati', *Times of*

*India*, 25 October 1987, p. 3; Kumkum Sangari and Sudesh Vaid, 'Sati in Modern India: A Report', *Economic and Political Weekly*, 1 August 1981, pp. 1284–8; Gayatri Chakravorty Spivak, 'Can the Subaltern Speak?' in Cary Nelson and Lawrence Grossberg, eds., *Marxism and the Interpretation of Culture* (London, Macmillan, 1988), pp. 271–313; Dorothy K. Stein, 'Women to Burn: Suttee as Normative Practice', *Signs* 4, 2 (Winter 1978), pp. 253–68. An important early source for descriptions of sati is Edward Thompson, *Suttee: A Historical and Philosophical Enquiry Into The Hindu Rite Of Widow Burning* (London, George Allen and Unwin, 1928).

23 Mani, 'Contentious Traditions', p. 117.
24 Spivak, 'Can the Subaltern Speak?', p. 299.
25 Edward Said, *Orientalism* ( London, Routledge and Kegan Paul, 1978).
26 Rajan, *Real and Imagined Women*, p. 8.
27 W. H. Sleeman, *Rambles and Recollections of an Indian Official* (London, Oxford University Press, 1915), pp. 22–3.
28 Mani, 'Contentious Traditions,' p. 110.
29 Thompson, *Suttee,* p. 40.
30 Rajan, *Real and Imagined Women*, pp. 17–18.
31 Mani, 'Contentious Traditions,' p. 118.
32 Stein, 'Women to Burn', p. 262.
33 Sangari and Vaid, 'Sati in Modern India,' p. 1288.
34 Rajan, *Real and Imagined Women*, p. 18.
35 Wilson Harris, 'Adversarial Contexts and Creativity', *New Left Review,* 154 (November/December 1985), pp. 124–8.
36 Ralph J. Crane, 'Ruth Prawer Jhabvala: A Checklist of Primary and Secondary Sources', *Journal of Commonwealth Literature*, XX, 1 (1985), p. 200. See also N. S. Pradhan, 'The Problem of Focus in Jhabvala's *Heat and Dust*', *Indian Literary Review*, 1, 1 (1978), pp. 15–20.
37 For a full account of such parallels see Gooneratne, *Silence, Exile and Cunning.*
38 Shirley Chew comments percipiently on this incident as evidence of the narrator's development in 'Fictions of Princely States and Empire', *Ariel*, 17 (1986), pp. 103–17.

# 4

# Babytalk

## *Anita Desai*, Baumgartner's Bombay

In a fashion reminiscent of the genesis of *Heat and Dust*, *Baumgartner's Bombay* opens with a cache of old letters, in this case immediately associated with crime – the murder of Hugo Baumgartner, a Jew, by a young German, many years after Baumgartner's escape from Nazi Germany to India. As the recurrent image of the racetrack suggests ('the circular track that began in Berlin and ended here in Bombay', p. 194),[1] Baumgartner's story comes full circle and his trajectory is strongly marked by repetition. After being dispossessed in Germany as a Jew, narrowly avoiding the Nazi camps, he is seized in India as a German, and imprisoned for six years as an enemy alien in a British internment camp. When world war gives way to partition struggles, his Moslem business partner in Calcutta is dispossessed, in his turn, by Hindus, and flees east to Dacca. After Baumgartner's return to Bombay, however, the death of his new Hindu partner sees him booted out once more, into an independent India which has little use for a European. As fresh waves of refugees continually replace each other in Bombay, fleeing wars, droughts, famines and communal riots, the novel seems to imply that history is only a process of endless and meaningless reenactment, a story which repeats itself. The novel therefore appears to respect Salman Rushdie's dictum: 'Europe repeats itself, in India, as farce.'[2]

Throughout the novel Baumgartner, shabby, smelly, shortsighted, his nose a warty, wobbling purplish lump (*Baumgartner's Bombay*, p. 5), is established as a clown, known to his neighbours as 'pagal sahib, bille-wal-lah sahib' (p. 204), the madman of the cats, for his habit of adopting strays as scruffy as himself. Even his death is presented in a mode of black comedy, combining the effects of Keystone Cops slapstick with a chase sequence and lashings of melodrama. Bloodstained footprints are sighted, and the wrong man promptly arrested by stereotypically plodding policemen, who subsequently unleash two Dobermanns on Baumgartner's feline friends. As cats fly in all directions, one of them, defenestrated, narrowly missing the bald perspiring head of the landlord (p. 225), the appearance of the fire brigade only adds to the confusion which culminates in the arrival of Baumgartner's friend, Lotte, who flings herself headlong upon the corpse, much to the delight of the goggling crowd :

> Memsahib on her knees, dress rucked up to the thighs, red hair fly-ing forwards, face buried on the old man's chest, sobbing. Farrokh standing by, wringing his hands, whining like a character on stage .... The audience shivered with delight (p. 228).

But does the reader? The terms of the description emphasise the murder as a fact in the public domain, presided over by assorted officials, its stagey quality suggestive of a replay of a previously rehearsed event. Yet the final sequence is itself a reenactment of a tragic opening scene. The novel comes full circle in its last sentence as Lotte spreads out the letters found by Baumgartner's dead body: 'Each one stamped with the number: J 673/1. As if they provided her with clues to a puzzle, a meaning to the mean-ingless' (p. 230). It is with these same letters (in fact mostly postcards) that the novel opens. Repetition is therefore embedded in the fictional structure which encloses the story of Baumgartner's life (narrated in flash-backs) within the events of one day, itself framed as a flashback by the initial and final sequences. The effect is rather of a *mise en abyme* or infi-nite regress, in which the novel ends as Lotte begins to read the letters which will reopen the action and provide a meaning to the repetitive absur-dities of Baumgartner's existence.

As the novel opens, the process of reading is deliberately highlighted, by the presence of a fictional reader (Lotte) mediating between **the** reader and the letters. Lotte is the point of entry to both the letters and Desai's text. The action begins as she enters her room, fumbling with the lock with as much awkwardness as she later displays when decoding the unfa-miliar German of the letters. Inner sanctum and text are equated as she opens the door 'as though she had forgotten its grammar, her fingers numb, tongue-tied as it were' (p. 1). For the reader it remains to be seen whether this is an entrance into a fictional 'world', a historical story, or simply into language.

The scene also indicates a movement inwards. At first Lotte poses, clutching the letters to her breast 'in the theatrical manner that came nat-urally to her' (p. 1), much as previously she had pressed a flower to her bosom, on stage. Once alone, inside her room, the public persona falls away as she begins to read. From the very beginning the letters pose a riddle. Whereas Olivia's letters were glossed and transcribed by Miss Rivers, rather than directly presented, Desai makes us, as Lotte's co-read-ers, equal partners in the enterprise of decipherment. The dichotomy between private and public space also typifies the tension created for the reader between the fictive and the historical. As Lotte weeps over the letters, public farce appears to conceal private tragedy, as if Desai has directed the reader back from Rushdie to Hegel: 'All acts and personages of great importance in world history occur, as it were, twice . . . the first time as tragedy, the second as farce.'[3] Reduplication is as much a feature of the inner as the outer scene. When Lotte first reads the letters she is overcome by a combination of emotion and strong drink. Pulling herself together, she finds everything in a mess 'reflecting her face, reflecting herself. The coffee spilt, the cards scattered, the bottle emptied, the glass lying on its side. A scene in miniature, copying the scene at Hugo's that she had fled' (p. 3). Repetition is also the mark of the letters, both in the baby language of their address, and in the repeated phrases which reduce each to a quasi-facsimile of its predecessor: 'each line seemed like the other, each card alike: 'Are you well, my rabbit? Do not worry yourself. I am well. I have enough. But have you enough, my mouse, my darling? Do not worry . . .' (p. 3). From these empty repetitions Lotte looks away towards the glass of her window: 'A blank sky, as always, with neither colour nor form. Empty. Afternoon light. Daylight. Perpetual light. And blankness' (p. 4). The image extends the emptiness represented by European letters into the Indian scene. World and text appear to mirror each other as if language and material reality were one indissoluble entity. Meaninglessness, perpetual recurrence, repetition and blankness are thus the initial impressions created by the letters. Moreover, in their sugary endearments they offer a sickly-sweet language of childhood which is construed as destructive. The image of the mother country is presented as fundamentally infantilising, fostering a dangerous dependence. As Lotte reads 'All the marzipan, all the barley sugar, the chocolates and toffees of childhood descended on her with their soft, sticking, suffocating sweetness. Enough to embrace her, enough to stifle her, enough to obliterate her . . . Lotte wept and drowned' (p. 5). As the novel continues, the letters become emblematic of both a stifling European textual world, itself linked to destructive illusions, and the tragic facts of recent history. Mirroring, copying and repeating are therefore important motifs in a novel which engages with history in all its particularity, while interrogating its moral relation to fictional discourse.

In this connection Baumgartner's experiences as a Jew in Nazi Germany are all-important. Anita Desai draws on her own background (her German mother left for India with her Bengali husband before the outbreak of war)[4] and on contemporary debates concerning language and its relation to history. In interview, Desai refused to consider her decision to write in English (rather than German or Bengali) as in any sense problematic: 'I believe with Karl Kraus that "Language is the universal whore whom I have made a virgin."'[5] In pre-war Vienna, Kraus made language the moral index of a dying way of life, his remarks on the subject anticipating the murderer's lexicon and dictionaries of the language of inhumanity (e.g.

'Final Solution'), which appeared after the end of Hitler's Reich. For Kraus, there was an absolute congruity between word and world, language and life. Language was a moral–linguistic imperative; the unworthiness of his age was defined by its treatment of language. Similarly, George Steiner has argued that a crisis of language exists in the modern world, beginning from concrete historical precedent in the dehumanisation of speech and the emptying of meaning in Nazi Germany.[6] In terms of post-Saussurean linguistics, the relation between literature and history has also become a closer one, with the recognition of language as a social fact. In the past Anita Desai has always sidestepped any such recognition, disavowing political intent and describing her work in 'universalist' terms. In interview she maintained that she had avoided many of the political problems created by the use of English, by not writing 'social document' novels: 'By writing novels that have been catalogued by critics as psychological, and that are purely subjective, I have been left free to employ, simply, the language of the interior.'[7] In *Baumgartner's Bombay,* however, Desai departs from her previous practice, in order to consider the relation of discourse to history, the language of the interior to that of the outer world.

In this connection, various intertextual devices are significant. The letters are not the only German texts reproduced within the novel. The first clues to their significance emerge in a long flashback to Baumgartner's prewar childhood in Berlin, a redolently textualised world which conjoins bitter-sweet imagery with a succession of intercalated German nursery rhymes and songs, set against the highly cultured background of Baumgartner's elegant Mutti, with her Goethe, Schiller and Heine. Because they are reproduced in German (largely without a gloss) these intertextual motifs create the impression of a thoroughly self-centred European society, an infantilised interior world which makes little concession to readers outside. They therefore function as a means of condemning the claustrophobic over-immersion in texts of that society, in order to reassert the importance of engagement with the sociohistorical world. Diana Brydon has noted that traditional criticism tends to see the imperial power as the mother country, the origin and nurturer of value.[8] In contrast, the colonised understand the imperial refusal to recognise the autonomy of other worlds as a species of infantile blindness – just as babies think the world exists only for their own omnipotent selves. In *Baumgartner's Bombay* Desai takes the imperial convention for representing the colonial mind (immaturity) and redefines it as a property of Europe.

At first the nursery rhymes merely emphasise the childish innocence of Hugo's world, which the adults mirror back to him, his father playfully imitating a horse ('Pferdchen lauf galopp', p. 25), for example. Slowly, however, they come to form a gloss on events, offering intertextual foreshadowings and commentary. As well as reflecting the action, they begin to project its full meaning. In a voice of 'precarious sweetness' (p. 28),

Mutti sings ('Kommt ein Vogel geflogen') of a bird bearing greetings from home, a song which ends on a note of regret when the singer is unable to accompany the bird back to mother. Meanwhile Hugo's mind moves to a baby hedgehog, separated from its mother, which he had 'rescued', only to kill it with kindness, overfeeding it until its corpse oozed warm milk. 'Then all the sweetness in the air had shattered into splinters of glass' (p. 28). The anecdote destroys any sentimental image of mother love, as previously presented by Mutti. The hedgehog died less because it was separated from its mother than from an excess of milky sweetness. As the reader is later to learn, had Baumgartner remained with his mother, he too would have died. The sentimental illusions of the song isolate Mutti from reality.

As the song cycle continues, the mood darkens. Sent out on an errand, Hugo finds the scene below less sunlit at close quarters than it had appeared from his upper windows: 'Coming loose from the window frame, it had crashed two storeys into darkness' (p. 29). Around him safe childhood certainties dissolve into a nightmare vision of the Berlin streets. Confronted with a world which is clearly falling apart, Hugo is taken by panic, forgets to buy himself his chocolate and arrives home having dropped both purse and coins in his terror. Mutti's comment, 'Your tongue lost its taste for sweets in the dark, did it?' (p. 32) has a deeper resonance, as does the song ('O du lieber Augustin'), which progresses from 'Geld ist weg/Beutel ist weg' (money and bag are gone) to 'alles ist hin!' – all is lost.[9] Most hideous of all in the episode is Hugo's encounter in the dark with 'something soft, warm, yielding' (p. 32) at the door, in fact the baker's cloth bag for rolls. Hugo's sensation of horror is clearly transferrable to his mother. Although she constantly attempts to shore up the illusion of a world of sweetness and light, Hugo comes to see the 'encirclement of her soft, sweet-smelling arms' (p. 33) as an imprisonment. His mother's attempt to play 'horsey' ('Hoppe, Hoppe, Reiter', p. 35) is no substitute for a longed-for excursion to the racetrack with his father. Desperate to accompany him, Hugo resorts to primitive linguistic magic, repeating 'Mick-muck-mo, Make-it-so ' (p. 34) as he formulates his wish. In pre-war Berlin, however, word and world fail to coalesce. Originally Hugo's mother had appeared to him as the entire universe. Her gilt-framed mirror 'held the whole room slightly tilted on its calm and shining surface' (p. 27). Downstairs, however, in his father's furniture showroom, the world is already more fragmentary and disquieting, reflecting the Fatherland's new definition of Jews as aliens. Amidst a wealth of rococo mirrors, Hugo is alarmed by the three-piece looking-glass which 'showed you unfamiliar aspects of your head, turning you into a stranger before your own eyes as you slowly rotated to find the recognisable' (p. 26). Mutti's enclosed world contrasts with the showroom, where 'the opulence of the interior' (p. 26) is none the less on display to – and dependent on – the public.

As time passes, the recognisable fades into the distance as a yawning fissure opens between the home world and that beyond it, between Mutti's literate culture and the realities of pre-war Germany. At Christmas, when there is no present for Hugo from the fir tree, his schoolteacher offers him instead the ornament which crowns the tree, 'a great ball of red glass in which all the light gathered together and danced' (p. 35). Earlier Hugo had thought that if he could own this all-reflecting globe, he would be the owner of the whole world. Now, when it is offered, he refuses, in the belief that 'he did not belong to the picture-book world of the fir tree, the gifts and the celebration' (p. 37). Instead he chooses to 'collapse into the dark ditch of his shame' (p. 36) fulfilling the image in the accompanying song of the rider who has come a cropper ('Fällt er in die Hecken', p. 35). For Hugo the gross mismatch between word and world is expressed in the contrast between the tales told by his mother and those of the former maidservant, now no longer willing to work for a Jewish family: 'his mother's gentle stories of the Red Rose and the White Rose lulled him to sleep too quickly so that he woke a little later and missed Berthe's stories of war and violence that had kept his nights lively' (p. 38). The next nursery song ('Hänschen klein, geht allein') bears witness to his new state. In the song little Hans goes out alone into the world, quite cheerfully, though his mother weeps. Hugo has now been sent to a Jewish school, dominated by 'strange large volumes' (p. 37) and a language which he has never heard before: 'the forbidding sound of the Torah' (p. 49). For all its strangeness, Hugo comes to appreciate its 'element of robust reality' (p. 50) in contrast to the bookish illusions of his maternal home.

By now, the wealthy Jews who patronised Herr Baumgartner's furniture shop have begun to invest their money in more portable assets, and the business is failing. In Hugo's dreams 'the brilliant mirrors tipped out their highly coloured and illuminated reflections like pools of water from unsteady basins, then slipped out of their frames and crashed' (pp. 39–40). The song 'Es tanzt ein Bibabutzemann' (a bogeyman dances in our house) introduces the character of Herr Pfuehl, the timber merchant from Hamburg who will eventually appropriate the business to his Aryan ownership. Isolated in her textual world, Mutti refuses to read the realities of Hitler's Germany, even when 'Jude' is painted in bold red letters on her windows. Soon, however, Hugo's dreams come true as (presumably in November 1938, on 'Kristallnacht') the salesroom is smashed up, and 'glass splintered, crashed, slid all over the floor in slanting, shining heaps' (p. 42). The following song, with its images of scarcity (the geese go barefoot, the shoemaker has no last) reflects the poverty and shortages of the time, in childish, nonsensical terms. The next day, when Herr Baumgartner is arrested, the description is also that of a nursery game:

The police car drew up at the curb, stilling its honking hooter, the stormtroopers in brown walked in, simply lifted Herr Baumgartner off his chair and carried him out; the hooting began again and the police car disappeared. Hugo might have been playing a game with his toy soldiers, marching them up, then marching them down (p. 43).

This is no game, however, nor are the 'honking' troopers geese. Herr Baumgartner returns from Dachau only to sign over his business to the not-so-foolish Herr Pfuehl. The following rhyme says it all: 'Fuchs, du hast die Gans gestohlen' (p. 44, Fox, you have stolen the goose).

Confronted with these visible horrors, Hugo's mother's reaction is to retreat, to pay a visit to her childhood friends, the Friedmanns, in the Grünewald, an excursion which is pastoral both in setting and in its representative texts. As well as enjoying cherry blossom and butterflies, Mutti sings of escape to 'the country where lemons flower' and reads verses 'about linden trees in Spring, about swallows in autumn skies, about butterflies, frost, children playing and, of course, the flowering cherry tree' (p. 48). One of the poems recited is entitled 'On Reading Tagore'; indeed the Friedmanns have been reading *Gitanjali* and show Hugo a photograph of the Bengali poet. The general escapism of the scene is reinforced by this image. The vogue for Tagore in Germany in the 1920s and 1930s has been persuasively accounted for as part of the German evolution towards the irrational and pseudomystic, reaching its climax in 1932 in democratic failure.[10] The fragility of the Friedmanns' world, suggested in the image of their globe lamp of red paper (p. 47), fills Hugo with foreboding. While his mother indulges in nostalgia, recalling a performance of *Lohengrin* in her schooldays, Hugo contemplates real rather than operatic swans, floating on the lake: 'somehow they reminded him of his father's rococo mirrors, gliding as they did upon the shining glass of their reflections in the still water, and he was silenced by the knowledge of their transience (p. 46). Mutti's magical memories of the Swan Knight are replaced by more disquieting, militaristic overtones; the swans' feathers are 'knitted together like chain mail' (p. 46). The Wagnerian connection of high art to mass brutality is significant. For Hugo, childhood provides little justification for nostalgia. In the lakeside woods

it seemed he was stumbling through the illustrations of a book of fairy stories, the forest where Hansel and Gretel followed a trail of breadcrumbs, or in which Sleeping Beauty lay hidden by a wall of thorns – beautiful, hushed and vaguely sinister (p. 47).

When Albert Friedmann begins to recite a poem about a deer entitled 'The Kaiser of the Woods', doubly anachronistic in both its political and its pastoral reference, Hugo calls his mother back from the world of texts to

the reality of Berlin, which destroys all the sweetness of their temporary
escape. Hugo's father is discovered, a suicide, in the sickening sweet odour
of gas. From now on, Hugo, isolated at home with Mutti, finds his copies
of 'Der Gute Kamerad' pure fantasy, 'its stories of camping in the forest
and journeys on the sea no more relevant to his life than a dream is to
daytime' (p. 50). Mutti's gift of a monumental 1906 *Kaiserbuch*, inscribed
with the imperial motto, is even less enticing. Virtually a prisoner, Hugo
is forced to exist entirely within the confines of the flat 'that was beginning to resemble that Kaiser-coffin of a book' (p. 50). The inefficacy of
Mutti's tactic of playing dead ('Totschweigentaktik', p. 54) is ironically
indicated in the song 'Haslein in der Grube sass' (p. 53, The baby hare
slept in the hollow . . . . Hop little hare). It is time now for Baumgartner
to hop away. Herr Pfuehl takes over the apartment and eventually dis-
patches Hugo to safety in India. Despite her enthusiasm for Tagore, Mutti
dismisses the idea of escape to India as a fairy tale: 'diese Märchen' (p.
56). Baumgartner's crude attempts to persuade her by word pictures of
new beginnings in the East, 'all tigers and palm trees and sunsets' (p. 55)
are quite unavailing. She is left behind with only her Goethe for company.
Her position recalls the unpalatable fact, learned after the Holocaust, that
'a man can read Goethe or Rilke in the evening, that he can play Bach
and Schubert and go to his day's work at Auschwitz in the morning'.[11]
All the polite letters in the world could not prevent the atrocity which
now hangs over Mutti. Baumgartner's Berlin appears to expose all texts
to the irony of history, and underlines the danger of over-immersion in an
interior realm of books which may reflect but which fail to act upon the
world about them. Mutti's old-fashioned Weimar high culture no longer
bears any relation to its circumambient society. The world reflected in her
mirrors has gone to smash.

The harmony between word and world, broken in Germany with tragic
consequences, features initially in India as a disjunction between language
and reality which offers new potentialities to Baumgartner. In his passage
to India, Hugo appears at first to have merely traded one illusion for
another: Hansel and Gretel for Aladdin. In Venice he feels as if 'already
transported to the East' (p. 59), comparing San Marco to 'an Oriental
potentate's palace' (p. 63). Yet Desai measures the distance here between
her protagonist and his predecessors. Returning from India, Forster's
Fielding saw in Venice a perfect harmony of nature and culture, and found
'tender romantic fancies' reawakening in him.[12] Baumgartner is travelling
in the other direction, and is happy to leave Venice behind: 'he felt himself to be inside a chocolate box, surfeited with sweetness and richness,
and tore away to breathe freely' (p. 60).

When he arrives in India, the Orientalist romance swiftly fades. The
Taj Hotel, previously envisaged as an Eastern palace, following lyrical
descriptions of its luxury from Baumgartner's fellow travellers, turns out

to be a seedy house with no lighting. It is, of course, the wrong Taj Hotel. Sign and referent do not accord. The proprietor's comment, 'I say Taj Hotel, then **this** Taj Hotel' (p. 85) introduces a world in which language creates new realities. All at sea, Baumgartner finds himself longing for a guidebook: 'Or at least a signboard. In a familiar language. A face with a familiar expression. He could not read these faces' (p. 83). Yet, although Baumgartner feels tricked by India, specifically in his misdirection to the hotel, although his language no longer controls his world, the 'unreadable' quality of Bombay has some positive consequences. If language is no longer mimetic, if it can no longer map the world according to Baumgartner's expectations, it may none the less offer a way out of the claustrophobia of Baumgartner's past into a world which is both multiple and syncretic:

> Was it not India's way of revealing the world that lay on the other side of the mirror? India flashed the mirror in your face . . . . You could be blinded by it. But if you refused to look into it, if you insisted on walking around to the back, then India stood aside, admitting you where you had not thought you could go. India was two worlds, or ten (p. 85).

Although Baumgartner's looking-glass world has given way to a less than enchanting Eastern Wonderland, the blindness of Berlin is not to be repeated.

Representing the new reality to Mutti is exceptionally difficult, however. On his travels in India, Baumgartner himself feels so incongruous as to doubt his own reality: 'If he were real, then surely the scene, the setting, was not. The match was improbable beyond belief' (p. 93). As a result he sets to work 'to build a new language to suit these new conditions' (p. 92), a syncretic language which expresses his own peculiar relation to India:

> Languages sprouted around him like tropical foliage and he picked words from it without knowing if they were English or Hindi or Bengali – they were simply words he needed . . . what was this language he was wrestling out of the air, wrenching around to his own purposes? He suspected it was not Indian, but India's, the India he was marking out for himself (p. 92).

Describing the scene to Mutti, however, is akin to 'doing heavy labour' (p. 91). Baumgartner resorts to previous discursive practices, converting the unreadable into a conventional traveller's tale, editing out the naked Indian children and starving cows, in favour of papayas and a picturesque snake charmer. Tragically, Mutti's letters appear to follow a similar pattern of omission, providing endless reassurances but no hard facts. Neither has a language which matches their experience, and the result is an inter-

rupted correspondence. When Baumgartner's last letter is returned to him
marked 'address unknown', he finds his travellers' tales met only by
silence. At Prince's, the European club whose members revel in similar
tales of elephant hunts, tiger shoots and fabulous banquets (pp. 99–100),
history catches up with him and he is arrested as an enemy alien.

This arrest, coinciding with the cessation of letters, suggests both a psychological state of interrupted development, as Baumgartner is put 'on
hold' for the duration of the war, and a more generalised condition of
deferred political autonomy. Where Mutti's story has obviously ended in
tragedy, Hugo's now moves into farcical repetition. Two points of special
significance emerge from Baumgartner's internment. The parodic nature of
the camp, which repeats the past in a species of Europe-in-India, provides
a critique of Europe in its imperial self-replication. In addition, the episode
focuses upon the status of silence as a tactic of response to the repeated
horrors of history. The first effect of his internment is to interrupt
Baumgartner's heterogeneous linguistic and cultural transformation, and
to replace him in a world which replicates the world of his childhood and
of pre-war German culture. With its camp orchestra, lectures on theo-
sophy, demonstrations of eurythmics, and opportunities for private study,
organised by the 'Kulturabteilung' or 'culture department', the camp provides a facsimile of German culture up to and including the hostilities
between Nazi and Jewish inmates, which eventually culminate in their separation by the British into two camps. (A transplanted Jewish inmate asks
bitterly, 'What shall we call our new home? Auschwitz or Theresienstadt?'
p. 117.) At the same time, Europe once more infantilises Baumgartner.
When first apprehended, he had resisted violently, striking out as he had
not done 'since he was a schoolboy' (p. 103), and finding himself 'so far
back in infancy' (p. 103) as to bite and draw blood ('warm, sweet, dis-
gusting') from his assailant. Once in camp he finds its discipline akin to
that of a school, with the inmates expected to eat, wash and sleep to a
timetable, as if in a 'comical dream – grown men finding themselves
returned to their school' (p. 108). In his carefully washed and pressed
white linen, Hugo's friend, Julius, looks 'like a figure from a pre-war
Sunday picnic, or coffee party' (p. 122), and his picture-books of furniture and antiques recall Herr Baumgartner. Hugo helps him to sketch furniture, 'recreating his father's elegant, well-lit, stylish showroom' (p. 124).
In fact, however, Julius's sketches are 'of objects and artefacts so far
removed from their actual environment as to seem bizzarre and fantastic'
(p. 120), as fantastic as Baumgartner originally felt in India. Within this
ersatz enclave, Baumgartner's own image of Germany becomes progressively distanced from reality. In the camp he finds himself yearning for a
motherland which he had never really known, as represented by a pale
Nordic blonde in the adjoining women's camp: 'she seemed to embody his
German childhood – at least, he chose to see her as such an embodiment,

it was so pleasant to do so, like humming a children's song' (p. 127). Baumgartner's pleasant reverie is fleshed out when the children play a game of 'Backe, backe Kuchen' in the background, creating the impression that 'Deutschland, the Heimat, was alive here' (p. 127). Baumgartner even dreams of the woman, holding a great glass globe between her fingers in which candlelight is reflected: a perfect 'Norse goddess of the camp' (p. 129). The illusion is rudely shattered when she speaks, in a language which Baumgartner cannot even recognise. Mrs Bruckner, a missionary's wife, has adapted completely to India and forgotten her German.

Nor is Baumgartner alone in living in a fantasy world. The camp inmates all enjoy constructing fictions about their respective backgrounds 'no matter how often such carefully constructed scenes were sent crashing by the truth' (p. 129). Cut off from history, the men resort to fictions of an increasingly fantastic nature. Thus they react to the discovery that the camp doctor is actually a veterinarian specialising in pigs, by weaving ever more preposterous tales about their own pasts. (Julius is said to have been a transvestite, for example.) Their practice is only a minor exaggeration of the outside world in which people live in fictions of their own creating, constructing themselves through successive revisions of their life stories and identity. Lotte points out that in India 'Lola' (one of her own 'exotic' stagenames) can have blue eyes and blonde hair and speak Yiddish. Name and cultural referent can be quite unrelated. Lotte's own successive transformations – from cabaret artiste to respectable memsahib to Hindu widow – are as nothing compared with those of her friend Gisela, who poses as a Russian aristocrat, the Lily of Shanghai, a prima ballerina, and finally as Gala Von Roth, wife of Julius (now renamed Julian). The unreality of these fictional identities may be comic or tragic. Gisela's 'dying swan' is a travesty of Pavlova; Lotte, driven from her apartment when her Hindu husband dies, and exiled to a miserable room, becomes a sad parody of Baumgartner's Mutti. Baumgartner, however, avoids a fabricated past; he has had enough of fictions. During their internment his other friend, Emil Schwarz, a bookish scholar, comments that the events in the camp have all happened before: 'Mann has described it all . . . in *The Magic Mountain*' (p. 132). Baumgartner remains unconvinced: 'it was just like Schwarz to refer everything in life to books as though that were the natural solution and end of it all' (p. 132).

Instead of taking refuge in fictions, Baumgartner eschews tale-telling. Silence becomes his response to events in the camp. When the radio announcements of German victories (in German) yield to reports of allied successes (in English), as if two languages rather than two cultures were vying for supremacy on the airwaves, the defiant Nazi prisoners insist on shouting 'Heil Hitler' after the National Anthem. When the Jews refuse, 'Baumgartner gratefully joined their silence. He realised at that instant that silence was his natural condition' (p. 117). Yet although silence can be a weapon, to submit to the finality of silence is to confirm the nihilism of Nazism. Mutti has also been silenced; no more letters have arrived from her. In order to shut out thoughts of his mother's fate, Baumgartner builds a defensive barrier against all information about the situation of the Jews in Germany, retreating from history as well as fiction:

> as if his mind were trying to construct a wall against history, a wall behind which he could crouch and hide, holding him to a desperate wish that Germany were still what he had known as a child and that in that dream-country his mother continued to live the life they had lived there together (p. 118).

As long as he has no replies to his letters, this illusion can persist. Even when it is shattered, on his departure from the camp, Baumgartner remains predisposed to silence. By the time in which the novel opens, on the last day of his life, he has come to realise that 'the habits of a hermit were growing upon him like some crustaceous effluent; it required an effort, an almost physical effort to crack it, to break through to the liquidity and flow and shift and kinesis of language' (p. 11).

It is a silence which is eventually shattered by Kurt, the young German, who recalls Baumgartner both to his native language and to the world of his youth. Two images of horror are juxtaposed before the close of the novel – the travellers' tales told by Kurt, and the letters from Mutti, presented in flashback after the reader has been introduced to Kurt. In broad terms they represent the powers of destructive fantasy (Kurt), as opposed to historical reality (Mutti). Before Mutti's fate is revealed to the reader, the action returns from the internment camp to the present, and to Baumgartner's adoption of Kurt. Initially, on first meeting Kurt in the Café de Paris, Hugo gives him a wide berth. For him, the Teutonic boy in shorts, 'a fair Aryan German' (p. 141), suggests only the horrors of the past in potentially repetitive form:

> The *Lieder* and the campfire. The campfire and the beer.
> The beer and the yodelling. The yodelling and the marching.
> The marching and the shooting. The shooting and the killing.
> The killing and the killing and the killing (p. 21).

Later, however, he decides that 'to think of Nazi Germany now, after all these years, in faraway Bombay, it was absurd after all' (p. 142). History does repeat itself, however, and when Baumgartner takes Kurt home he is promptly murdered for his racing trophies, as a source of cash to support Kurt's drug habit.

The explanation for Baumgartner's sudden charity may lie in the café proprietor's introduction of Kurt as one of the 'baby-men' (p. 15) who had come to India 'uninvited' (p. 14) and have now turned beggar. In a long disquisition, Farrokh describes the young German as representative of a type – 'men who remain children' (p. 13) – who has probably 'kicked his parents in the face' (p. 13) in order to visit India and now expects to be supported by others.

> Soon they need money. Go to post office. Has letter come from my dear mummy, my darling daddy? No? Must have, please look, look again, they must send ! No, no letter, no money . . . . Next day, again post office, again: My money come? No? Look again, you pig, you swine, you Indian ass, they shout, my money must come, my daddy will send, he love me, my mummy love me. But no letter (p. 16).

Baumgartner, listening, is irked by the 'personal references' (p. 16) in Farrokh's diatribe. Baumgartner, similarly uninvited, also came to India in his youth, and has been reduced to begging scraps in the café (for his cats). He, too, left a parent behind, fled to India, waited in vain for letters. Reversing the conventional colonial metaphor of 'mother country' and dependency, Desai pictures Europe as child, Europe as the place of illusion, whether tragic (in pre-war Germany) or wilfully cultivated (as in Kurt's use of drugs as a means to an alternative reality). Baumgartner's own arrested development, his paralysis by a European past, reappears in the young German's infantilism. At Baumgartner's flat he behaves 'like a naughty child', hurling beer about the room, amused by Baumgartner 'as a fairground might amuse a high-spirited child' (p. 154). The historical parallels make Baumgartner vulnerable to Kurt, who is a nightmarish projection of the retribution which Baumgartner, a guilty survivor, expects. He is eventually destroyed by an awful *alter ego* – a mirror self become a mirror enemy. In hard fact, the perceived resemblances are illusory. Baumgartner is not at all like Kurt; their specific historical situations are quite different. Baumgartner could not have saved his mother, and was an unwilling victim of the Aryan cult of strength, not, as Kurt is, its devotee. Baumgartner is too ready to see himself as guilty (in the psychological condition known as 'survival guilt'); it is this illusion of generalised guilt which exposes him to Kurt, much as fancied resemblances placed Miss Rivers under the spell of her double, Olivia.

Kurt, however, has little use for fact. Baumgartner's silence is suddenly filled by the German's flood of Indian horror stories, involving cannibalism, ritual sacrifice, wholesale slaughter, leprosy, flagellation, excess both erotic and narcotic, and finally, farcically, a yeti. Where the flashback to Berlin illustrated the inefficacy of high culture to defend itself against the grossest forms of inhumanity, demonstrating that books could not prevent atrocity, Kurt's tales dramatise a counter-truth – that those who begin by burning books end by burning men. Kurt's cult of strength has led him to murder. A would-be Tantric, he has eaten human flesh and burned men (though in Benares in the burning ghats). Where Baumgartner was almost smothered by love, Kurt has set out 'to destroy that love' (p. 158), to live for himself alone, on a quest for identity in temples, pilgrimages and shrines. He is wilfully out of touch with the ordinary world, and his tales reflect that fact; they are clearly neither mimetic nor true. Quite apart from the presence of a yeti, they involve a sword-shaped plant topped with a cockerel's head, which crows at dawn, sea serpents, a guest appearance from the devil, and Tibetan magicians flying into the sky on a streak of lightning. Baumgartner's 'mick-muck-mo, make it so' appears to be Kurt's watchword. Moreover, in each of his tales – almost vignettes – the reader feels the force of a gathering repetition, a sickening excess. 'In Goa he had lived on the beach in a hut made of coconut tree fronds. In Goa he had bought and sold and lived on opium, on marijuana, on cannabis, on heroin' (p. 158). 'In Delhi . . . he had stood with his feet in blood, his hands in blood, all of him covered with blood' (p. 159). 'In Lucknow he had walked in the procession at Mohurrum . . . chanting 'Hassan – Hosain – Hassan – Hosain', while he cut and lashed his body till the blood ran' (p. 159). 'In Mathura . . . . they had drunk opium in milk, eaten opium in sweets, smoked opium in pipes' (p. 159).

The repeated termination of a vignette with Baumgartner's incredulous question and Kurt's response, almost a refrain, further reinforces the impression of stylised repetition leading further and further from ordinary human experiences. Playing fast and loose with material reality on Kurt's part, transforming his life into a series of fictions, independent of truth or history, initiates a process of destructive fantasy which culminates in the murder of Baumgartner (appropriately in pursuit of the latter's racing trophies, the symbols of his own past magical desires) in order to procure fresh supplies of illusion-producing substances. The title of the novel, therefore, with its echoes of travelogue (compare *Fodor's Beijing*)[13] is deeply ironic. Baumgartner's Bombay has not been very different from his Berlin after all. He is murdered by an *alter ego* deeply enclosed within fictions, much as his own earlier self had been. Fairy stories and nursery rhymes have yielded to travellers' tales and thence to a horror story. Fictions appear to have triumphed over fact, and the reader is left with an image of history as textual repetition, and of repetition as horror.

A different story is told, nevertheless, by the postcards and letters discovered by Baumgartner's body. When Baumgartner first reads them he finds them 'strangely empty, repetitive and cryptic' (p. 164), a continual reprise of the same phrases 'Are you well? I am well. Do not worry. I have enough. Have you enough?' (p. 164). Resistant to textual interpretation, these letters cannot be glossed or decoded. Their explanation, indicated by the numbers on the postcards, which stop abruptly in February 1941, depends upon historical knowledge: in the early days of the war it was possible for the inmates of concentration camps to send and receive mail. The letters thus offer an emblematic opposition between endless rehearsal and an untold story, repeated horrors and a paralysed silence, which cannot in the end itself avoid repetition. Baumgartner is frozen in the horror of Mutti's untold story, his silence typical of the Holocaust survivor who lives in loss to the extent that even speaking of it is impossible.[14] He cannot go forward and therefore can only repeat. In themselves the letters have no content (the rules permitted inmates to say very little)[15] but their material reality is crushingly significant, bearing witness to the worst horrors of recent history. Imagination baulks at filling in Mutti's silences, or fleshing out her untold story. For some stories there can be no revisions. In the words of George Steiner, 'The world of Auschwitz lies outside speech.'[16]

Importantly, it was the discovery of a similar cache of real letters in Bombay, passed to Anita Desai for translation, which triggered the novel. She remarked that, 'Perhaps because they had been so empty they teased my mind. I had to supply the missing history to them.'[17] To the reader who has moved through flashback within flashback across Baumgartner's last day on earth, the letters are now fully significant. **Their** history will not pass into oblivion; their gaps and silences, paradoxically, say everything. In the double sense of 'Mutti's letters' – the polite letters (literature) which failed to save her, the correspondence which for all its sparsity bears witness to inhumanity – Desai interrogates the potential importance of European letters in India, as tragically irrelevant or, in their very absences and omissions, historically significant. The authority of fiction is therefore simultaneously affirmed and undercut.

It is striking that it is only **after** both Kurt's horror stories and the revelation of Mutti's fate, when the relative merits and demerits of the relation of the Indian writer to European literature and history have been problematised, that *Baumgartner's Bombay,* a hitherto freestanding novel, reestablishes a link with Forster which had apparently been broken. In Desai's case, the connection between the new fiction and its predecessor in the past is less one of critical rewriting than of fidelity to history, conjoined with firm opposition to its uncritical reproduction. It is worth noting that Desai is on record as deploring the David Lean film of *A Passage to India* for its divergence from the original. She particularly condemned Lean's rewriting of the ending, in order to make Indian and Englishman clasp hands in friendship. In Desai's opinion, Lean believed he had 'improved' Forster. 'What he is admitting is that he feels he has improved history as well.'[18] For Desai the facts of history cannot be too scrupulously preserved.

When, therefore, Desai rewrites Forster, the effect is tellingly different from Ruth Prawer Jhabvala's revisionings. In a reprise of the Marabar Caves incident in *A Passage to India*, Baumgartner enters a cave where he hears **not** a repetitive echo (Forster's 'ou-boum') but an absolute silence. Rather than being presented as a symbolic image of the encounter with an all-consuming transcendental deity, Desai's cave is fully historicised. In the internment camp Baumgartner had tried to keep his mind occupied by watching ants entering a crevice, described as 'the dark cave in a crack between the floor and the wall' (p. 119). But the tactic failed:

> The trouble with such fascinating sights was their silence, their tedium, the endless repetition of forms and actions that blurred and turned into an endless labour of human forms – bent, driven into black caves from which they did not reemerge.

> *Nacht und Nebel.* Night and Fog. Into which, once cast, there was no return (p. 119).

The German phrase[19] repeats the term applied by the Nazis to prisoners destined for death, for disappearance into 'night and fog' whether in labour camps, transports or extermination blocks. In the later incident when Baumgartner squeezes through the narrow crack which gives entry to the cave, he has a moment of panic, struggling with the fear of having his face clawed by escaping birds or bats. Unlike Forster's heroines, however, he overcomes these purely imaginary horrors. History has taught Baumgartner that there is more to fear in life than birds or bats. Within the cave he finds blackness, silence and a complete absence of explanatory text: 'No voice, no song, not even a dim inscription' (p. 189). Some things are lost to history.The shrine in the cave is invisible, unnamed and unexplained; the cave figures forth the absence, silence and untold horrors of the letters, the night into which Mutti disappeared. Despite the emptiness, a real sense of evil none the less communicates itself to Baumgartner, who runs various possibilities through his mind, including human sacrifice and Tantric rites. 'Had some drugged creature, animal or human, been dragged up here to be decapitated', he wonders (p. 190). The imagistic link to Kurt with his catalogue of gloating horrors is firmly rejected, however. Baumgartner declines to expand precise historical horror into totalising negativity. Refusing any vision of nothingness, he makes a rapid exit from the cave. Unlike Mrs Moore, 'Baumgartner would not have its no' (p. 190). Without minimising the real horrors of the past, Desai emphasises the need not to be complicit with those forces that would erase historical truth, reducing events to myth, fantasy or silence. Although the Holocaust was an enactment of absolute evil, it was so because of particular crimes against particular people. In counter-distinction to the image of history as meaningless repetition, the cave incident, like the letters, asserts the specificity of history and the necessity of maintaining its silences and omissions in full view, rather than placing past horrors in a generalised history of evil for which nobody in particular, or everyone in general, may be held accountable.

As Baumgartner sinks into his last sleep, losing his hold on Mutti's letters, he is left with a puzzle:

he lay with his arm over his eyes and in the dark could still see the script, spidery and fine. Gradually the words ran into each other, became garbled. They made no sense. Nothing made sense. Germany there, India here, – India there, Germany here. Impossible to capture, to hold, to read them, to make sense of them. They all fell away from him, into an abyss . . . he shut his eyes to receive the darkness that flooded in, poured in and filled the vacuum with the thick black ink of oblivion, of *Nacht und Nebel* (pp. 215–16).

Although Baumgartner's life appears to have come full circle, the letters remain, to reawaken Lotte to her past (in the time of fiction) and to memorialise their originals (in actual history). After the war Baumgartner had never been willing to think back to the past: 'That time was a closed book, or like a pack of cards – finite in number' (p. 172). Mutti's letters, however, also a small collection of cards, are finite yet infinite in their implications. For Desai, history cannot be a closed book, a silenced story, but neither can it be reopened and rewritten at random. Some women have been lost to history and to literature, and no amount of revisionings can call them back. Where Jhabvala's Miss Rivers attempted to close the gap in time between Europe and India, imperial and independent, erasing the distance originally traversed by letters, and very nearly succeeding in anachronistically reenacting Olivia, Desai recognises that only a sense of the historical violence which traversed that distance can supply its full meaning. Where Jhabvala emphasises the danger of the generic 'Indian horror story' as a conditioning force on history, Desai acknowledges the need to recognise that some horrors are historically true. Rather than operating as a conditioning force, letters may resist any accommodation to cultural coercions, bear witness to uncomfortable historical truths, and act as a continually renewed warning to the present. Just as the novel ends with Lotte, the surrogate reader, beginning to read the letters which will reopen the action, so it leaves the reader haunted by both their silences and their meaning. At the close, writing recognises no ending, perpetuating itself as if in a labyrinth of mirrors. Paradoxically, therefore, Mutti's letters reveal both the insufficiency of literature in the face of history – and its absolute necessity.

# Notes

1 Anita Desai, *Baumgartner's Bombay* (London, Heinemann, 1988). Page references follow quotations in parentheses.
2 Salman Rushdie, *Midnight's Children* (London, Picador, 1982), p. 185.
3 Karl Marx and Friedrich Engels, *Selected Works* (London, Lawrence and Wishart, 1968), p. 96.

4  For biographical material see Corinne Demas Bliss, 'Against the Current: A Conversation with Anita Desai', *Massachusetts Review* (Fall 1988), 521–37.

5  Ramesh K. Srivasta, 'Anita Desai At Work : An Interview', in Ramesh K. Srivasta, *Perspectives on Anita Desai* (Ghaziabad, Vimal Prakashan, 1984), p. 210. See also Frank Field, *The Last Days of Mankind: Karl Kraus and his Vienna* (London, Macmillan, 1967).

6  George Steiner, *Language and Silence: Essays on Language, Literature and the Inhuman* (New York, Atheneum, 1967).

7  Anita Desai, 'The Indian Writer's Problems', in Srivasta, *Perspectives*, p. 3.

8  See Diana Brydon, 'The Myths That Write Us', *Commonwealth*, 10, 1 (1987), pp. 4–5.

9  My translation, as in the examples which follow.

10  Alex Aronson, *Rabindranath Through Western Eyes* (Calcutta, RDDHI – India, 1943).

11  Steiner, *Language and Silence*, p. ix.

12  E. M. Forster, *A Passage to India* (London, Penguin, 1969), pp. 275–6 (Chapter 32).

13  Paul West, 'The Man Who Didn't Belong', *New York Times Book Review*, 9 April 1989, p. 3.

14  Helen Epstein, *Children of the Holocaust* (New York, G. P. Putnam's Sons, 1979), p. 103.

15  Konnilyn G. Feig, *Hitler's Death Camps* (London, Holmes and Meier, 1981), p. 52. The rules for correspondents in Dachau limited postcard messages to ten lines of legible German.

16  Steiner, *Language and Silence*, p. 123.

17  Andrew Robinson, 'Out of Custody', *The Observer*, 3 July 1988, p. 42.

18  Anita Desai, 'The Rage for the Raj', *New Republic*, 25 November 1985, p. 28.

19  Feig notes that a block at Ravensbruck, the women's camp, was known as 'Nacht und Nebel'. *Night and Fog* is also the title of Alain Resnais' celebrated film.

# 5

# *Postcolonial Gothic*

## Ruth Prawer Jhabvala and the Sobhraj Case

It will not have escaped the reader that, in some sense, all the texts considered up to this point have been horror stories of one sort or another. Gothic motifs are exceptionally prevalent in postcolonial fiction, even from very different locations.[1] Classic postcolonial transformations of Gothic emanate from the Caribbean (*Wide Sargasso Sea*), Africa (Bessie Head's *A Question of Power*) and India (*Heat and Dust*). In Canada, Gothic is almost the norm: whether in Margaret Atwood's comic *Lady Oracle*, or Anne Hébert's *Héloise* (the Québecois tale of a vampire who haunts the Paris Metro). Unsurprisingly, when the heroine of Alice Munro's *Lives of Girls and Women* thinks of writing about Jubilee, Ontario, she promptly chooses to begin a Gothic novel. Nearer home, ghosts wander the pages of Paul Scott's *Raj Quartet*, and J. G. Farrell begins his *Empire Trilogy* in a decaying Great House, complete with mysteriously fading heroine, demonic cats, and ever-widening crack in the external wall. Further afield, what is Isak Dinesen doing on a coffee farm in Kenya in 1931 but writing *Seven Gothic Tales*?

Gothic has a particular relation to issues of language and history, and to the silencing of the Other, though it may function to conservative as well as subversive effect. Margaret Atwood's *Lady Oracle* features a heroine who writes costume Gothics, exploiting the socially conditioned and manipulative nature of a genre which provides socially sanctioned stories for unliberated women. Atwood's project – to argue that the premises of Gothic are true and that men are out to kill women – rebounds, however, into historical Gothic as the parody spiritualism of her opening suddenly produces the ghost of the heroine's mother, as presage of danger. The process is uncomfortably reminiscent of that use of occultism which Patrick Brantlinger has termed 'imperial Gothic', in which the ghosts of Empire come home to roost, following the protagonist back from some 'farther shore' which may equally be construed as Empire or spirit world.

Brantlinger notes that late Victorian and Edwardian spiritualist literature is filled with metaphors of exploration, immigration, conquest and colonisation, tending to describe the passage to the 'other side' as a voyage of emigration.[2] As a result, Atwood's parody of the norms of popular Gothic reinscribes some of the original conventions within its apparent contestation. Toni Morrison runs some of the same risks in *Beloved*, conflating Africa with the 'other side', though her ambiguity is more productive. Under slavery the disembodied are a political reality. Those who do not own their own bodies will constitute space, time and the future quite differently.[3] Under these circumstances, who is not a ghost?

Postcolonial Gothic is therefore Janus-faced. At its heart lies the unresolved conflict between the imperial power and the former colony, which the mystery at the centre of its plot both figures and conceals. Its discourse therefore establishes a dynamic between the unspoken and the 'spoken for' – on the one hand the silenced colonial subject rendered inadmissible to discourse, on the other that discourse itself which keeps telling the story again and again on its own terms. As a European genre, Gothic cannot unbind all its historical ties to the West. Conversely, its ability to retrace the unseen and unsaid of culture renders it peculiarly well adapted to articulating the untold stories of the colonial experience. Eve Kosofsky Sedgwick has analysed the Gothic emphasis on the 'unspeakable', both in the intensificatory sense of 'nameless horrors', and in the play of the narrative structure itself, with its illegible manuscripts, stories within stories, secret confessions, and general difficulty in getting the story told at all. As Sedgwick puts it, Gothic novels are 'like Watergate transcripts. The story does get through, but in a muffled form, with a distorted time sense, and accompanied by a kind of despair about any direct use of language.'[4] In her analysis, a central privation of Gothic is that of language. When the linguistic safety valve between inside and outside is closed off, all knowledge becomes solitary, furtive and explosive. As a result, dire knowledge may be shared, but it cannot be acknowledged to be shared, and is therefore 'shared separately', as the barrier of unspeakableness separates those who know the same thing. This Gothic apartheid is almost a classic definition of imperialism's hidden discourse – the collaboration in a surreptitious relationship, never openly articulated, which is that of coloniser and colonised. Again in Sedgwick's account, Gothic offers an image of language as live burial. The notion that one's life is a text in an incomprehensible language opens the possibility that one is being placed in another's text, interpreted as the figural realisation of another's consciousness, a figure in somebody else's dream. Naipaul's *Guerrillas* exploits this aspect of textualisation, of being 'spoken for', whereas *Wide Sargasso Sea* concentrates its attention on the unspeakable and the silenced.

It is possible, however, for a novel to exploit both strategies – to politicise Gothic by overcoming the taboo on speaking, without slippage into the dominant discourse. A symptomatic reading of Ruth Prawer Jhabvala's *Three Continents* is instructive. *Three Continents* is situated at the sharp end of the Gothic generic transfer, not least because of its Indian subject matter. It is also explicitly related to one of the West's oldest Indian horror stories. Patrick Brantlinger has commented that:

> In the late 1830s . . . new revelations about a destructive offshoot of Hinduism provided another sensational focus for reformist writing, and served as the subject of the first best-selling Anglo-Indian novel, Philip Meadows Taylor's *Confessions of a Thug* (1839).[5]

Thuggee, the secret cult of professional murderers and robbers who worshipped Kali and preyed on unsuspecting travellers, became in Taylor's hands the central theme of a highly successful crime novel – as it was also to do for Jhabvala. In 1979 Jhabvala referred to thuggee in the context of modern muggers, remarking that areas of New York were now as deserted 'as though they were infested by those thugs that throttled wayfarers in the deserts of Rajasthan or the ravines of Madhya Pradesh'.[6] In *Three Continents*, Jhabvala's central character, Crishi, is based upon a modern 'thug', Charles Sobhraj, the Indian 'drug and rob' man and serial killer who preyed upon Western travellers who had set out on the 'hippy trail' in search of mystic enlightenment in the timeless East. In modelling her hero on Sobhraj, Jhabvala contests a dominant cultural narrative while she avoids buying into the cultural stereotype of the exotic Gothic villain. Rather than shifting the problem of violence on to universal grounds (Gothic evil), Jhabvala emphasises the mutual implication of literary, cultural and political texts in its production. Social dislocation and socioeconomic dispossession in the wake of the end of Empire become determining factors in the representation of the Gothic protagonist.

A strong strain of Gothic has been identified in the works of Jhabvala which feature demon lovers, mysterious Indian palaces with intricately concealed secrets, ruined forts, poison, willing victims, plus the eroticisation of spirituality, with gurus standing in for sinister monks, and ashrams for convents.[7] Jhabvala is, of course, influenced by eighteenth-century European literature. Among other topics, her London University MA thesis discussed the Oriental tale and the falseness of its 'East' which was based on preconceived literary notions. Jhabvala also lamented the prevalence of the tale of the 'unfortunate maiden fallen into the hands of a dusky seducer'.[8] This is none the less precisely the plot of *Three Continents*, in which Harriet Wishwell, the scion of a wealthy, if now declining, American clan, stands to inherit a fortune with her twin, Michael, on their twenty-first birthday. When the pair fall under the spell of the mysterious Rawul, one of Jhabvala's ambivalent guru figures, the horrible possibility looms that their legacy will pass swiftly through his hands and into those of his charismatic second-in-command, Crishi,

Harriet's husband, whose sexual favours she shares with homosexual Michael and the Rawul's mistress, Rani. Like Atwood, Jhabvala conflates historical Gothic with the plot of modern Gothic. As defined by Joanna Russ,[9] the latter involves a young, shy, passive heroine, with absent or ineffectual parents and a friend or ally in the pale, bloodless 'shadow male'. She travels to an exotic setting, forms a connection with a dark, magnetic 'supermale', finds herself up against 'another woman', and has to solve a 'buried ominous secret', usually, in modern Gothic, a criminal activity centred on money. The plot generally ends in attempted murder. In *Three Continents* the exotic area is India; the persecuted Harriet is totally passive and after an initial ambivalence towards dark, super-phallic Crishi, becomes his sexual slave, disregarding sinister rumours. (There was, of course, a first wife with a nameless fate.) Rani features as the other woman. (She makes Harriet think of 'stories of intrigue and poison and other hidden deeds taking place in the harem' (p. 199)[10] and has a child who may or may not be Crishi's adulterous offspring.) Harriet's family includes a conventionally vapid mother (in this case also fully occupied with a girlish Lesbian affair) and a pathologically spendthrift father, neither of whom is much help to her. The pallid Michael fulfils the textbook role of the 'shadow male', apparently representing the security of childhood, but actually inducting Harriet into the Rawul's 'Sixth World' movement. The 'buried ominous secret' turns out to be an international smuggling ring, masterminded by Crishi who transports jewels and *objets d'art* across borders, under cover of the movement. Throughout the novel the reader is afforded glimpses of the real situation, with recurrent dark hints and a veritable anthology of half-told stories and half-heard conversations in the wings, creating an atmosphere of sustained menace.

Elements of historical Gothic are self-consciously introduced, often in a fashion which suggests the conditioning force of the literary genre on Harriet. Her first encounter with Crishi, in her brother's room, is presented as an erotic shock 'as of a live wire suddenly coming in contact with an innermost part of one's being' (p. 16), though the demon-lover has appeared only to borrow some shaving cream. Later he succeeds in binding Harriet to him, forcing her body to move in unison with his 'as if my body obeyed him more than it did me' (p. 59), until she makes good her escape and flees, in true Gothic heroine mode: 'I didn't stop running till I was in the house' (p. 60). The scene is somewhat undercut by the fact that what Crishi was enjoying was a three-legged race at a Fourth of July party. None the less Harriet soon awakens in the night 'suddenly as if someone had called me' (p. 111). As a matter of fact, somebody has – Crishi – who is standing by her bed. (No Jane Eyre long-distance telepathy here.) The couple repair to the emblematic locale of the ruined Linton house, where, after peering through the windows at its ruined splendours (Cathy and Heathcliff), Crishi seduces Harriet. Later, exulting in passion,

Harriet describes herself as 'a woman savage running to her mate' (p. 115), when in fact she has been despatched to fetch Crishi's trousers. Quite clearly Jhabvala is consciously exploiting Gothic conventions while under-lining the distinction between the conditioning force of literary genre and the resistant fact of Crishi. A group of 'bhais', the Rawul's henchmen, rival any eighteenth-century group of banditti, and Rani takes to haunting Harriet's bedroom by night, 'her reflection ghostlike in the mirror' (p. 304) like some madwoman in the attic. After a journey through 'uncharted regions' (p. 366), sealed in a small chamber lit by a ghostly blue light (the sleeping coupé of an Indian train, an interesting variation on the idea of live burial), the novel ends with the ascent of a winding stair to a crenel-lated roof terrace reminiscent of Thornfield Hall where all is revealed by the villain. The twist upon the tale lies in Harriet's transition from vic-timhood to complicity. At the close, Harriet joins with her demon-lover to conceal Michael's murder and to forge the suicide note which will ensure that his fortune passes to them.

As a smuggler of art objects, Crishi is explicitly connected to the cyn-ical and exploitative transfer of art from one culture to another, in his case via the plundering of the East to the benefit of the West. The ques-tions raised by generic transfer are therefore thematised within the action itself. Artistic transfer is none the less a two-way traffic, as Jhabvala's exploitation of European conventions in a postcolonial environment demonstrates. Is this use of Asian Gothic merely a Eurocentric, Orientalist strategy, to adopt Edward Said's terminology? Or does it offer the post-colonial writer opportunities to criticise European textual and ideological practices by strategies unavailable to the realist novel? Does it merely con-tribute to the already abundant literature of India as horror story? Or can it illuminate the roots of violence in the postcolonial situation?

The answer to these questions depends upon an informed awareness of another story within the novel. Jhabvala indicates the relationship of the 'unspoken' of Gothic with the activity of 'speaking for' of culture, by firmly connecting the 'unspeakable' nature of events (dark hints, half-told stories) to a story which has already been told so often as to be recog-nisably a product of Western hegemonic discourse – that of Charles Sobhraj, the Asian serial killer, who is the model for Crishi.

In the 1970s, Sobhraj left a trail of bodies across India, Thailand and Nepal; he specialised in smuggling gems for which he needed a constant supply of fresh passports, bought or stolen from overlanders on the hippy trail. He then graduated to the *modus operandi* of a 'drug and rob' man, first surreptitiously administering laxatives and other drugs, then 'medi-cines' which reduced his victims to helplessness. Many of his targets, like Harriet and Michael, were seeking mystic enlightenment in the East. While planning to rob the jewellery store in Delhi's Imperial Hotel in 1976, Sobhraj was finally caught when he drugged an entire package tour of sixty French graduate engineers, whose instantaneous and simultaneous collapse in their hotel lobby finally aroused suspicion. Sobhraj was at various points arrested and gaoled in Kabul, Teheran, Greece and Paris, and made several daring escapes, notably following an unnecessary appendectomy, from which he bore identifying scars. A man of considerable charisma, he often gained the sympathy of his victims and accomplices by tales of his awful youth (as Crishi does with Harriet). His main female accomplice, a young Canadian, appears to have been kept in total sexual thrall to him. Other parallels with the fictitious Crishi are legion. Both men spend part of their youth in Bombay (p. 110), live by jewel smuggling and participate in murder. The hotel jewellery shop is the locus of mystery in *Three Continents*. Crishi goes in for martial exercises (for Sobhraj it was karate), has abdominal scars (p. 139), prison sentences in Teheran and elsewhere (p. 139), and has carried out gaolbreaks (p. 176). Both Sobhraj and Crishi relish media exposure, the former after his arrest, the latter in connection with the 'Sixth World' movement. At the close, when Harriet is looking for Michael, she encounters Paul, one of the Westerners, who is clearly very unwell. Like others in the group (p. 353), he has given Crishi his passport and is begging for its return. It is an exact replication of the means by which Sobhraj surrounded himself with couriers, targets and accomplices. Paul came to India 'to get away from home, from his family, from himself . . . not to be bound by anything' (p. 353). Boundless freedom has left him, however, without the means to move on, in a position of statelessness.

Despite the fact that Charles Sobhraj is still in gaol in India and that there are therefore legal impediments to the enterprise, his story has already been told several times, in two works of 'faction', one since revised and updated, in a TV mini-series, and in various newspapers and magazines, quite sufficient to suggest that the Sobhraj case is one of those 'Orientalist' horror stories which the West likes to repeat. From the first the story served ideological purposes. In India it broke at an opportune moment during the Emergency Rule powers of Indira Gandhi, when the Maintenance of Internal Security Act meant that anyone suspected of 'subversion' could be gaoled indefinitely. In India the international dimension of the story was insisted upon:

> India's newspapers, subdued and fearful under Indira Gandhi's dictatorial powers, relished a story that had no political overtones. The 'notorious gang' and 'international killers' were profiled endlessly, mug shots decorating Sunday feature pages.[11]

In the West the evolution of the story was classically hegemonic, its political complexities steadily watered down in favour of a stereotypically Orientalist tale. One of the first in the field, Thomas Thompson, in his faction, *Serpentine,* drew explicit parallels between the events of Sobhraj's life and the dismantling of the French colonial Empire. As the illegitimate offspring of a Vietnamese mother and an Indian father, born in Saigon when it was under Japanese occupation, but Vichy French administration, Sobhraj's early experiences included kidnap by the Viet Minh, rescue by the British, abandonment by his mother who married a French army officer, and life on the streets of Saigon. Reclaimed, he moved to Dakar, French West Africa, then France, whence he ran away by ship to Saigon, only to be promptly sent to Bombay by his father in a vain attempt to gain Indian citizenship. Stateless, institutionalised at several points, Sobhraj shuttled between countries until adulthood. Thompson's portrayal of him as a casualty of Empire, lacking roots, security and identity, ends on a note that appears to have offered Jhabvala the cue for the American opening of her novel. In gaol in India, Sobhraj was apparently considering his future:

> He required a country in which he was neither known nor wanted by police, one in which riches abounded, one whose boundaries were easy to traverse illegally, one whose residents were generous with attention and applause. At last report, the serpentine roads of destiny – he believed – would lead him to the United States.[12]

Thompson's implicit recourse, here, to the 'invasion scare' model of Gothic is very much the emphasis of other works, which have tended to minimise the postcolonial background. In *Bad Blood* Richard Neville and Julie Clarke read Sobhraj in terms of a paradigm of early rejection and deprivation. Neville, a veteran of the *Oz* 'Schoolkids Edition' obscenity trial had no great reverence for authority, and went to Delhi to interview Sobhraj with a theory 'of Charles as a child of colonialism, revenging himself on the counterculture'.[13] He concluded, however, that Sobhraj's claims to anti-imperialist motivation were groundless, and that the story was that of an individual of great potential, whose life resembled the form of Shakespearian tragedy. Updating the book ten years later as a TV tie-in, Neville revealed that his relationship with his co-author had been severely threatened by their involvement in the case, and that they had come close to being polarised into victim and accomplice. Julie Clarke's sympathies had remained with the victims; Neville, however, admitted that when interviewing Sobhraj he came to feel 'like a conspirator'.[14] The TV mini-series (*Shadow of the Cobra*) developed the hint, focusing its plot on the threat to one romantic relationship (two young journalists) and transforming Sobhraj from child of colonialism into diabolical villain. In an artistic trajectory which says much for the extent to which the rage for the Raj has been transformed into the redemonisation of the East, the role of Sobhraj was taken by Art Malik, veteran of *The Jewel in the Crown, The Far Pavilions* and *Passage to India*. The blurb to the reissued tie-in said it all: 'An audience with psychopathic mass murderer Charles Sobhraj. It was like having supper with the devil.' Reviewers concurred that Sobhraj was a 'plausible, Bruce Lee style, Asian fiend'[15] operating in, the 'dangerous jungle'[16] of Asia. There, this 'diabolically charismatic'[17] villain took his victim on a 'descent into hell'.[18] The evolution of the various accounts shows the West writing and rewriting Sobhraj into the norms of the snakey Oriental villain, with socioeconomic readings excised in favour of (at best) popular psychoanalysis, and (at worst) elements of *Vathek*, Milton's Satan and Fu Man Chu.

In contrast, Jhabvala's understanding of the socioeconomic dimension of the story is already evident in her first attempt at the theme. In her short story 'Expiation', the plot centres upon a *nouveau riche* Indian family who have made a fortune in textiles, and their son's fatal involvement with Sachu, a criminal from a deprived background. Sachu's target for kidnap, ransom and murder is the child of an Indian military family, described as light-skinned educated gentry who speak Hindi with an accent 'like Sahibs'.[19] Arrested, Sachu boasts of his philosophy to the press, much as Sobhraj did. Commentators on the Sobhraj case have frequently expressed bewilderment at the lack of motivation for many of the crimes. In 'Expiation', however, the crime is less the product of a fiendish Oriental torturer than a revenge across both class and race, against the preceding imperial norms (the Sahibs) and their replication in a newly industrialised India.

The account chimes with recent research on the serial killer, which contextualises his motivation in socioeconomic terms. Anthropologist Elliott Leyton has argued that serial killers are intensely class conscious and obsessed with status. The majority are adopted, illegitimate or institutionalised in youth, and seek a sense of identity in international celebrity. Typically, their victims are drawn from a social category which is some social bands above the killer, and the prime mission is to wreak revenge on the established order. (Ted Bundy, for example, took the most valuable 'possessions' of the American middle class, their beautiful and talented university women.) In 'Expiation' the fictitious Sachu wreaks revenge simultaneously on the Eurocentric army officers **and** the new entrepreneurial class via the deaths of both their offspring. For Leyton, as for Jhabvala, serial killers are the dark consequences of the social and economic formations that pattern our lives. Killings of this nature are a protest against a perceived exclusion from society, and constitute a form of utterance on the part of those who have looked at their lives and pronounced them unliveable.

> The killings are thus also a form of suicide note (literally so with most mass murderers, who expect to die before the day or week is out; metaphorically so for most serial murderers, who sacrifice the remainder of their lives to the 'cause'), in which the killer states clearly which social category has excluded him.[20]

The act itself is therefore the 'note' – an unspeakable crime which is none the less a message that society must learn to read. Unlike mass murderers, serial killers tend to want to live to tell their stories and bask in fame. Once society has read the message the story will be retold by press and media, and become a means to identity. Two other factors cited by Leyton in the formation of the serial killer have a bearing on *Three Continents*: first he must be inculcated with a dream or ambition which society betrays, and second there must be the necessary existence of cultural forms that can mediate killer and victim in a special sense, ridding victims of humanity and killer of responsibility. (Leyton cites the social validation of violent identity in modern films, television and fiction.) In retelling the story, Jhabvala's daring strategy is to recast it in Gothic mould – apparently redundantly. As Thompson remarked, the case already 'contained enough sex and betrayal and intrigue to fill the darkest scenario'.[21] By exploiting the silences of Gothic, however, Jhabvala avoids contributing to the social validation of the killer. In addition, she is able to repoliticise the story, revealing its horrors without stereotypical demonisation by insisting on the interrelationship of the Gothic 'unspeakable' and the 'spoken for' of culture – the discourse from which the postcolonial is excluded, and into which the postcolonial subject feels that he can break only by violence.

Where the Sobhraj case was used in India as a diversion from the increasingly dictatorial nature of the political settlement, Jhabvala supplies a public political dimension by the introduction of the Rawul's militaristic 'Sixth World' movement, which dehumanises its followers and legitimises brutality on the basis of a vaguely transcendental cult. Ostensibly devoted to the unification of the globe by 'transcendental internationalism', the Rawul plans its transformation into a 'stateless, casteless, countryless' (p. 201) world by transcending not so much spiritual as national and political bounds, and with them 'the tiny concepts, geographical or other, of an earlier humanity' (p. 241). Linda Bayer-Berenbaum has connected the resurgence of twentieth-century Gothic with the waning of 1960s' cults, arguing that both movements were motivated by the search for an expanded and intensified consciousness. She therefore likened the Gothic revival to 'a variety of religious cults that have grown in popularity, be they Christian fundamentalist, Hari Krishna, the Sufis, or most recently, the Moonies. Unlike these movements though, Gothicism asserts that transcendence is primarily evil'.[22] In *Three Continents* the Gothic 'secret' provides an ironic revelation of the real import of the Rawul's transcendental activities, in the political world, and the extent to which they operate as a legitimising cover for Crishi, the excluded. Natural and political boundaries **are** crossed, but for criminal reasons. The movement towards being citizens of the world depends heavily for its day-to-day activities upon stolen passports. The plan to unite the best of all civilisations translates into the pillaging of material artefacts. Harriet and Michael throw off Western materialism, only for it to come back to haunt them from the Third World. Mobility is the mark of both the Western truthseeker and the serial killer. Just as the latter links the culturally spoken and the unspeakable, so Crishi reveals in his actions the revenge of the excluded. Sobhraj, the stateless exile, killed those whose wilful deracination parodied his own state, just as Crishi, who has had disinheritance forced upon him, sees to it that his condition is shared.

In addition to reflecting the Rawul's project in a dark mirror, so the Gothic structure dramatises Harriet's surreptitious slippage from a counter-cultural to a collusive position, from victim to accomplice, and implicitly from a readerly to a writerly role. At the beginning of the novel, Harriet's stunned silence, as the Rawul takes over, is such as to make her almost a voyeur, watching her story unfold and guessing its outcome from the same hints available to the reader. Again and again the text tells us that Harriet can get no explanations from the men: 'What was it all about? Who were they, and why had they come? I waited for Michael to tell me, but he had no time to tell me anything. "You'll find out," was all he said' (p. 15). The reader is thus brought into close affective proximity to events, while being simultaneously warned off from any uncritical suspension of disbelief. (Rani and Crishi present themselves as mother and son in an 'indifferent, believe-it-or-not way' p. 23.) Originally Harriet and Michael communicate wordlessly, the one often completing the other's thoughts (p. 14). Crishi, however, appropriates their private language (specifically the term 'neti' meaning 'phoney') and deprives them of it. Though each is enjoying Crishi's sexual favours neither feels able to discuss the matter, converting their former spiritual communion into a shared secret, separately held. They welcome the noise of the swimming hole, because there 'conversation was impossible' (p. 72). Later when Harriet shares her bed with Rani as well, she feels Michael 'willing me not to speak', so that the act remains 'unmentioned, rather than unmentionable' (p. 215). The prohibition on speech even extends to Crishi's marriage proposal. He manages to propose by proxy, through Rani, so that Harriet becomes 'spoken for' without ever being spoken to.

The secret engagement and muffling of events is in strong contrast to the ever more publicity-conscious movement, which develops to the point at which 'interviews became the central activity of the house' (p. 133). The Rawul has a tendency to convert all his utterances into speeches for public consumption, even to his small daughters (p. 268). Linguistic and political structures evolve together. A chat with the Rawul becomes 'more in the nature of an audience. Everything around the Rawul was taking on more formality' (p. 119). The movement to transcend all boundaries begins to use security guards and checkpoints and to beat up intruders. Even Michael's speech patterns change, so that instead of groping for thoughts he becomes brisk and unreflective: 'he no longer had to think . . . . It was all there, all formulated' (p. 223). Where Gothic mystery preserves the possibility of unvoiced stories, the Sixth World movement accretes everything to one public formulation, assisted by Anna Sultan, a journalist who provides their first 'major media exposure' (p.182). Harriet's difficulty in getting at her story contrasts with Anna's ease. Harriet notes that: 'Everything I had only guessed at Anna seemed to know for sure' (p. 138). Anna's account none the less includes a highly fanciful tale of the Rawul's initial encounter with Crishi, first in his dreams, then promptly discovered asleep in a poet's tomb. Over the others' protests, Rani and Crishi endorse the story: '"it's what the common reader wants," Crishi said. "Ask Harriet . . . . Harriet liked it and she's a very common reader. You have to give them these sort of stories."' (p. 184). The incident provides an explicit comment on the way in which cultural formations function to legitimise exploitation. Anna Sultan herself turns the personal into the public, making her name with a daring profile of a Lebanese leader: 'daring because she had recorded his private along with his public activities, and had not drawn back from chronicling her own affair with him (p. 133). For Anna any assignment involves a love affair, which is speedily terminated when her story is finished. In Crishi, however, she meets her match as the postcolonial subject refuses textualisation except on his own terms. Crishi's only interest is the book which will publicise, authenticate and create his identity, whereas Anna becomes personally attached and exploited in her turn – the fate which threatened Richard Neville at Sobhraj's hands. It is a telling image of the revenge of the excluded subject, who turns his own exploitation against his exploiters, to write his own social message.

It is not for nothing that the group are compared to a movie company (p. 40); their lives are being swallowed up by public performance. The Rawul even stages appropriate public ceremonies to authenticate the movement. Harriet's wedding is briskly converted into a symbol of the synthesis of East and West, so symbolic indeed that Crishi spends the wedding night with Rani. The Rawul's idea that the new movement must find a mode of expression 'emancipated from all outworn forms' (p. 143) backfires into irony, however, as the couple symbolise their transcendent unity by sharing a loving-cup of a more sinister Gothic nature: 'This vessel had crossed deserts and dried-up riverbeds, had been secretly buried, lost for a generation or two, murdered for by sword and poison – it had a lot of history and legend behind it' (p. 148). Appropriately the wine turns out to be spoiled, but Harriet swallows it almost as willingly as the legends. From perceiving herself with Michael as 'blank pages no one had ever written on' (p. 259), Harriet is being steadily scripted into a public role.

A second ceremony which involves the public weighing of the Rawul against a pile of books, supposedly representing the wisdom of the ages, reveals both the totalising project of the movement, and its amorality. Like

Crishi, the Rawul intends to textualise himself on his own terms. Michael had wanted to buy bound sets of volumes, but Crishi exercises a financial veto so that the Rawul is actually outweighed by a motley collection of tattered secondhand copies of the Bible, Plato, *The Tibetan Book of the Dead*, Carlos Castaneda and Kierkegaard. The form of this attempt to appropriate all cultures to one universal meaning is ludicrously parodic; several volumes have to be removed from the scales to balance the Rawul. Significantly 'it was at Kierkegaard that the Rawul started to swing up' (p. 279) – appropriately, given Kierkegaard's separation of the religious and the ethical spheres. The twins, however, react uncritically. For Michael the event is a summation of 'everything he had thought and read and experienced . . . It was all summed up for him in the pile of books on the one hand . . . and the Rawul on the other' (p. 279). Meanwhile Harriet uses the mythologising process in order to put a high gloss on Crishi's activities, reflecting that 'it doesn't seem to matter that sometimes these gods don't behave too well, Venus running off with Mars, Krishna cheating on Radha – they still remain gods' (pp. 277–8).

Once on Indian soil, however, Crishi lives up to Krishna, his trickily elusive namesake, and naked power emerges from behind the myths and legends, as the Rawul's movement swiftly modulates into a conventional political party. Far from transporting his followers into a boundless world, he moves the party into an airconditioned hotel, completely cut off from the outside world. Harriet and Michael are once more linguistically isolated – they speak no Indian languages. Michael's death is the direct result of the clash between the spoken and the unspoken. Impatiently he demands that the Rawul make a religious oration, rather than merely entertaining influential politicos: 'When's he going to speak?' 'He's got to speak,' he insists (p. 331). Michael is slow to realise that (to quote Christine Brooke-Rose):

> everyone knows that real power, whether political, economic, social, psychological or even mystical, functions silently and has no need of the semblance of speech, even though it never ceases to use that semblance to persuade that we participate.[23]

Secure in his power base, the Rawul dispenses with the mediating forms which had previously legitimised him. Instead his wife speaks, giving secret instructions in her own language to her henchmen who promptly remove Michael. The power to which Michael contributed by his rhetorical formulations is unleashed to silence him, and to consign him to the unspoken of Gothic.

In contrast, Harriet's movement into collusion with crime is rendered as a progression from the unspoken to the fully discursive, as Jhabvala demonstrates that the final horror is equally located in the process of 'speaking for'. When Michael disappears, Harriet is taken aback by the sudden silence which meets all her enquiries – the English of the hotel staff evaporates, the Rawul is so concerned with the universal that he cannot stoop to the particular to answer a personal question (p. 348), the jeweller provides only partial and guarded replies. Yet she continues the process of speaking for Michael, pretending to her grandmother that he is on the other end of a phone line, and doing some very fast talking of her own. Harriet's collusion with both the unspeakable and the textual is ambiguously dramatised at the close, in the suicide note which she co-authors with the presumed killer. Harriet knows very well that Crishi's account of Michael's suicide is a lie. (The supposed suicide note is too badly spelled to be his.) She collaborates none the less in rewriting the note in more convincing fashion, revising a visibly false story to make it more believable. Revision becomes replication-as-falsity. Harriet would have been truer to the facts of murder if she had allowed the gaps and absences in the original to speak for themselves. No longer a common reader, Harriet has progressed to writing – writing as complicity and betrayal. She writes 'with ease' (p. 383), almost with enjoyment, as if becoming Michael, speaking for him, constructing a fiction of defeated dreams as his motive.

> I said that I – that is, I, Michael – was going away because there was nothing in this world that was good enough for me . . . . I said that if once you have these expectations – that is, of Beauty, Truth, and Justice – then you feel cheated by everything that falls short of them; and everything here – that is, here, in this world – does fall short of them. It is all neti, neti (p. 383).

As that last word indicates, Harriet uses their private language to authenticate a public document. Spiritual communion becomes the unspeakable. Framed to meet legal requirements, the note is multiply authored – ostensibly by Michael, actually by Harriet, partly at Crishi's dictation – and is the product of multiple silencing, that of the postcolonial subject, that of the woman excluded from knowledge, and – fatally – of the representative of the society which excluded them. At the close, Crishi has carried out the action which communicates a social message of defeated hopes, while Harriet, writing as a male and at the same time writing off a male, has produced a socially legitimising text. The note therefore conceals – and sanctions – an act of violence.

This chapter began with a question – whether the Gothic novel is an accomplice in the process of Eurocentric textualisation of the East, or whether it may serve to reveal the sources of violence in the colonial encounter. In counter-cultural Harriet, who slips into the position of accomplice, Jhabvala provides a searching investigation of the psychopathology of power, the process of domination and its relation to mediating cultural forms. The complicity of the writer in generic manipulation and transfer may indeed amount to collusion in violence and exploitation, but may also reveal the bases of such violence in silencing and exclusion. The duplicity of Gothic – its propensity for crossing boundaries, violating taboos, transgressing limits, together with its sense of blockage, privation and prohibition against utterance – makes it the perfect means to dramatise the horrors of the relationship between the social group which sanctions its actions by cultural forms, and those excluded from discourse, who speak by deeds. The Gothic undermines the Rawul's pretensions to one-ness, universality and totalisation at the same time as it preserves the unspeakable quality of the killer's actions. By its intertextual nature, its ability to translate from one text to another and back, it prevents the univocal from holding sway. At the close, therefore, Jhabvala offers a multiple text, a piece of writing which conceals a secret and reveals a silenced story, which demonstrates the writer's complicity and (by highlighting issues of fictionality) separates the reader from affective collusion. As the original suicide note showed, truth for the postcolonial writer may be measured as much by its failure to represent itself as by its social production. What the Gothic does not say – its half-told stories – constitutes the evidence of a contrary project undermining public formulations. By preserving the unspoken within the text, Jhabvala remains true to the events of both political and social history.

# Notes

1 Examples include Jean Rhys, *Wide Sargasso Sea* (1966); Bessie Head, *A Question of Power* (London, Heinemann, 1973); Ruth Prawer Jhabvala, *Heat and Dust* (1975); Margaret Atwood, *Lady Oracle* (Toronto, McCleland and Stewart, 1976); Anne Hébert, *Héloïse* (Paris, Seuil, 1980); Alice Munro, *Lives of Girls and Women* (Toronto, McGraw Hill Ryerson, 1971); Isak Dinesen (Karen Blixen), *Seven Gothic Tales* (London, Putnam, 1934); V. S. Naipaul, *Guerrillas* (London, Deutsch, 1975); Paul Scott, *The Raj Quartet* (London, Heinemann, 1966–75); J. G. Farrell, *Troubles* (London, Cape, 1970); Toni Morrison, *Beloved* (London, Chatto and Windus, 1987).
2 Patrick Brantlinger, *Rule of Darkness: British Literature and Imperialism, 1830–1914* (Ithaca, Cornell University Press, 1988), Chapter 8. For a sympathetic and illuminating discussion of *Lady Oracle* as Gothic novel see Molly Hite, *The Other Side of the Story* (Ithaca, Cornell University Press, 1989), Chapter 4.
3 I am indebted for this observation to Mary Gordon, 'Where Women Come In: Whose Realism Is It Anyway?', Belgian-Luxembourg American Studies Association Conference on Neo-Realism in Contemporary American Fiction, Ghent, 1991.
4 Eve Kosofsky Sedgwick, *The Coherence of Gothic Conventions* (London, Methuen, 1986), p. 13.

5 See Brantlinger, *Rule of Darkness*, Chapter 3.
6 Ruth Prawer Jhabvala, 'Disinheritance', *Blackwoods*, April 1979, p. 14.
7 Laurie Sucher, *The Fiction of Ruth Prawer Jhabvala: The Politics of Passion* (London, Macmillan, 1989).
8 Ruth Prawer, 'The Short-Story in England, 1700–1750', London University MA thesis, 1950, p. 42. (I am grateful to Ruth Prawer Jhabvala for permission to quote this passage.)
9 Joanna Russ, 'Somebody's Trying To Kill Me And I Think It's My Husband: The Modern Gothic', in Juliann E. Fleenor, ed., *The Female Gothic* (Montreal, Eden Press, 1983), pp. 31–56.
10 Ruth Prawer Jhabvala, *Three Continents* (London, Penguin, 1988). First published by John Murray, 1987. Page references which follow quotations in parentheses are to the Penguin edition.
11 Thomas Thompson, *Serpentine* (London, Macdonald, 1980), pp. 565–6.
12 Thompson, *Serpentine*, p. 659.
13 Richard Neville and Julie Clarke, *Bad Blood: The Life and Crimes of Charles Sobhraj* (London, Pan, 1979), p. 350.
14 Richard Neville and Julie Clarke, *Shadow of the Cobra: The Life and Crimes of Charles Sobhraj* (London; Penguin, 1989), p. 343. For an account of the mini-series see *Radio Times*, 15–21 July 1989, pp. 4–5 and the *Listener*, 13 July 1989, p. 33.
15 *Books and Bookmen*, February 1980, p. 11.
16 *Far Eastern Economic Review*, 13 August 1976, p. 10.
17 *Books and Bookmen*, February 1980, p. 11.
18 *Bestsellers*, January 1980, p. 383.
19 Ruth Prawer Jhabvala, 'Expiation', *New Yorker*, 10 October 1982, p. 49.
20 Elliott Leyton, *Hunting Humans: The Rise of the Modern Multiple Murderer* (London, Penguin, 1989), pp. 26–7, first published as *Compulsive Killers* (New York University Press, 1986). I am grateful to Bruce Babington of the University of Newcastle upon Tyne for drawing this book to my attention, despite the sleepless night it occasioned.
21 Thompson, *Serpentine*, p. xi.
22 Linda Bayer-Berenbaum, *The Gothic Imagination* (London and Toronto, Associated University Presses, 1982), pp. 12–13.
23 Christine Brooke-Rose, *A Rhetoric of the Unreal: Studies in Narrative and Structure, especially of the fantastic* (Cambridge University Press, 1983), p. 389.

# |6|

# *Empire as a dirty story*

## J. M. Coetzee,
## Waiting for the Barbarians *and* Foe

Where Rhys, Jhabvala and Desai are concerned as much with issues of history or 'herstory' as with the 'literary', other postcolonial writers engage with the past in less specifically historical fashion, constructing consciously atemporal fictions (Coetzee), or dystopian fable (Emecheta), consciously eliding the realities of time and place (Naipaul), and actively embracing the attractions of the limitless (Mukherjee). J. M. Coetzee's opposition to the 'colonisation of the novel by the discourse of history' is a matter of record.[1] Writing in 1988 he inveighed against the tendency in South Africa to subsume fiction under history, to read novels as imaginative investigations of real historical circumstances, and to treat those which do not perform such investigations as lacking in seriousness. Critics, however, have defined the writer's apparent distance from his immediate sociopolitical context as a weakness. David Attwell's is a representative objection. Noting that the 'people's culture' campaign led by the United Democratic Front during the 1985 and 1986 States of Emergency encouraged a concern with the accessibility of art to underclass audiences and readerships, the need to build a national culture, and an emphasis on documentary realism produced by the artist as cultural worker, Attwell argues that Coetzee, in contrast, opposes to any historical narrative various intertextual configurations, which participate explicitly in the international affiliations of intellectual, literary–critical or, at best, literary–historical culture. 'The intertextual networks of literature seem to provide Coetzee with a kind of guarantee of the possibility of . . . freedom, even if this means only the freedom to rethink . . . the categories of dominance'.[2] Yet for Attwell the intertextuality that is sought after as a free area, independent of the history-governed aesthetics of oppositional South Africa, also constitutes a potential limitation. Coetzee does not seek non-metropolitan, African forms of affiliation, but rather European or American. Michael K is closer to Beckett or Kafka than to any revolutionary; the subject matter of *Foe* speaks for itself.

*Waiting for the Barbarians* has been no exception to the critical consensus, its lack of specific location in time and place, its emphasis on the cyclical time of the seasons, its narrative present tense, all making it susceptible to ahistorical and apolitical readings. *Waiting for the Barbarians* is also richly intertextual with echoes of Kafka ('In the Penal Colony'), Hawthorne and the ubiquitous Beckett. For many readers such self-conscious literary reflexivity militates against political content. Intertextuality turns in upon itself – interestingly, perhaps – but as a substitute for focusing its powers on the real world. Yet *Waiting for the Barbarians* is in fact a novel which directly thematises intertextuality in a careful strategy of repoliticisation. Key intertexts are rewritten and deployed in order to underline specific political points, within an overall framework which reconstrues the literary technique itself to subversive ends, by drawing upon a specific nexus of ideas concerning pollution behaviour and its anthropological analysis.

The novel owes its general situation to Dino Buzzati's *Il Deserto Dei Tartari* (1945) translated into English in 1952 as *The Tartar Steppe*. Giovanni Drogo, a young officer in an unnamed country, is posted to Fort Bastiani, located in a dead stretch of frontier, beyond which lies a great desert, the Tartar Steppe. Long ago there may have been Tartars but, as in *Waiting for the Barbarians*, none have appeared in living memory. None the less Colonel Filimore is 'still waiting for them' (Buzzati, p. 48).[3] Even Colonel Ortiz, who describes the legend of the Tartars as just that – a legend – comments: 'The Tartars, the Tartars. At first it sounds like nonsense, naturally, then you end up believing it yourself.' (Buzzati, p. 158). Waiting for the Tartars, like waiting for Godot, is something of an absurdist activity. The first death of the novel emphasises both the futility of militarism and the extent to which the Tartars exist only in the soldiers' projections. When a stray horse appears outside the fort, Private Lazzari defies the rules in order to catch it, and, not having the password for reentry, is promptly shot as an 'enemy' by his friend Moretto. Unlike Coetzee, however, Buzzati does eventually confirm the reality of the external threat: an invading army is spotted, crossing the desert. To his chagrin, Drogo, dying of a liver complaint, is invalided out at the very moment when glory beckons, after thirty years 'merely waiting for the enemy' (Buzzati, p. 207). Futile as his personal fate appears, the fact remains that an enemy does appear, and that the fort's defensive function is justified.

In remodelling *The Tartar Steppe*, therefore, Coetzee turns to an African intertext – Constantin Cavafy's 'Waiting for the Barbarians'. In the poem, the Emperor, Praetors and Consuls have been waiting, splendidly apparelled, for the arrival at the city gates of the barbarians – who never appear. Discomfited they return to their homes, suddenly aware that Empire has no meaning without a subject to oppress, a subject by which to define itself. The concluding lines draw the moral explicitly:

Why are all the streets and squares emptying so quickly?
And everybody turning home again so full of thought?
Because night has fallen and the barbarians have not come.
And some people have arrived from the frontier;
They said there are no barbarians any more.
And now what will become of us without Barbarians?
Those people were some sort of a solution.[4]

In *Waiting for the Barbarians,* as in Cavafy, no barbarians ever appear, only fisher people and nomads, and the latter only briefly. To the barbarous proponents of Empire, however, they are very necessary, regularly invoked in scare stories, in a procedure reminiscent of the well-known South African tactic of 'swartgevaar' (black danger). Nadine Gordimer's novella 'Something Out There' focuses on precisely this use of 'bogeyman' tactics as a means to hold together a fractured polity by an invented external threat[5] (see Chapter 10). Both Cavafy and Coetzee, therefore, define the category 'barbarian' as a political invention, the recourse of the imperialist and the racist throughout the centuries.

In both cases, of course, an objection remains. The intertext is European (Buzzati) or 'white African' (a Greek-speaking Alexandrian) and is accessible only to the well-educated metropolitan reader. Coetzee's intertextual frame, Mary Douglas's *Purity and Danger,* raises no such reservations, drawing as it does upon ideas which will communicate readily to members of most human groups. By situating the phenomenon of intertextuality within the anthropological analysis of the discourse of pollution, Coetzee facilitates the establishment of a literary technique on altogether broader grounds, allowing both its thematisation and the contestation of its ahistorical nature. The method is adopted precisely in order to implicate the reader in the dirty story of Empire, and informs the major concerns of the novel: the frontier, the 'Other', pollution, torture, purificatory rituals, social systems, punishment and dreams. As method and theme conjoin, so the reasons why readers resist intertextuality become disquietingly apparent.

Mary Douglas's *Purity and Danger* announces itself in its subtitle as 'An Analysis of Concepts of Pollution and Taboo'.[6] Sturdily anthropological, the essential argument is that:

> Ideas about separating, purifying, demarcating and punishing transgressions have as their main function to impose system on an inherently untidy experience. It is only by exaggerating the difference between within and without, above and below, male and female, with and against, that a semblance of order is created (Douglas, p. 4).

Douglas offers a definition of dirt as essentially disorder. Dirt is relative. (Shoes are not dirty in themselves, but it is dirty to place them on a table.

Food is dirt if spattered on clothing.) Our pollution behaviour is the reaction which condemns any object or idea which is likely to confuse or contradict cherished classifications: 'Reflection on dirt involves reflection on the relation of order to disorder, being to non-being, form to formlessness, life to death' (Douglas, p. 5). Ideas of dirt therefore lead us straight into the symbolic order; where there is dirt there is system. 'Dirt is the byproduct of a systematic ordering and classification of matter' (Douglas, p. 35).

Since culture (in the sense of the public, standardised values of a community) mediates the experiences of individuals by providing basic categories into which ideas and values are ordered, culture will always tend to evolve rules for avoiding anomalous things, in order to affirm and strengthen the definitions to which they do not conform. In a case study of the abominations of Leviticus, Douglas argues that definitions of 'holiness' depend upon the notion of wholeness or completeness. In this context holiness means keeping distinct the categories of creation and therefore involves correct definition, discrimination and order. In dietary taboos the underlying principle of cleanness in animals is that they should conform fully to their class. Thus four-footed animals that fly are unclean; birds are clean. Scaly fish swim with fins in water; anything in water without fins or scales is unclean. And almost anything that creeps, crawls or swarms tends to be unclean because the movement itself is of an indeterminate nature. Holiness demands that individuals conform completely to the class to which they belong, and requires that different classes of things should not be confused. Any blurring of the lines between species will constitute pollution, uncleanness.

In a broader sense, all margins may come to be perceived as dangerous. People in a marginal state, placeless, left out of the social patterning, become sources of danger because their status is undefinable, whether they are social outsiders, offenders against the bounded wholeness of the human body, or in some way positioned between the living and the dead. (Douglas cites the unborn child, menstrual blood, the monstrous birth as examples of such interstitial forms; we might wish to add the racial minority, the physically handicapped or the sexually ambiguous.) At the same time, power goes hand in hand with danger. Danger lies in marginal states because transition is neither one state nor the next, but undefinable. To have been in the margins is to have been in contact with danger, to have been at the source of power. To enter the disordered regions of the mind, in dreams, faints and frenzies, is often seen as revealing unconscious truths. Similarly, in physical rituals, venturing into uncharted areas beyond the confines of society may convey power and status on the return from initiation. Even the attraction of works of art may be understood in terms of their function in enabling us to go beyond the explicit structures of our normal experience. Formlessness, indeterminacy, indefinability are therefore credited with powers, some dangerous, some good.

In 'normal' society, however, pollution arises from the interplay of form with formlessness. Pollution dangers strike when form has been attacked.

> A polluting person is always in the wrong. He has developed some wrong condition or simply crossed some line which should not have been crossed and this displacement unleashes danger for someone (Douglas, p. 113).

Often, of course, the main danger is to the polluting person himself, and in this respect the parallelism between the body and its society is of crucial import.

> The body is a model which can stand for any bounded system. Its boundaries can represent any boundaries which are threatened or precarious (Douglas, p. 115).

Since the body is a symbol of society's oneness, the powers and dangers credited to social structures may be reproduced in little on the human body, whether in public rituals, attitudes to bodily refuse, or in the treatment of bodily margins or thresholds as invested with power and danger (eyes, mouth, sexual or evacuatory orifices). People think of society as consisting of other people joined or separated by lines that must be respected. In consequence, whenever the lines are threatened, Douglas finds pollution ideas coming to their support. Any transgression of a social barrier is treated as a dangerous pollution, with the polluter becoming the object of reprobation. Purity is the enemy of change, ambiguity or compromise; the yearning for rigidity is in us all.

As this brief paraphrase indicates, Douglas's ideas inform the plot, imagery, structure and politics of *Waiting for the Barbarians*. Images of pollution proliferate in the novel, within a narrative in which frontiers, marginality, the mutilated and violated body express political and cultural realities. The action falls into representative phases: an initial movement, dominated by the presence of a crippled 'barbarian' girl, in which a liberal magistrate attempts to maintain the status quo, via ritual cleansings, but is drawn towards a deeper truth by the unconscious life of his dreams; and a second, after his excursion into the uncharted areas across the frontier, in which the state unleashes its powers to dramatise its symbolic structures on his physical body. There are few direct references to South Africa, though we may wish to consider that 'apartheid' (separateness) with its systems of classification of racial purity stands implicitly condemned.

From its opening chapter, *Waiting for the Barbarians* emphasises the opposition between the rigidity of form and the powers and dangers of formlessness. The magistrate, a representative liberal, is concerned only with maintaining the status quo, keeping his own hands clean by due observance. Confronted with two extremely smelly prisoners, the one bearing a suppurating sore, his reaction is 'Get these men to clean them-selves'[7] after which he abandons them to the sinister ministrations of Colonel Joll of the Third Bureau. The boy has come to the fort to have the sore treated, to be restored to wholeness. Ironically, however, by cross-ing the line between desert and fort, he has placed himself automatically in the role of the polluter. After Colonel Joll's 'interrogation' and the death of the older man (modelled on Steve Biko's) the magistrate is horrified to discover corpse and boy in the same cell. Again he appears to be more outraged by the lack of respect for due forms, the transgression of the boundaries between the living and the dead (the torturers have threatened to sew the boy into his uncle's shroud) than with the survivor's continued exposure to torture. In a phrase which recalls Douglas's discussion of the nature of taboo as involving both power and danger, sacred and unclean, he comments that the gaol has become 'holy or unholy ground, if there is any difference, preserve of the mysteries of the State' (p. 6).

At this point, however, the first of the magistrate's many dreams pro-vides a different perspective. In the dream, clean snow obliterates bound-aries, the sun has dissolved into mist, the square blurs at its edges into the sky. 'Walls, trees, houses have dwindled, lost their solidity, retired over the rim of the world' (p. 9). Children building a snowcastle are similarly muffled and faceless, melting away as he approaches. In the dream the clean and the formless go together. The text then moves to the tortured body of the boy, and to the magistrate's dawning awareness that unclean-ness resides with Empire:

> is it only in the provinces that headsmen and torturers are still thought of as unclean? . . . I find myself wondering too whether he [Joll] has a private ritual of purification, carried out behind closed doors, to enable him to return and break bread with other men . . . or has the Bureau created new men who can pass without disquiet between the unclean and the clean? (p.12).

The subsequent dream presents an indeterminately sexed body, its pubic apertures swarming with bees, an image of the uncleanness resulting from the simultaneous blurring of bodily, sexual and species boundaries. Clearly, while in his conscious behaviour the magistrate equates the imperial mis-sion with due form and ritual, his unconscious reverses the terms to reveal the imperial state as unclean, the formless expanse as pure.

The intuition remains a buried one, however. When Joll sends back more prisoners (fisher people) the magistrate finds them just as filthy as the townspeople do, repelled by their public defecation (no latrines have been provided): 'all together we lose sympathy with them. The filth, the smell' (p.19). Rumours fly that they are diseased; both their food and a dead cat are flung indiscriminately amongst them, a woman suffers a rape attempt. The definition of dirt is clearly a relative one, however. The removal and burial of a dead child, secreted under its mother's clothes, renders her unclean to **her** people who shun her. The magistrate wonders: 'Have we violated some custom of theirs . . . by taking the child and burying it?' (p. 20).

Yet the moment that Joll departs, he reverts almost comically to type: 'I want everything cleaned up! Soap and water! I want everything as it was before' (p. 24). In his desire to erase the dirty story of what has been happening, he is even tempted to resort to the type of purification which in the balkanised former Yugoslavia would be termed 'ethnic cleansing' – to make a fresh start by marching the prisoners out to the desert and burying them there. The temptation is resisted:

> that will not be my way. The new men of Empire are the ones who believe in fresh starts, new chapters, clean pages; I struggle on with the old story, hoping that before it is finished it will reveal to me why it was that I thought it worth the trouble (p. 25).

The comment is intensely revelatory, both in political and aesthetic terms. Readers' impatience with Coetzee's intertextual methods depends upon an uncomfortable awareness that his page is not clean, blank or fresh, that there is already an old story – *Robinson Crusoe* or *Waiting for Godot* – the outlines of which are being blurred and reshaped into the new, with the result a hybrid creation. Coetzee's generic crossovers (poem, drama, novel) exacerbate the awareness that category is not being respected, that the lines have been crossed illegitimately, and that things have not been kept in their 'right place'. Literary history has been defied in favour of imaginative reinvention, story privileged over history. Intertextuality is also, of course, a technique for initiates. The reader who recognises an allusion feels complicity with the author and with fellow-members of an interpretive community. It is therefore the ideal strategy with which to dramatise the attraction of category membership **and** the extent to which the desire for such rigid categorisations implicates the reader in the dirty story of Empire. *Waiting for the Barbarians* exposes the reader to the same kinds of pollution anxiety which threaten the magistrate, attaching the reader to the same motive forces which drive imperialism, while simultaneously condemning the rigidity of such cultural definitions.

As the magistrate is to discover, there are no clean pages. In his relationship with the abandoned 'barbarian' girl, he finds himself attracted by her awkward creeping movement and her misshapen feet. The connection to the unclean is heightened by her other mutilations. Because she has been half-blinded she bears a scar by her eye 'as though a caterpillar lay there with its head under her eyelid, grazing' (p. 31) – another image of an unclean, creeping animal violating the bounds of the body. A ritual is speedily established in which the magistrate washes and massages the girl's feet, frequently interrupted by waves of sleep, 'like death to me, or enchantment, blank, outside time' (p. 31). Ritual offers both a fantasy of atonement and a means of symbolically negating or reformulating the past. The girl's gender is also significant. Toril Moi has noted that patriarchy's definition of woman as marginal within the symbolic order, as on the frontier between men and chaos, means that it is appropriate for her to be perceived as the link to the 'outside': 'Women seen as the limit of the symbolic order will in other words share in the disconcerting properties of all frontiers: they will be neither inside nor outside, neither known nor unknown.'[8] It is this status which the girl defies, however. The magistrate attempts to define her as marginal. He argues that sex with her would be out of place: 'Lodging my dry old man's member in that blood-hot sheath makes me think of acid in milk, ashes in honey, chalk in bread' (p. 34). Mentally characterising her as damaged, unclean, he compares her to an animal, the untrained silver fox cub which he keeps inappropriately as a house pet. Yet he finds that she refuses to conform to the definition. With another woman, sexual desire has meant 'to pierce her surface and stir the quiet of her interior into an ecstatic storm' (p. 43). With the girl, however, 'it is as if there is no interior, only a surface across which I hunt back and forth seeking entry' (p. 43). The parallelism between the woman's body and the colonised land is also a parallel between body and story. While the girl remains mute, the narrator hunts for the truth of her story, examining the signs of torture on her body and repeatedly questioning her. Hunting, however, has already been equated with pollution, in Colonel Joll's heap of animal carcasses, left to rot (p. 1), and the magistrate has found himself unable as a result to hunt waterbuck (p. 39). Now he senses an obscure correspondence between his own quest for the truth and the interrogations of Colonel Joll. For a brief period the girl's lack of verbal or sexual responsiveness drives him to a young prostitute in whose arms he finds it a pleasure 'to be lied to so flatteringly' (p. 42). But sex with the playacting prostitute is only an attempt 'to obliterate the girl' (p. 47), to wipe clean the slate. Pleasant fictions of erotic desire cannot rival the girl's untold story. By holding back its details, she refuses to initiate him fully, leaving **him** in an interstitial position, aware of his complicity with the torturers, and yet unable to move on, to turn the page. Now he finds himself recalling unsettling occasions when, in the middle of the sexual act, he found himself 'losing my way like a storyteller losing the thread of his story' (p. 45). When he tries to write a history of his thirty years on the frontier he finds himself similarly stalled: 'It seems appropriate that a man who does not know what to do with the woman in his bed should not know what to write' (p. 58). It is the magistrate's fear of being rewritten or even ignored by future history which is at the root of his sexual and writerly block. When two deserters are found frozen to death in the desert he insists that they are brought back to have the appropriate rites, to demonstrate that 'we survive as filiations in the memory of those we knew' (p. 54), aware that he is comforting himself against the vision of a future 'barbarian' triumph which would mark the end of his history. Again and again he dreams of the girl, now with clearly defined features, building a snow fort 'empty of life' (p. 53). The dreams express his anxiety that there will come a time when **his** story will be the missing one, the blank and absence, when **his** people will be gone but the girl's vividly present. Ironically, to the half-blind girl he has always been 'a blur, a blank' (p. 31), lacking distinct outlines. In response, she remains stubbornly physical, refusing to reduce herself to his language, his categorisations,[9] symbolically enacting in her own body her own structures of meaning. As Douglas noted, there is power as well as danger in marginal status.

To enter the girl the magistrate must enter the interstitial formlessness of the desert, crossing the line to return her to her own people. The journey, beset by danger, is described as a venture into formlessness, outside categories. 'Dust rather than air becomes the medium in which we live. We swim through dust like fish through water' (p. 60). Even the ground beneath their feet turns out to be a frozen lake. In this new medium, sexual possession suddenly becomes possible, and the appearance of the 'barbarians' swiftly follows. Both magistrate and girl are, for once, in the same category. When the girl menstruates she is rendered unclean in the eyes of the men. 'It is the old story: a woman's flux is bad luck, bad for the crops, bad for the hunt, bad for the horses' (p. 69). In response, the magistrate invents a ceremony of purification for them both ('for I have made myself unclean by sleeping in her bed', p. 70). With a stick he draws a line in the sand, leads her across, washes her hands, then leads her back across the line into the camp. Almost immediately, the nomads appear from behind the rocks and the magistrate realises that 'We have crossed the limits of the Empire' (p. 70). The sequence of events reveals just how far the magistrate has come. He is now prepared to 'contaminate' himself with the girl, to cross the frontier, and to recognise the illusory nature of social boundaries, mere lines drawn in the sand, the product of cultural projections. After the sexual act with the girl, the magistrate contemplates two alternative realisations: 'Perhaps whatever can be articulated is falsely put. Or perhaps it is the case that only that which has not been articulated has to be lived through' (p. 63). Where the prostitute's fictions were well articulated, but false, the girl's untold story of marginalisation, torture and resistance remains unarticulated, and it is the magistrate's fate to live it through. If the first movement of the novel bears out the first alternative, insisting that truth lies outside categorisations, in the indeterminate, the hybrid, the half-articulated, the second movement bears out the other alternative, as the magistrate lives out in his own body the truths which entry into the margins has brought.

On his return to the fort, the magistrate finds himself seen as the polluter. By entering the desert he has made himself unclean, and society promptly mobilises to cast him in the appropriate symbolic role which dramatises its own values. To Colonel Joll he is now 'the enemy' (p. 77) and is swiftly reduced to an unwashed, sick and smelly prisoner. For a moment the magistrate reverts to type, wondering, 'Have I truly enjoyed the unbounded freedom of this past year in which more than ever before my life has been mine to make up as I go along?' (p. 78). In his dreams the girl appears once more as an image of monstrosity, her feet 'disembodied, monstrous', her figure evolving into massive shapes of horror (p. 87). Where in the first part of the novel the magistrate had been ambivalent to Empire, expressing his resistance subconsciously through symbolic reorganisation of its rules, his venture beyond the frontier, though a source of power, can only be a temporary excursion. Now he must both come out from behind symbolic structures, and return from the uncharted realms of the desert. Rethinking the categories of dominance is not enough. Active intervention in events is called for.

Three key incidents make Coetzee's point. When Colonel Joll displays prisoners, to prove that the 'barbarians' are real, the men are linked into a line by a loop of wire running through their hands and cheeks, so that, to minimise pain, they are forced to move as one cohesive body. In addition to this overt image of the enforced oneness of the body politic, the word 'enemy' is written in charcoal on each naked, dusty back. The ensuing purificatory ritual will involve beating them 'till their backs are washed clean' (p. 105), by blood and sweat. The magistrate objects, insisting upon the wholeness and the holiness of the human being: 'We are the great miracle of creation' (p. 107). Empire, however, is swift to take the magistrate at his word, dramatising the state's concern for its own wholeness, firstly by the use of torture, then by mimicry of the magistrate's own inversions of the symbolic order. Importantly the torture is not directed at eliciting confession but rather at 'demonstrating to me what it meant to live in a body, as a body, a body which can entertain notions of justice only as long as it is whole and well' (p. 115). Threatened itself with fragmentation, the state organises to dramatise the attractions of unity and wholeness on the human body. Earlier in the novel the magistrate's concern to wipe out the dirty story of the visit from the Third Bureau emerged in imagery of a potentially reunified body, cleansed and healed by ritual washings. Now personal rituals of atonement move to the public stage, as the state revivifies a fragmented polity by the example of the magistrate's body. At the risk of stating the obvious, the nexus at which the parallel between body and body politic becomes most apparent is the moment of judicial torture, which expresses the power of the body politic on the human body, violating or extending its boundaries, replicating the conditions of pollution and inversion of category, in order to make the victim welcome re-insertion into the category – wholeness of self and state. In the successive acts of public torture to which he is subjected, the

magistrate undergoes a series of inversions – from adult authority to childish clown, forced to jump to and fro over a line of rope; from male to
female, dressed in a woman's smock; and from human being to bird or
insect, hoisted into the air and forced to 'fly' upside down. Forcibly
inverted, bellowing with pain, simultaneously an image of woman, animal, insect, 'Other', his incoherent howls recall an etymological origin:
'"He is calling his barbarian friends," someone observes. "That is barbarian language"' (p. 121). In public, therefore, the magistrate enters a
state of liminality, inhabiting a space on the margins of male and female,
human and animal, an area seen as prelinguistic, outside the categories of
language. While the audience vicariously participate in this inversion of
established forms they are also satisfied by the punishment visited upon
the dangerous polluter, a punishment which they have evaded.[10] The town
now closes ranks, subscribing *en masse* to a wave of scare stories about
the barbarians, to whom they attribute thefts, rapes, and every chance violation of their irrigation channels and earthworks. As the audience to the
magistrate's humiliation, their membership of a clear category has been
reinforced.

Where, then, does this leave Coetzee's audience – his readership?
*Waiting for the Barbarians* is not a comfortable novel in this respect,
incriminating its readers through its intertextual techniques, exposing us
to the feeling that we have assisted in the creation of a hybrid. Yet our
input as readers is also potentially powerful and liberating, as one scene
demonstrates. When Colonel Joll interrogates the magistrate as to the
meaning of the inscribed poplar slips, discovered in archaeological investigations, the magistrate can offer no historical explanation. Instead he
offers a story. In his capacity as reader, he chooses not to construe them
as mere blanks, nor does he offer a reading of them which would gener-
ate an entirely new story. Instead he operates intertextually, retelling the
events of *Waiting for the Barbarians* in coded, reshaped and oppositional
form. One slip, interpreted as a father's greeting to his daughter, expresses
the loving care and protection which the girl's tortured father was prevented from providing. A second and third supposedly recount the abduc-
tion, beating and death of a brother, recalling the events of the opening
of the novel. An invented detail, a stitch through the dead man's eyelid,
underlines the extent to which Empire cultivates and enforces blindness to
alternative truths. Colonel Joll's military exploits are also a target. The
last slip, a single character, is decoded as 'the barbarian character *war*,
but it has other senses too. It can stand for *vengeance* and if you turn it
upside down like this, it can be made to read *Justice*' (p. 112). The inversion suggests V. N. Volosinov's point, that members of a society may share
a common linguistic system but that their differing social and economic
positions mean that they will interpret signs in different ways: what is freedom for one group is oppression for another.[11]

The magistrate had come to recognise that he has been complicit in the work of Empire, that his hands are not clean:

> For I was not, as I liked to think, the indulgent, pleasure-loving opposite to the cold, rigid Colonel. I was the lie that Empire tells when times are easy, he the truth that Empire tells when harsh winds blow. Two sides of imperial rule, no more, no less (p. 135).

Yet the slips reveal that, although he and Colonel Joll may share membership of a common category, Empire, categories can be not merely inverted but reinvented and imaginatively reshaped. Intertextuality does not simply rethink the categories of dominance, but also argues for imaginative intervention in events, for avoiding fresh starts in favour of reshaping an old story, even at the price of getting one's hands dirty. Readers may be fellow-initiates in one interpretive community, able to recognise Beckett, Buzzati and Kafka, and disquieted by the pollution offered by intertextuality, yet such group membership also permits change, reversal of definitions, militating against rigidity. It also facilitates action. Near the close, the magistrate finds himself able to ask the question of Colonel Joll which he had earlier only imagined:

> Do you find it easy to take food afterwards? I have imagined that one would want to wash one's hands. But no ordinary washing would be enough, one would require priestly intervention, a ceremonial of cleansing (p. 126).

The novel ends on a note of indeterminacy. The magistrate is still unable to set down any organised record of his times, and feels that 'There has been something staring me in the face, and still I do not see it' (p. 155). Yet indeterminacy also offers a fragile possibility. In a final dream the magistrate, merged with snow and wind, flies once more, swooping down on the girl. No damage is done by their collision, however, which has become a meeting of like with like. He is left with a vivid impression of her smiling, healthy face, and a feeling of relief. The dream becomes a kind of reality in the novel's final pages. Once more the magistrate watches children at play in the snow, but this time far from constructing a defensive fort, they are building a snowman. Though the figure is armless and misshapen, the magistrate does not intervene to correct it. Just as each dream scene reshaped and imaginatively reformulated the categories in which he had found himself confined, so now the image of a human body, not fully defined, is accepted as a tentative image of hope.

If *Waiting for the Barbarians* caters to some extent to an elite of intertextual initiates in its literary referents, Coetzee's later novel, *Foe*, opens the issues to the widest possible readership, by engaging with that Ur-novel of the colonising process, now a cultural myth, *Robinson Crusoe*. As the title suggests, *Foe* raises the question of the relation of the postcolonial to the metropolitan text in even more explicit terms as a relationship apparently inescapably antagonistic. 'The enemy is the imperial text through which the writer shuts the racial and cultural otherness of colonized peoples into closed European myth systems and orders of interpretation.'[12] In the plot of the novel, Daniel Defoe, bearing his ungentrified patronymic of Foe, figures as the enemy both of Susan Barton ('Mrs Cruso') the narrator, and of Friday, whom she has rescued from the desert isle. Importantly, Susan's island bears little relation to that of Robinson Crusoe. Coetzee's Cruso is an illustration of the futility of Empire: he keeps no journal and is impervious to Susan's suggestion that they dive into the wreck in search of tools. His refusal is an index of the extent to which he has turned his back on his cultural inheritance. Friday is equally distinct from Defoe's 'handsome Carib youth with near-European features'.[13] He is a black African, apparently voiceless. The story of the island boils down to wind, rain and rough weather. It is a tale which, as Susan recognises, would need some spicing up were it to become a fully-fledged fiction: 'Are these enough strange circumstances to make a story of? How long before I am driven to invent new and stranger circumstances: the salvage of tools and muskets from Cruso's ship; the building of a boat . . . a landing by cannibals.'[14] When she passes on the tale to Foe, she anticipates his objections: 'Better had there been only Cruso and Friday. Better without the woman' (p. 72).

As later readers of *Robinson Crusoe* know only too well, Foe fulfils her worst fears, hijacking her story, excising her presence on the island, transforming Friday into a happy slave and Cruso into a colonist and protocapitalist. Defoe is the enemy, however, in a more complex sense. *Robinson Crusoe* is cryptonomic of another of Defoe's fictions, *Roxana*. When Susan Barton presents herself to Foe as 'a figure of fortune' (p. 48), she evokes its alternative title: *The Fortunate Mistress*. Susan Barton is the real name of both Roxana and her daughter, whose pursuit of her mother, the last third of Defoe's plot, spills over into Coetzee's novel. Foe, then, is an enemy twice over, removing Susan from her own story ('The Female Castaway', p. 67) in order to script her as Roxana, an adventuress who lives by whoring, her life of deceit culminating in the murder of her daughter who threatens to expose her past history. On the surface, therefore, Coetzee's novel appears to be a relatively straightforward oppositional text, in which an imperialist author (Foe) appropriates the story of the colonial subject, rewrites it to his own ends, inserts stereotypical images of the Other (cannibalism) and, in a form of gender apartheid, removes the female from the male adventure genre, to insert her into an all too familiar gendered story of sexual relationships and (in the shape of the daughter) biological determinism. The reader may well conclude, with Coetzee's Cruso, that there is little to salvage from the wreck of Empire, and that Friday pursues the correct course of action. Friday floats silently over the wreck, scattering petals. For him, as a slaveship, the wreck is a mass grave, on which one does not dive. Coetzee's intertextuality thus appears decidedly toothless, in its creation of one more Robinsonnade. One wonders whether he might not have been better advised, unlike the magistrate, in beginning a new story from a blank page. In choosing, however, to insert into *Robinson Crusoe* the story of a mutilated Friday, a sexually transgressive woman, and a Cruso who spends his time building walls around nothing, Coetzee develops the intertextual framework, established in his preceding novel, to different ends. Like *Waiting for the Barbarians*, *Foe* exposes its readers to the feeling that we have assisted at the creation of a hybrid.[15] In the novel Foe is envisaged as separating the events related to him, in all their disorder, by Susan Barton into two stories, the one a male story of Empire, the other a 'dirty' female story of an adventuress. Key images – mutilation, pollution, taboo, transgression, boundaries – derive their significance from Douglas's analysis.

Coetzee's revision of *Roxana* demonstrates both the powers and dangers of intertextuality. Defoe's Roxana is herself an intertextual creation.[16] Although she begins life as Susan Barton, she is transformed into a character, scripted into a role by 'society'. In the celebrated scene in which she performs an exotic 'Turkish' dance, Susan is hailed by the audience as 'Roxana!'[17] and the name sticks. Roxana's dance (actually French) mirrors the male audience's preconceptions. They already know Roxana's story. Racine's play *Bajazet* (1672), Montesquieu's epistolary novel *Lettres persanes* (1721) and Diderot's essay 'Sur les Femmes' had all contributed to her creation. As Katie Trumpener remarks,

> Roxane, the historical figure . . . had by the early eighteenth century become Roxane, the literary character, an oriental queen who always, no matter what the plot in which she appeared, embodied ambition, sexuality, revenge, exoticism; in fact, in the eighteenth century she came to personify womanhood itself: mysterious, sensual, resentful.[18]

In Defoe's novel, Susan Barton's initial declarations of sturdy female independence founder, in Trumpener's view, upon the intertextual discourse of Orientalism; her abandoned daughter is able to track her down via the clue of the 'Turkish' costume, thus threatening the new beginning which her mother has made. As the younger Susan's quest becomes increasingly desperate, Roxana becomes an accessory to her murder, in order to preserve that fresh start.

In contrast, in *Foe*, Susan Barton never becomes a Roxana, or even the Roxana of Defoe. When Foe introduces characters from *Roxana*, including the alleged daughter, Susan rejects her angrily: 'She is not my daughter. Do you think women drop children and forget them as snakes lay eggs? Only a man could entertain such a fancy' (p. 75). Instead, Coetzee's Susan begins the novel herself desperately seeking Susan, in quest of her daughter who has been abducted by 'a factor and agent in the carrying trade' (p. 10). The point specifically undercuts Defoe's authority. After his death, Defoe's novel was itself rewritten: in 1740 (with a happy ending), in 1745 (ending punitively), in 1775 (sentimentally) and in 1807, as a tragedy by William Godwin.[19] In the second rewriting the daughter married and went abroad with 'a gentleman who is going factor for the Dutch East India Company'.[20] Defoe may have trapped his heroine in a preexistent web of textuality; later writers, however, anticipated Coetzee and set her free. Coetzee's Susan does fear becoming a mere character in someone else's story, a person without 'substance' (p. 51), a mere ghost. But she puts up a vigorous resistance, taking over Foe's house, pen and paper and declaring her right to her own story, untold by others:

> a story I do not choose to tell. I choose not to tell it because to no one, not even to you, do I owe proof that I am a substantial being with a substantial history in the world . . . . I am a free woman who asserts her freedom by telling her story according to her own desire (p. 131).

It is only Defoe who translates 'free woman' into the patriarchal coding as adventuress.

Where Susan's story illustrates the powers of metropolitan intertextualisation of the Other, Friday's apparently demonstrates the reverse: the danger posed by one's story remaining forever untold. Without words, Friday has 'no defence against being re-shaped, day by day, in conformity with the desires of others' (p. 121). Importantly, because of the seraglio setting, early versions of the Roxana story proliferate with eunuchs and slaves, with attendant meditations on the rights of women, male mastery, womanhood as slavery. If the seraglio offers an extreme example of the closing off of one group from another, the eunuch may be read as a liminal figure; male in his ability to command the women, but physically emasculated, neither quite male nor female, master or slave.[21] When Coetzee revisions Friday, it is as just such an interstitial figure. According to Cruso, Friday's tongue has been cut out by slavers. Susan's reaction is a classic example of pollution anxiety. Regarding Friday 'with the horror we reserve for the mutilated' (p. 24) she finds herself 'flinching when he came near, or holding my breath so as not to have to smell him. Behind his back I wiped the utensils his hands had touched' (p. 25). In an explicitly Douglassian reference, Friday reminds her how easily 'wholeness' (p. 85) is destroyed; she entertains the possibility that his tongue was severed as a punishment for transgression – for eating forbidden foods. In no time at all her mind has run to cannibalism and castration: is the lost tongue merely a euphemism, she wonders, 'for a more atrocious mutilation . . . a slave unmanned' (p. 119). In short, Friday encapsulates the social outsider, as a member of a racial minority, physically handicapped, sexually ambiguous, and an eater of the ultimate in unclean foods.

As literally placeless people, the castaways find themselves on a desert island which challenges categorisations – a place of swarming insect life, stinking seaweed, rocks white with guano, a place where only ash is available as cleansing agent. Where Susan's reaction is to focus her anxieties on Friday as transgressor/polluter, Cruso spends his time building walls, boundaries around nothing. Futile in practical terms (there is no seedcorn), the terraces are entirely comprehensible as expressions of the need for bounded systems.

On their return to London, Susan continues to attempt to integrate Friday into her own systems. She teaches him to cut boundary hedges 'in a clean line' (p. 60) and trains him as a laundryman. Finally she undertakes a trip to Bristol, in an attempt to return Friday to Africa, his 'proper place'. Susan finances this attempt to repair history by selling books: Pakenham's *Travels in Abyssinia* and Purchas's *Pilgrimages*. Friday, however, cannot be returned: his silence offers no defence against reenslavement. Susan's failure indicates that we cannot simply exchange Eurocentric books for African freedom. Disposing of the exotic travelogues of the past is quite unproductive of Friday's liberty. The journey, however, dissolves the easy distinctions between Susan and Friday. On the road she is mistaken for a placeless outsider, a gypsy. The pair are ejected from an inn: 'This is a clean house', objects the innkeeper (p. 102). Susan had seen Friday as outsider and polluter; now she is forced to share that role. When she discovers the 'cast out' (p. 105) body of a child, at the edge of the road, 'stillborn, or perhaps stifled, all bloody with the afterbirth' (p. 105), a baby which existed only on the margins between life and death, Susan is moved by the parallel between this interstitially positioned being and herself: 'Who was the child but I, in another life?' (p. 105). Contemplating Friday, she recognises that 'We cannot shrink in disgust from our neighbour's touch because his hands, that are clean now, were once dirty' (p. 106). As a result she revises her opinion of Friday, realising that his apparently 'savage' dancing and repetitive flute playing have the power to transport him, entranced, beyond the realm of the ordinary. She comes to understand that 'what we needed from the wreck was not a chest of tools but a case of flutes' (p. 97). Art, even in 'dirty' hands, has transformative potential. Slowly a possibility emerges: that Friday's position is not so much a source of danger as of power. Friday first appears with bleeding feet, and a 'halo' (p. 5) of light: as holy, if not whole. When he dances, revealing his nakedness, Susan comments 'I saw and believed I had seen, though afterwards I remembered Thomas, who also saw, but could not be brought to believe till he had put his hand in the wound' (pp. 119–20). Friday's mutilation, then, may be construed not as a punishment for transgression, but as a source of future power. Coetzee's refusal to tell the reader what Susan saw – whether potency or emasculation – underlines the irremediable doubleness of the wound, as both power and danger.

In addition Susan's subsequent comment returns the reader to the question of taboo: 'I do not know how these matters can be written of in a book unless they are covered up again in figures' (p. 120). She is unable to violate the taboo on the representation of the sex organs. The scene points to Coetzee's own consideration of taboo in relation to the experience of reading. At the close of the novel, the narrator (unnamed, ungendered, no longer Susan Barton) finally dives into the wreck – a composite wreck composed in equal parts of Cruso's original ship, Friday's slaveship, the mutineers' ship which marooned Susan, and the rescue ship.[22] Coetzee's literary 'craft' unites the disparate elements of rescue, enslavement, resource and rebellion which make up culture. Mysterious and much debated, the ending goes beyond the explicit structures of the preceding text into an indeterminate world of flux and dissolution. More than one reader has noted the intertextual reference to Adrienne Rich's 'Diving into the Wreck'.[23] In this poem a diver descends into the wreck of history to survey the damage and the treasures, to salvage what meanings survive from the old myths of patriarchy. Rich's description of culture as:

a book of myths
in which
our names do not appear

clearly chimes with Susan Barton's desperate quest for her own identity, and for the continuation of independent female agency in the shape of her identically named daughter. The male culture of the past makes no place for independent women. In the poem, however, the diver, androgynous, neither male nor female, returns to a primordial point of origin, undifferentiated, before language or gender, in order to seek

the thing I came for:
the wreck and not the story of the wreck
the thing itself and not the myth.

In contrast, Coetzee's diver eschews any attempt to wipe the slate clean of story and return to a primordial point of origin. In Coetzee's dive three features are particularly noteworthy: the sea is dirty; it is the haunt of a mythological monster, the kraken; and it is intensely textual, drawing upon one last intertext, another story of mutilated man, sexually free woman and taboos transgressed, *Lady Chatterley's Lover*. Discussing Lawrence's treatment of taboo in *Lady Chatterley's Lover*, Coetzee highlighted the basis of taboo in the notion of pollution: of class (lady and gamekeeper), of body (sodomy); and of mind. (Mellors pollutes Connie's mind by teaching her taboo words. He teaches her 'how to curse' in a sense.) Coetzee then places the novel in the context of Lawrence's concept of the excremental experience of sex: in healthy human beings two kinds of flow take place: an excremental downward flow in which form is dissolved and living matter becomes dirt, and a sexual upward flow that is procreative and form-giving. In

Lawrence's view, in most human beings the instinct to hold the polarities apart has collapsed; all the flow is downward, issuing in dirt. Lawrence therefore argues for a return to a time of primal innocence, before taboos on the representation of sexuality, before sex acts became 'dirty'. All taboos should be abolished. In the anal sex scene in *Lady Chatterley's Lover*, therefore, 'The excremental taboo is destroyed in its lair. The god-phallus disappears into the labyrinth of the underworld, hunts out the monster, slays it there and emerges triumphant.'[24] If we turn to the ending of *Foe*, we will note that the diver enters a sexualised sea, moving through a 'great bed' of seaweed, where something 'gropes' a leg, 'caresses' an arm (p. 155). Descending the 'trunks', the diver goes below deck: 'The timbers are black, the hole even blacker that gives entry. If the kraken lurks anywhere it lurks here . . . . I enter the hole' (p. 156). Making his way past rotting obstructions, the diver comments: 'I had not thought the sea could be so dirty. But the sand under my hands is soft, dank, slimy . . . . It is like the mud of Flanders' (p. 156). The comparison explicitly conjures up the mud of the Great War, a powerful image of the wreck of Western imperial civilisation. Here is no fresh beginning; the past is usable only if the dirt and damage are kept in view. Earlier in the novel, Susan had recalled a description of eternity as resembling 'a bath-house . . . any Sunday in the country' (p. 114). Now the narrator remarks, 'It is not a country bath-house' (p. 156). The image is not of a return to cleanness, primal innocence, a state of nature, but of immersion in history as death, dirt, decay.

For the reader it is also an experience of intertextual repetition. The diver immerses her/himself in Susan's story, as it appeared on the first page of the novel, and as repeated in paraphrase to Cruso (p. 11). Reading Lawrence, Coetzee had raised a fundamental objection, both to his novel and to his exegesis: 'What is the fate of the monster?' Connie may become 'one of the purified' after her rite of initiation, but 'What do the purified do the night after their initiation?' Do they return to the genital rite? Or continue hunting out the monster night after night? In short, Coetzee wonders, is the taboo annihilated once it is transgressed – or is it revived every time we re-read, only to be vanquished anew. For Coetzee, the novel demonstrates the durability of taboo. *Lady Chatterley's Lover* is 'a tale about the transgression of boundaries – sexual boundaries and sexualized social boundaries – a tale whose local tensions and dramatic force depend on the continuing viability of taboos'.[25] Above all, therefore, even Lawrence's novel reveals the impossibility of clean pages. Coetzee notes that Lawrence could only elaborate his anti-excremental, oppositionist views because he himself was alert to pollution, to smelling out taint.

> Is any reading at all possible to a man without a nose? Where would such a man begin reading? . . . Is there not a direct connection between reading, curiosity and a nose for dirt?[26]

We might translate: is any reading possible without previous readings, intertextual readings? As intertextuality signals overtly, are we not all 'dirty' readers of 'dirty' books?

In refusing to separate the formlessness and variety of experience into two stories – *Robinson Crusoe, Roxana* – Coetzee explicitly rejects Lawrence's notion of polarities between innocence and degeneration, clean and unclean. At the close of the novel the reader is re-reading, setting out to conquer the monster of taboo again. The diver approaches Friday, overcomes the taboo on mutilation, and touches him, releasing a flow which is unending. For many readers of *Foe*, Friday's silence, his mutilation, is his power. Friday being taught to write would be the equivalent of Caliban being taught to curse – a way of appropriating his fundamental Otherness into metropolitan discourse, much as intertextuality is seen as a metropolitan tactic. Coetzee, however, closes Susan's narrative with the image of Friday replacing Foe at his writing table, in Foe's robes and with his wig 'filthy as a bird's nest' on his head. Susan objects: 'He will foul your papers.' Foe's reply is telling: 'My papers are foul enough, he can make them no worse' (p. 151). Friday is writing, over and over again, the letter o. Foe comments: 'It is a beginning. Tomorrow we must teach him a' (p. 152). Coetzee's point is, of course, that o (omega) is not a beginning but an end. Friday must move backwards, as writing in some ways always begins at the end, on a page that is already 'foul'. Coetzee's novel is not about the need to avoid telling the black story; rather it concerns the necessity for repeated efforts to overcome divisions and categorisations – apartheid – even in the knowledge that there can be no return to innocence or wholeness. At the risk of stating the obvious, in South Africa sexualised and social boundaries are often the same; racial 'taint' is an obsession,[27] and the country's political history pullulates with classifications of racial purity, bounded homelands, bantustans, white areas. Coetzee wrote *Foe* before the dismantling of the walls of apartheid and his vision is prophetic. As the novel indicates, the dissolution of such boundaries may involve danger, but it is a danger which grants its own powers.

# Notes

1 J. M. Coetzee, 'The Novel Today', *Upstream* 6, 1 (1988), p. 3.
2 David Attwell, 'The Problem of History in the Fiction of J. M. Coetzee', in Martin Trump, ed., *Rendering Things Visible: Essays on South African Literary Culture*, (Athens, Ohio University Press, 1990), p. 117. See also Stephen Watson, 'Colonialism and the Novels of J. M. Coetzee', *Research in African*

*Literatures* 17, 3 (1986), pp. 370–92; Susan Van Zanten Gallagher, 'Torture and the Novel: J. M. Coetzee's *Waiting for the Barbarians*', *Contemporary Literature* XXIX, 2 (1988), pp. 277–85. Watson sees Coetzee's plurality of meaning as floating his fiction free of time and place; Gallagher construes indeterminacy (a significant term in the light of my argument) as opposed to sociopolitical commitment.

3 Dino Buzzati, *The Tartar Steppe*, trans. Stuart Hood (Manchester, Carcanet, 1985). First published as *Il Deserto Dei Tartari* (Milan, Arnoldo Mondadore Editore SPA, 1945), trans. Stuart Hood (London, Secker and Warburg, 1952). I am grateful to Dennis Walder of the Open University for drawing my attention to this source.

4 Constantin Cavafy, *Poems by C. P. Cavafy*, trans. John Mavrogordato (London, Chatto and Windus, 1971), pp. 28–9.

5 Judie Newman, 'Nadine Gordimer and the Naked Southern Ape: "Something Out There"', *Journal of the Short Story in English*, 15 (1990), pp. 55–73.

6 Mary Douglas, *Purity and Danger: An Analysis of Concepts of Pollution and Taboo* (London, Routledge and Kegan Paul, 1966). I am not suggesting that anthropology offers a universalist foundation, merely a broader frame of reference. For a critique of (and response to) classical anthropology see Louis A. Sass, 'Anthropology's Native Problems: Revisionism in the Field', *Harper's* 272, 1632 (1986), pp. 49–57.

7 J. M. Coetzee, *Waiting for the Barbarians* (London , Penguin, 1982), p. 2.

8 Toril Moi, 'Feminist Literary Criticism', in Ann Jefferson and David Robey, eds., *Modern Literary Theory* (London, Batsford, 1986), p. 213.

9 The point is made by Debra A. Castillo, 'The Composition of the Self in Coetzee's *Waiting for the Barbarians*', *Critique* 27, 2 (1987), pp. 78–90.

10 The scene bears comparison with the discussion of aioresis as a festival of metamorphosis in Hélène Cixous and Catherine Clément, *The Newly Born Woman* (Minneapolis, University of Minnesota Press, 1986), pp. 20–2, first published as *La Jeune Née* (Paris, Union Générale d'Editions, 1975).

11 V. N. Volosinov, *Marxism and the Philosophy of Language* (Seminar, 1973).

12 Derek Wright, 'Fiction as Foe: The Novels of J. M. Coetzee', *International Fiction Review* 15 (Summer 1989), p. 118.

13 Tony Morphet, 'Two Interviews with J. M. Coetzee, 1983 and 1987', *Tri-Quarterly* 69 (1987), p. 463.

14 J. M. Coetzee, *Foe* (London, Penguin, 1987), p. 67. Subsequent references follow quotations in parentheses.

15 An impression strengthened by echoes of other works by Defoe, and by slight but deliberate inaccuracies of nomenclature. See Derek Attridge, 'Oppressive Silence: J. M. Coetzee's *Foe* and the Politics of the Canon', in Karen R. Lawrence, ed., *Decolonizing Tradition* (Urbana and Chicago, University of Illinois Press, 1992).

16 I am enormously indebted here to Katie Trumpener, 'Rewriting Roxane: Orientalism And Intertextuality in Montesquieu's *Lettres persanes* and Defoe's *The Fortunate Mistress*', *Stanford French Review* II, 2 (1987), pp. 177–91.

17 Daniel Defoe, *Roxana* (London, Penguin, 1982), p. 217.

18 Trumpener, 'Rewriting Roxane', p. 178.

19 Bram Dijkstra, *Defoe and Economics* (London, Macmillan, 1987), Chapter 5.

20 Dijkstra, *Defoe and Economics*, p. 98.

21 Trumpener, 'Rewriting Roxane', p. 182. See also Roland Barthes, *Sur Racine* (Paris, Seuil, 1963).

22 The ship encloses Susan and her dead captain (mutineers' ship), Friday in chains (slaveship) but 'under the transoms' (rescue ship, p. 41). Above it float

     the petals scattered on Cruso's ship.
23 Beginning with Nina Auerbach, 'A Novel of Her Own', *New Republic*, 9 March
     1987, pp. 36–8. For the poem and a selection of critical readings see Barbara
     Charlesworth Gelpi and Albert Gelpi, eds., *Adrienne Rich's Poetry* (London,
     W. W. Norton, 1975).
24 J. M. Coetzee, 'The Taint of the Pornographic' (1988) in J. M. Coetzee,
     *Doubling The Point: Essays and Interviews,* ed. David Attwell (Cambridge,
     Mass., Harvard University Press, 1992), p. 313.
25 Coetzee, 'The Taint of the Pornographic' , p. 313.
26 Coetzee, 'The Taint of the Pornographic,' p. 310.
27 J. M. Coetzee discusses the notion of racial 'taint' in 'Blood, Taint, Flaw,
     Degeneration: The Novels of Sarah Gertrude Millin' (1980) in J. M. Coetzee,
     *White Writing: On the Culture of Letters in South Africa* (New Haven,Yale
     University Press, 1988), pp. 136–62.

# 7

# *He neo-Tarzan, she Jane?*

## *Buchi Emecheta*, The Rape of Shavi

Although Buchi Emecheta's fiction has attracted considerable interest and attention, one novel, *The Rape of Shavi* (1983), has been passed over in critical silence. Reviewers were nevertheless not slow to recognise the quality of the novel.[1] For the *London Review of Books* it was:

a very good story artfully told: the rational, provoking arguments about multi-racial societies and military law, are dropped into the narrative with a natural, unobtrusive cunning, rare in modern fiction.

The *New York Times Book Review* applauded her 'provocative storytelling'; the *Listener* commented that her sense of irony was 'finely balanced'. Reviewers, however, divided on the question of the novel's treatment of tradition, describing it in one case as equally scornful of both African tradition and Western development (*World Literature Today*), as emphasising 'a people's stoic traditionalism' (*New York Times Book Review*), and even as embracing development: 'The Kingdom of Shavi is pretty thoroughly raped by the white visitors before the book's ending – and Miss Emecheta's story seems to suggest that this rape might be all for the best (*London Review of Books*). Indeed, for the *Listener*, 'Western civilisation [was] not totally to blame.' The *New York Times Book Review*, on the other hand, described Emecheta's prose as 'like that of a community singer of tales . . . steeped in the tradition of a difficult rural African life'. The reviewers' differences suggest a productive ambiguity in Emecheta's tale, which thematises the postcolonial debate between nativists and universalists, purists and appropriators, within its fictional frame. In the context of postcolonial writing the notion of tradition (often linked to discussions of orature) is highly problematic, not least in relation to the status of women.

Set in an ostensibly postnuclear future, in the imaginary kingdom of

Shavi somewhere in the Saharan region, Emecheta's dystopian fable pits Western and African forms of feminism against each other, in order to determine how far feminism may go in Africa, and what might be its most productive relation to African traditions. Although critics have been much engaged with Emecheta's relationship to feminism, their silence in this context may not be unrelated to the fact that the major representative of political thought in the novel, although a figure thoroughly identified with feminism, is both European and a man: George Bernard Shaw. Shaw's vigorous defence of women's right to liberate themselves, whether expressed in tough polemical writing or in the gallery of emancipated women who feature in his dramatic works, is almost too well known to need rehearsal.[2] Two examples worth recalling in connection with Emecheta's African subject matter are *The Adventures of the Black Girl in Her Search for God* (in which Shaw rejects the patriarchal God, and ends the search by having the heroine find her god within herself) and *Captain Brassbound's Conversion*, which was inspired by Mary Kingsley's *Travels in West Africa* (1897), and by the contrast between her non-racist, egalitarian relationship to Africans, and the guns and aggression of male explorers. For Kingsley, as for pacifist Shaw, respect for another's culture worked better than a revolver.[3] As Emecheta's title suggests, the novel draws upon Shavian beliefs in its exposure of the myths of man-as-breadwinner, militarism and nationalism. Shaw's discussion of capitalist civilisation as a disease also gains fresh relevance in post-Aids Africa, as a community of women struggle to repair the damage done by the rape of their traditional culture by Western capitalists.

In order to problematise the notion of tradition, Emecheta adopts a daringly intertextual strategy. Inevitably the play on Shaw's name in the creation of the imaginary kingdom of Shavi invites a reading of the novel as Eurocentric, importing European literary and political standards into Africa, and overlaying the specificity of an African culture with the false universals which earned Chinua Achebe's sarcastic attack:

> In the nature of things the work of the western writer is automatically informed by universality. It is only some others who must strive to achieve it. As though universality were some distant bend in the road you must take if you travel far enough in the direction of America or Europe.[4]

Emecheta's references to Shaw are explicit. The novel opens with an emblematically Shavian scene, in the council of King Patayon, whose sobriquet 'The Slow One' recalls Fabius ('The Delayer'), the Roman general whose policy of tactical delay inspired Fabianism as a political movement built upon a strategy of cautious advance. Similarly, for the African Shavians, the pace of change is slow in their kingdom, 'a place of democratic freedom' (p. 24),[5] reached only after the escape from a previous history of enslavement. Just as Shaw favoured the abolition of the party system, with power proceeding directly from below, from the people, so in Shavi decisions are taken in communal fashion, with direct access to the king:

> They had learnt though their ancestors what it was to be enslaved, and Shavi prided herself on being the only place in the whole of the Sahara, where a child was free to tell the king where it was that he had gone wrong (p. 3).

One lesson, however, has yet to be learned. Despite the fact that the tutelary deity of Shavi (appropriately, given Shaw's interest in eugenics) is Ogene, the river goddess, Shavian women appear to have been left out of the open society. When Queen Shoshovi enters the council of elders, her form of address leaves nothing to doubt: 'My owners', she begins (p. 4). Around her neck she wears the close-fitting 'ehulu' neckband, four layers deep, as obligatory to queens as the slave-collar. 'She had to wear it until the day she died' (p. 6). King Patayon has apparently not benefited from Shaw's understanding that, by ignoring the value of women's work, by casting man as the sole breadwinner, the system

> made a slave of the man, and then, by paying the woman through him, made her his slave, [so that] she became the slave of a slave, which is the worst sort of slavery.[6]

In point of fact, Queen Shoshovi is in the council in order to demand payment, a payment which illustrates the workings of Shavian patriarchy to the full. Patayon plans to celebrate the end of a long drought in traditional fashion by taking a new queen, a plan with which he has failed to acquaint his first wife. Nor has he provided her with the traditional gift – a cow. Matters degenerate further when the council's least tactful member, Mensa (so named, ironically, after the British society for those with high 'IQ' ratings), handles her complaint in a brusque fashion. Shoshovi's son, Asogba, witnesses his mother's humiliation and her angry reaction. With the initial maltreatment of a mother, Emecheta strikes a characteristic note, in the opening scene, initiating a novel in which mothers are to become a focal point. Eyeing Shoshovi, Patayon reflects, 'Women! When they are angered they forget how deeply they have loved. They throw all caution and reason into the empty air' (p. 8). His comment is immediately proleptic as the air explodes about him:

> A big fast-moving cloud suddenly loomed and tore itself from the sky, one minute a cloud, the next looking like an unusually long house, another minute the shape of a bird . . . . The bird of fire arched and crashed (p. 9).

To the spectators the catastrophe indicates a female revenge: 'Has the

Queen's anger become so great that she's summoned Ogene to send a mysterious bird of fire into Shavi?' (p. 9). As the occupants of the crashed aircraft emerge, refugees from a threatened nuclear conflict in Europe, the scene is set for an encounter between Western and African women which explores the relation of metropolitan feminism to African traditional society. The dynamics of the opening scene suggest, fairly overtly, that feminism may have an important role to play in relation to apparently oppressed African women, that Western intervention may be construed as a rescue mission, and that traditional beliefs (here, in Ogene) risk subordination to the notion of white men as gods.

Things are not quite so simple, however. For the alert reader a cautionary note is struck by the description of the plane as a bird of fire. Emecheta's political fable of the relation between tradition and modernity refers explicitly to a male-dominated literary debate on the same subject, the celebrated clash between the so-called neo-Tarzanists and their critics. By invoking this debate, Emecheta deliberately lays down the gauntlet to the West, foregrounding the problematic status of both traditionalism and modernity, not merely in literary but also in highly politicised terms. The salient points of the debate are easily summarised. Writing in 1975, Wole Soyinka coined the term 'neo-Tarzanism' in order to characterise the poetics of pseudo-tradition. Soyinka was responding to three African literary critics, the 'troika' of Chinweizu, Onwuchekwa Jemie and Ihechukwu Madubuike, whose views (subsequently expanded in *Toward the Decolonization of African Literature*) emphatically rejected European universalism. Known also as 'bolekaja', meaning 'come down and fight', the troika denounced the standards used to evaluate contemporary African literature as Eurocentric and inappropriate, particularly in the imposition of realist norms upon the novel. They argued for a return to African traditions and a revalorisation of earlier African orature, as a first step to the decolonisation of African literature. Emecheta's adoption of the fable form, her deliberately unrealistic evocation of an imaginary kingdom, is buttressed by references to kriors and by the citation of the Shavian 'Song of Freedom' (p. 17). Chinweizu also approved the adoption of 'a language of African particulars' as a source of poetic power, applauding

> an African poetic landscape with its flora and fauna – a landscape of elephants, beggars, calabashes, serpents, pumpkins, baskets, town-criers, iron bells, slit drums, iron masks, hares, snakes, squirrels; a landscape that is no longer used as an exoticism for background effect . . . a landscape portrayed with native eyes to which aeroplanes naturally appear as iron birds.[7]

Soyinka's response was withering: 'I am not at all certain how this proves more acceptable than the traditional Hollywood image of the pop-eyed African in the jungle – 'Bwana, bwana, me see big iron bird.'[8] Soyinka's

African world is altogether more intricate than Chinweizu's landscape model, embracing technology and macroeconomics, and crossed by railway trains rather than iron snakes. In his view, neo-Tarzanism is the inevitable result of the espousal (or even the creation) of pseudo-traditions. Commenting on the debate, Gareth Griffiths and David Moody pointed out that, although Soyinka had been promptly cast as a conservative Euromodernist patriarch, with the troika as radical *enfants terribles*, neither side had taken very much account of the specific determining forces of social and cultural practice. Oversimplifications apart, however, Griffiths and Moody agreed with Soyinka that the contemporary African intellectual actually inhabits a world of profound and inescapable hybridity, in which African ontology, the mask, or the Ogun cult (Soyinka's examples) are not sealed off from the discursive practices of such African phenomena as engineering. In Soyinka's terms, 'Sango is today's god of electricity, not of white-man-magic-light. Ogun is today's god of precision technology, oil-rigs and space rockets, not a benighted rustic cowering at the "iron bird".'[9] The question raised by such hybridity is inevitably that of cultural allegiance. Are such hybridities as Greek and Yoruba heroes (Soyinka) or, in Emecheta's case, that of Shaw in the Sahara, signs of cultural betrayal? For Griffiths and Moody the possibility at least exists of reading them

> as the characteristic marks of the possibilities inherent in post-colonial discourse to escape the simplicity of binary opposition and to generate a new, powerful and creative synthesis of disparate and contradictory elements – a synthesis which embraces difference as a sign of possibility, not as a marker of closure.[10]

It is a hypothesis rigorously tested in *The Rape of Shavi* in relation to that possibility left out of the equation – women. In choosing a non-realist form, Emecheta sets her discussion of feminism within the context of a specifically African literary debate concerning the relation of tradition to modernity, in order to promote a political engagement with the facts of recent Nigerian history.

By engineering her plot as catalysed by the nuclear threat, Emecheta makes an initial anti-separatist point, arguing (if not for universalism) at least for the notion of 'one world'. None the less, in the action which follows, responsibility for disaster is laid fair and square at the feet of men. Ironically the pacifists whose plane lands in Shavi are ultimately responsible not only for the destruction of Shavian culture, but also for two wars, the one male-led, the other a 'women's war' (p. 96). In the male sphere, events are triggered when Philip (Flip) Wagner, former nuclear scientist, discovers the commercial value of Shavian mineral crystals. The younger male Shavians, led by Asogba, export the crystals in return for imported foodstuffs, abandon their traditional agricultural practices, arm themselves, and make war on their neighbours, whom they enslave. With the collapse of the market in crystals, coincidental with another drought, the kingdom of Shavi is decimated by famine. In general terms the tale is therefore a sadly familiar one of development, exploitation of mineral resources, and aid-induced dependency, culminating in disaster.

More specifically, the young men's enthusiastic adoption of militarism in the attempted establishment of the nation state is explicitly reminiscent of Emecheta's analysis of recent Nigerian history. In *Destination Biafra* (1983), her novel of the Nigerian Civil War (1967–70), Emecheta set out to attack Britain as having promoted militarism, trained the army officers, and supplied arms in order to safeguard its own investments in Nigerian oil. The parallel with Mendoza's supply of arms to Asogba in order to maintain a monopoly of the crystals could hardly be clearer. The heroine of *Destination Biafra*, Debbie Ogedemgbe, is writing a book about her experience of the war, to avoid the women's story being lost to history. (The novel foregrounds rape, including the gang rape of the heroine by her own comrades, as one of the hidden facts of the conflict.) Emecheta's research for the novel concentrated particularly on the background role of the British military training establishment at Sandhurst. In her foreword to the published novel, Emecheta noted that the result of her labours was not entirely satisfactory. Production costs had reduced the manuscript to half its original size. In addition, as Emecheta drily noted, 'One of the mysteries connected with this work is that the enlightening chapter based on my visit to Sandhurst where most of my military characters were trained disappeared into thin air when the ms. was with my literary agent.'[11] *The Rape of Shavi*, it is worth highlighting, was produced by Emecheta's own publishing operation, Ogwugwu Afor, in Nigeria. Thwarted in attempting to make her point through the realist novel and the metropolitan publisher, Emecheta therefore transforms events into a fable, a non-Eurocentric form which gets the political message across in a more direct fashion.

In Emecheta's novel, the young men are the foes of tradition. Patayon's policy of cautious advance founders on the enthusiasm of the young for modernity, as power passes from the conservative patriarchs into the hands of the militarised young. Militarisation is also neoimperialism. Eurocentric in a different sense, Asogba sets out to 'make Shavi great' by a series of raids modelled on European history: 'Hadn't he been told that this was how England's Empire was established? He and his men would start their expansion likewise' (p. 162). The action of the novel therefore brings together literary and political activity, its political events shadowed by the neo-Tarzanist debate. Michael Valdez Moses has argued persuasively that the Soyinka/Chinweizu clash exposes the fact that Western literary history changes its features when seen in relation to the emerging literatures of the Third World. In particular, the notion of the novel as an inert object of literary-historical interest gives way to a sharper perception of fiction as effecting a cultural task and as a work of historical agency. Emecheta's active engagement with Nigerian history tallies with the 'troika's' political agenda:

> The ultimate standard for judging the appropriateness of cultural syncretism is their conception of what would constitute the best possible regime for contemporary Nigeria. Behind their objection to Western cultural or literary standards being imposed on non-Western cultures is a much more basic objection to the inappropriateness of those regimes as comprehensive models for contemporary African states.[12]

In the action of her novel Emecheta foregrounds the issue which underlies the literary debate – the end of the Shavian form of African socialism, and the rise of the neoimperialist nation state.

For the Shavian women, however, unlike their men, tradition is not so lightly abandoned. Much of the action of the novel dramatises a continuing debate between Western feminists (Andria, Ista) and African traditionalists (Shoshovi, Siegbo, Iyalode). Cynthia Ward has commented on the tendency of Western feminism to reenact colonial intervention into other cultures, by appropriating Emecheta's writing to a universalist liberating discourse. Thus 'a feminist reading frequently reinscribes the image of Africa as the dark continent where "primitive" cultural practices must be guided into productive paths by enlightened Europeans.'[13] Like the troika's, such readings may also risk constructing a pseudo-traditional image of African culture as source of women's oppression, in order to validate Western interference. Is Emecheta's case similarly an instance of culturally assigned binary roles, in this case female rather than male? He Tarzan she Jane? The rape of Ayoko, Asogba's betrothed, by Ronje, a white incomer, is a case in point. Ronje rapes, in part, because he perceives Ayoko as an oppressed victim: 'Here women are used as chattels' (p. 41). In fact, as the future queen of Shavi, Ayoko enjoys maximum status. Ronje's act stands as a metaphor for the despoilment of an entire culture: 'Ayoko is the symbolic Mother of Shavi. If you rape her, you rape Shavi' (p. 104). The rape is also the product of Eurocentric preconceptions. For Ronje, 'Flip had started their relationship with the people of Shavi on the wrong footing. They were Europeans, after all, and it had always been the duty of Europeans to impose their culture on whomever they came in contact with' (p. 105). Far from acceding to the status of victim, however, Ayoko turns to the community of women for assistance. When she informs Siegbo of events, 'she saw her mother transformed into a warrior' (p. 98). Resolutely insisting that 'this is a case beyond men' (p. 96), the women briskly define Ronje as an 'uthang' rather than a human being (so much for his claims to superior culture) and ambush him, abandoning him, trapped in their nets, to the mercy of wild animals. Commenting in interview on the scene, Emecheta drew attention to its origins in cultural practices founded in the tradition of African female communal action. Sex offenders, in her native culture, were similarly executed by women.[14] Far from being in need of a white feminist rescue mission, the Shavian women are more than capable of defending themselves. The incomers are at a distinct disadvantage, compared with the strength offered to the Shavians by their traditional culture.

The two groups clash on several occasions over such issues as arranged marriage, child-bearing practices, polygamy and cliterectomy. In each case, Emecheta avoids any simplification of the complexities involved. The topic of arranged marriage, for example, is approached from several angles. Ayoko has been destined from birth to be the wife of Asogba, as a result of the machinations of her father, Anoku, the power-hungry chief priest. She has little choice in the matter. On the other hand when 'marriages' are arranged (by the administration of large quantities of barley beer) between Ista and Mendoza and Andria and Flip, the results are surprisingly harmonious. Ista, formerly a champion of Western ways, finds herself acquiescing to Mendoza's dominance, though the relationship ends on their return to Britain. Flip and Andria, however, remarry in a formal ceremony. The role of Western medicine also comes in for scrutiny. When a Shavian woman goes into labour, Ista, a trained gynaecologist, instantly pushes past Shoshovi and attempts to take charge. While Ista is arguing furiously that a breech birth demands a Caesarean, Shoshovi quietly supports the mother in the traditional squatting position. The result is something of an advertisement for natural childbirth, as opposed to Western interventionism: 'The baby came out according to gravity, so the mother didn't have to bear down horizontally the way we do' (p. 133).

On the other hand Emecheta does not glorify Shavi. Flip notes the absence of deformity or handicap in the population, and supposes that it is the ideal climatic conditions which produce perfection in this Shangri-La. Perfection, however, is bought at a price:

> They had no mongols or deformed people, because they got rid of them at birth, and those that lived by accident never survived that long. They had no means of artificially prolonging life. Every living being had to be able to contribute something to the community (p. 76).

In this communal ethos, it appears that women are called upon to make more painful contributions. When Flip and Mendoza succeed in restoring their aircraft and perform a demonstration flight, the Shavians celebrate in traditional fashion, by presenting them with wives. 'This was the way Shavi repaid her heroes' (p. 136). Over the Western men's objections, and against a background of rending screams, the brides are clitorised. In interview Emecheta has described cliterectomy as indefensible, but as more likely to pass away gradually in response to education, than to respond to heavy-handed Western intervention. Patayon-like, Emecheta argued instead for gradualism. In her view, a major problem, potentially a source of hardening attitudes rather than enlightenment, is that of Western feminist arrogance. For Emecheta, Western feminism easily becomes another form of ideological colonisation, with the white feminist as 'Lady Bountiful'. Feminism in this mould is, she argued, 'a luxury I cannot at the moment afford'. In global terms, only a relation of mutual respect for difference could impact upon the situation. 'Until the Western woman swallows her arrogance and takes the hand of the woman from the developing world, to try to save the world . . . there's not going to be any peace.'[15] Ironically, in *The Rape of Shavi*, the custom of cliterectomy does end. Ronje's rape reveals to Ayoko that the traditional belief system is ill-founded: 'Hadn't they told her that if a girl was not clitorised a man couldn't enter her? . . . That again was not true' (p. 122). Ayoko's arranged marriage to Asogba is also put off. After the rape Ronje had determined to see Ayoko again: 'He would civilize her' (p. 106). In fact he infects her with syphilis. For the Shavians, civilisation and syphilisation become homophonic. Shaw's pronouncement that 'The civilisation produced by capitalism is a disease'[16] is horribly borne out in the conclusion. When Asogba marries an apparently recovered Ayoko, it is to discover that 'time couldn't eradicate the albino disease' (p. 178). Neither Asogba nor Ayoko live long. By the close of the novel the Shavians have returned entirely to their traditions, in reaction to their encounter with the West. Western interventionism, both violently male and condescendingly female, has ended in disaster.

In its denouement, therefore, the tale may appear to validate the retreat from hybridity, and a move towards a new isolationism. Throughout the novel, however, Emecheta has been careful to avoid the simplicity of a binary opposition between African tradition and European modernity, a process encapsulated in the application of the term 'Shavian' both to a set of European literary-political beliefs, and to a sub-Saharan kingdom. The notion of hybridity is kept in view by the mixture of styles. Chapter titles alternate between the two cultures. 'The Drinks Party', for example, is a Western description of a barley beer feast; 'The Leper Creatures' is a black response to the arrival of whites. Similarly, if Mensa is a fine example of Shavian idiocy, he has his counterpart in Flip, a classic illustration of Shaw's conception of the scientist as amoral, led by his intellect to the untenable proposition that scientific research must go on, whatever the cost. Flip's initial belief in nuclear power is successfully challenged by Andria, but his conversion is only temporary. By the end of the novel he has returned to the munitions business (now in the field of conventional weapons) and has consigned his Shavian agricultural project to the experts:

'Flip didn't feel guilty at all that he had in a way disturbed the Shavians' quiet life. He was an academic and a scientist. His work was to invent, to discover, and that was where his responsibility ended' (p. 167). It is of course Flip who identifies the value of the Shavian crystals: ultimately it is his intelligence which rapes Shavi.

In addition Emecheta makes the point that traditionalism is not limited to Africa: the equation of the West with modern progress does not go unchallenged. One incident is particularly revealing. When the aircraft crashes, discussion at the council of elders centres upon the fate of the mysterious 'albinos' saved from the wreckage. Are they human? For Anoku 'the priest with the skull-like head' (p. 36) they are not and should be sacrificed promptly to Ogene. When the others demur at the prospect of 'killing people who are immigrant in our society' (p. 36) Anoku works himself into a frenzy of demagoguery, declaiming:

> I see the Ogene river bubbling with blood instead of clear water. The Ogene is very angry. These people are not humans and will bring us destruction. They may look like humans but they have no souls. They should be used as slaves or killed or driven away (p. 38).

The reference to Enoch Powell's anti-immigrant 'rivers of blood' speech is overt. Emecheta is on record as having been deeply upset by the speech, with its attendant visions of compulsory repatriation, and the inevitable escalation of racial tensions. In her autobiography she describes Powell's failure to reach the highest political office (the goal, in her analysis, of his racist policies) as a miracle.[17] (Anoku has his eyes on a similar preeminence via his daughter's marriage.) The Shavian 'skull-headed priest' (a fair description of Powell) demonstrates that conservatism is not always on the side of the angels. As a traditionalist, Anoku is a racist as pernicious as his namesake. Though Shavi is destroyed by the forces of modernism, Anoku's example invokes the demise of another democratic, socialist state, Great Britain, at the hands of so-called 'traditional' conservative values.

The Shavian council, fortunately, are not easily swayed by racist rhetoric. 'Are we not all immigrants in Shavi, and even on the face of the earth? We're all members of the human race' (p. 39). The statement should not, however, be read as merely a declaration of blanket universalism. Emecheta is swift to draw Britain and Africa together, but she does so in a fashion designed to emphasise the value of hybridity. The Shavians, themselves, reached Shavi only after a trek from slavery to freedom and are therefore happy to welcome the white refugees, perceiving in difference a value to be embraced. The white group is itself distinctly heterogeneous, comprising Flip and Andria (Canadians), Mendoza (Spanish-Jewish), Ista (German via the Sudan and Nepal) and Ronje (Danish). Comically, their fate on arrival in Shavi is reminiscent of that of black British immigrants in the 1950s and 1960s, offered only menial jobs, whatever their qualifications. Andria and Ista find themselves sweeping the compound, though the Shavians have, at least, the justification that their culture is not, as yet, able to utilise the two women's highly specialised skills. In the pairing of Flip/Mensa, Enoch/Anoku, Shaw and Sahara, the satirical current is continually being reversed, the irony double-edged.

One doubling, however, escapes satire. Flip's original change of heart was occasioned by the spectacle of 'A determined mother' (p. 62) at an anti-nuclear demonstration, intent on saving the world. Emecheta redefines political action as emerging from a common concern for the welfare of children, and thus the need to save the world. Similarly Asogba decides that the 'albinos' are human only when he recognises the same woman's concern for her injured child: 'That is the cry of a mother . . . . I must go and see if they need our help. We must talk about their humanity later' (p. 15).

At the close of the novel the male population of Shavi has been decimated, the elders dead in the drought, the younger men in the war. Shoshovi is now the mentor of the survivors: 'We've lost all our men, our way of life and our privacy. We have to start all over again. There are no more than fifty men in the whole of Shavi, but we have at least kept all the children alive' (p. 177). The woman-centred politics which has evolved here is Shavian in both senses of the term: a testimony to richness in difference and hybridity. Shaw inveighed against the fashion in which men had got into the way of accepting the ferocities of war as substitutes for courage, whereas women, in his view, know that

> communities live not by slaughter and by doing death but by creating life and nursing it to its highest possibilities. When Ibsen said that the hope of the world lay in the women and the workers he was neither a sentimentalist nor a demagogue . . . . Women are not angels . . . but they have had to devote themselves to life whilst men have had to devote themselves to death.[18]

When, at the close of the novel, Asogba ponders 'what exactly is civilisation?' (p. 178), the Shavian women appear to come closest to a living definition. Without necessarily embracing an essentialist approach which would take for granted the supreme value of the mother as civiliser, Emecheta clearly endorses the vision offered by Shaw of women's autonomous communal activity as a source of strength, both in the past and for the future.

# Notes

1 Major reviews appeared in the *Listener*, 111 (22 March 1984), p. 25; *London Review of Books*, 2–15 February 1984, pp. 17–18 ; *New York Times*, 134 (23 February 1985), p. 6; *New York Times Book Review* 90 (5 May 1985), p. 24; *Women's Review of Books*, 2 (1985), pp. 6–7; *World Literature Today* 58 (1984), p. 657.

2 Rodelle Weintraub, ed., *Fabian Feminist: Bernard Shaw and Women* (London, Pennsylvania State University Press, 1977), p. 194.

3 On Shaw's thought in relation to women and society see particularly Eric Bentley, *Bernard Shaw* (New York, 1976); Barbara Bellow Watson, *A Shavian Guide to the Intelligent Woman* (London, Chatto, 1964); and Rodelle Weintraub, ed., *Fabian Feminist*. See also *Captain Brassbound's Conversion*, in *Three Plays For Puritans* (London, Constable, 1931) and *The Adventures of the Black Girl in her Search for God* (London, Constable, 1932).

4 Chinua Achebe, *Morning Yet on Creation Day* (London, Heinemann, 1975), p. 9.

5 Buchi Emecheta, *The Rape of Shavi* (London and Ibuza, Nigeria, Ogwugwu Afor, 1983). Subsequent page references follow quotations in parentheses.

6 George Bernard Shaw, *The Intelligent Woman's Guide to Socialism, Capitalism, Sovietism and Fascism* (London, Penguin, 1971), p. 219.

7 Chinweizu, 'Prodigals, Come Home!' *Okike* (1973), p. 4. See also Chinweizu, Onwuchekwa Jemie and Ihechukwu Madubuike, *Toward the Decolonization of African Literature* (Enugu, Nigeria, Fourth Estate, 1980).

8 Wole Soyinka, 'Neo-Tarzanism: The Poetics of Pseudo-Tradition', *Transition* 48 (1975), p. 38.

9 Soyinka, 'Neo-Tarzanism', p. 44.

10 Gareth Griffiths, and David Moody, 'Of Marx and Missionaries: Soyinka and the Survival of Universalism in Post-Colonial Literary Theory', *Kunapipi* XI (1989), p. 78.

11 Buchi Emecheta, *Destination Biafra* (London, Fontana, 1983), p. vii.

12 Michael Valdez Moses, 'Caliban and His Precursors: The Politics of Literary History and the Third World', in David Perkins, ed., *Harvard English Studies 16. Theoretical Issues in Literary History* (Cambridge, Mass., Harvard University Press, 1991), p. 221.

13 Cynthia Ward, 'What They Told Buchi Emecheta: Oral Subjectivity and the Joys of "Otherhood" ', *PMLA* 105 (1990), p. 85.

14 'Guardian Conversation: Buchi Emecheta Talks to Susheila Nasta' (London, ICA Video, 1988).

15 'Guardian Conversation'.

16 Shaw, *The Intelligent Woman's Guide*, p. 155.

17 Buchi Emecheta, *Head Above Water* (London, Fontana, 1986), p. 115.

18 Shaw, *The Intelligent Woman's Guide*, p. 447.

# 8

# Don't cry for me Argentina –

## Jane Eyre as Evita Perón
## V. S. Naipaul, Guerrillas

The problem of origins, close cousin to foundationalism, has been several times referred to in the course of this study, without full-scale investigation. Foundationalism is decidedly unpopular in literary quarters today; it smells of the universal, the essential, in other words of the patriarchal, Eurocentric norm. The writer who provides the symptomatic case for study is, of course, V. S. Naipaul. Amongst Third World critics it has been open season on Naipaul since George Lamming attacked his 'castrated satire' in 1960.[1] Accusations of defeatism, racism, affiliation to 'universal' metropolitan values, and generally of being a lackey of neocolonialism have followed thick and fast, together with charges of anti-feminism in the creation of his female characters, and of setting himself up as the First World's favourite native informant. It is one of the odder phenomena of postcolonial literary criticism that so many people have been prepared to write lengthy, detailed and scholarly books about a writer whom they appear to deplore.

Perhaps rather consciously cocking a snook at his critics, Naipaul entitled a public lecture 'Our Universal Civilization'. In essence, however, Naipaul's lecture emphasised the social and economic mechanisms which operate beneath the 'universal':

> books are not created just in the mind. Books are physical objects .... To get your name on the spine of the created physical object, you need a vast apparatus outside yourself. You need publishers, editors, designers, printers, binders, booksellers, critics, newspapers, and magazines and television where the critics can say what they think of the book; and, of course, buyers and readers.
>
> I want to stress this mundane side of things, because it is easy to take for granted; it is easy to think of writing only in its personal, romantic aspect. Writing is a private act; but the published book,

when it starts to live, speaks of the cooperation of a particular kind of society.[2]

In what follows, Naipaul translates the term 'universal' (which he admits to finding an embarrassment) into a description of the community which has a major role in constituting the book: its audience, and those who produce it for that audience. In revealing the economic underpinnings of foundationalist assumptions, Naipaul therefore highlights the correlation between meanings and means.[3] The point has a special relevance to *Guerrillas*, in which Jimmy Ahmed (whose novel-in-progress remains romantic, personal, unpublished) colludes with Roche (the author of a carefully packaged, published memoir of sabotage in South Africa) to cover up the murder of Jane (who lists her occupation in her passport as 'publisher'). In this tale of the murder of a publisher by one writer who never finds an audience, and another whose book has been doctored by his publisher to skew it towards a particular target readership, Naipaul focuses on the related questions of audience and origin.

It probably goes without saying that a novel which opens as *Guerrillas* does, sets out to upset Eurocentric norms. 'After lunch, Jane and Roche left their house on the Ridge to drive to Thrushcross Grange' (p. 9).[4] As readers, we are immediately unsure where we are. Are we dealing with 'real' people, or with characters in a novel – Jane Eyre and Rochester? As the pair descend from the 'Heights' of the Ridge to the Grange, the reader is left to wonder whether they are moving across a physical reality (in this case an unnamed Caribbean island) or from one text (*Jane Eyre*) to another (*Wuthering Heights*). The characters' identities have been detached from their 'place' in fiction. As readers, entering a text for the first time, we usually get a handle on events by rehearsing the familiar, establishing a frame of the known around the new experience, colonising and grounding it in our own 'normal' assumptions. But how do we grapple with Naipaul's opening, which simultaneously invites and repels boarders, which both is, and is not, England, and in which the boundaries of text and world melt into each other?

In discussing the notion of 'frame', the theoretical work of Erving Goffman offers a helpful orientation.[5] Two of Goffman's notions are of special significance to *Guerrillas*: firstly that of the relation of self to role, and second that of 'frame analysis'. In the first, Goffman's most distinctive line of thought was to adopt a dramaturgical approach to social interaction, emphasising particularly the discrepancies between the self-image which the actor presents to others in an interactive process ('the presentation self') and his underlying private attitudes. Goffman's studies of such diverse groups as salesmen, hotel workers, surgical teams, games players and mental patients argue for pervasive roleplaying in social situations, suggesting that the individual is always acting within a fiction, a text, which is socially evolved. In this model, the autonomous bourgeois individual subject becomes more of a 'holding company' for a set of not relevantly connected selves. Some roles can be independently validated (Goffman cites that of law student), others cannot (Goffman cites the claim to be a true believer, or a friend). The reality of such claims will depend upon the establishment by group members of a shared conception of the horizon or frame of a situation, of shared symbolic systems. The notion of a shared horizon is obviously of intense interest to the margin/centre dynamic in postcolonial fiction in general, and to *Guerrillas* in particular, a novel in which landscapes are repeatedly framed or extended for the reader's inspection, and in which horizons – symbolic or physical – are a central focus.[6]

In addition, Goffman's sociological employment of frame analysis as a metaphor for the organisation of experience has been applied to the theory of literature. Intertextuality is the recognition of a frame, a context that allows the reader (of literature) or the actor (in a social situation) to orient himself, to distinguish 'text' from 'context', and to make sense of what would otherwise appear senseless. Just as a book offers a comprehensible **new** experience only because the reader has a framework of familiar points of contact between the self and the book, so in Goffman's analysis, everyday life depends upon the adumbration of a pattern or model, a conscious degree of roleplaying within the frame of situation, within the social text. Society is thus as much the **outcome** of situations as the **ground** for situations.[7] It is the result of our belief in intersubjectivity – that others are participating in the same reality. Deciding what degree of involvement is required, or what degree of role distance, mutually sustaining a definition of a situation – these are processes socially organised through rules of relevance and irrelevance, inclusion and exclusion, rules concerning 'what counts' as the reality of the situation. In Goffman's view, therefore, reality is sponsored by the team. Thus, almost identical actions may be transformed or transcribed by participants from one frame to another, via a systematic alteration which radically reconstitutes for participants 'what is going on'. An obvious example offered by Goffman is the distinction between fighting, and playing at fighting, in animal or human behaviour. When the reader becomes totally involved in fiction (a horror story, for example) he or she may check that involvement by saying that 'It's only a story', reframing events in order to take back their meaning or annul their emotional impact. Intertextual devices may function similarly, in order to reverse or undo the action, to establish that 'it doesn't count'.

Naipaul provides a creative enactment of such reframing in the actual beginning of his novel. In framing this critical discussion, in proposing the opening sentence as point of origin, the current writer has cheated. The novel in fact begins with an epigraph:

When everybody wants to fight there's nothing to fight for. Every-body wants to fight his own little war, everybody is a guerrilla.

James Ahmed

To the unwary (of whom the present writer admits to having been one) the quotation bears all the marks of authoritative political commentary, situ-ated on the 'outside' of the novel. It is a surprise to find (p. 87) that it is merely a quotation from a letter written by one of the main protagonists. It is also repeated, later in the novel, in paraphrase by Harry, a minor char-acter, commenting upon the failure of Jimmy Ahmed's popular uprising: 'They don't know who they fighting or who they fighting for. Everybody down there is a leader now' (p. 185). The intertextual Brontëan opening is not, therefore, the point at which we begin; it is inside a text initiated by Jimmy. We are Jimmy's readers before we are Naipaul's. We may not know this immediately (indeed many readers will simply have missed the epigraph, often consigned to liminal limbo), but when we do the relation between inner and outer will need readjustment. The frame is inside the novel; the novel is framing itself. What was 'out' is now 'in', what was margin has become centre. Frame implodes, and the boundary between world and book breaks down. Harry's later paraphrase repeats the process, retranscribing the quotation from the literary (Jimmy's letter) to the action 'proper' of the novel – though that is in itself a questionable distinction. By now the reader may have legitimate doubts about where the centre of the action might be said to be, in deeds or in words. In little, the special problems of the novel's opening introduce the dominant concerns of *Guerrillas*: origins (where does the action start?) and audience (who is acting and who is peripheral to the action?). In a novel intensely interested in notions of self and role, acting (theatre) and action (deeds), distance and involvement, performer and audi-ence, the question of who 'frames' whom, who establishes the horizon and ground of the social situation, excluding or including, defining as mean-ingful or meaningless, saturates plot, character and political agenda.

If we return to our 'opening' it is to find that Thrushcross Grange has more surprises in store: it is apparently a revolutionary commune. Its sign-boards bear an emblematic clenched fist and the words (typographically framed from the surrounding text):

THRUSHCROSS GRANGE
PEOPLE'S COMMUNE
FOR THE LAND AND THE REVOLUTION
Entry without prior permission strictly
forbidden at all times
By Order of the High Command
JAMES AHMED (Haji)
(p. 12)

When Jane and Roche meet Jimmy, he hands them an official communiqué which sets out his belief in the origins of revolution as land-based, and emphasises the foundationalist notions of virgin land and of birth rights (the statement is set off from the surrounding text by italicisation, another form of framing):

> *All revolutions begin with the land. Men are born on the earth, every man has his one spot, it is his birth right, and men must claim their portion of the earth in brotherhood and harmony. In this spirit we came an intrepid band to virgin forest, it is the life style and philosophy of Thrushcross Grange* (p. 17).

As Michael Neill has established, in a comprehensive discussion of Naipaul's gradually unfolding argument with, and debt to, Frantz Fanon, Jimmy's idea of the necessity of all revolutions to begin from the land is original not to himself, but to Fanon, whom he paraphrases (evoking the title of Fanon's *magnum opus*, *Black Skin, White Masks*): 'it's always a case of black faces white masks' (p. 86). In Jimmy's agricultural commune Naipaul criticises not only the proposition (specific to Fanon) that the peasantry, alone, outside the class system, could make a revolution, but also, much more generally, the idea that everything can and should be started from scratch, in some return to pre-industrial origins. Fanon's writings are suffused with the image of this return. Michael Neill has underlined the apocalyptic tenor of such 'fresh starts':

> The implications of this stance . . . are that the imperial past must be annihilated, and all present links with the controlling power severed. It can lead at one extreme to the self-destructive frenzy initiated by the Paris-trained intellectuals of Pol Pot's Kampuchea, Year Zero.[8]

While Naipaul certainly lambasts the cheap apocalyptic rhetoric of Jane and her fellow Home Counties 'radicals', his major target is the notion of origins, satirised unmercifully here. Jimmy's 'virgin forest', for example, is actually post-industrial. The Grange is established on what remains of an abandoned industrial estate from the first days of independence, its fields choked with weeds, it outbuildings derelict and half abandoned: 'already in the midst of bush, the effect was that of urban slum' (p. 19). Indeed, its inhabitants are slum boys, recruited by Roche. Fanon had also anticipated that, in the right conditions, the gangs of the towns could become the spearhead of revolution. In *The Wretched of the Earth* he cites the example of the city gangster, dying in conflict with the police, who becomes a heroic populist model.[9] In *Guerrillas*, however, the death of Stephens (gangster and former commune member) in a shoot-out with the police remains an off-stage anti-climax, without translating, despite Jimmy's efforts to capitalise on it, into enduring political consequences. Roche speaks the epitaph on the uprising in a radio interview when he comments 'I didn't believe in the guerrillas . . . . I believed in the gangs' (p. 213).

Rather like Coetzee *vis-à-vis* **his** 'barbarians', Naipaul is primarily concerned with an absence: the Grange is no guerrilla base, there are no guerrillas. Far from suggesting a step forward, Jimmy's desire to foster a land-based revolution actually seems to be turning the clock back. His 'intrepid band' (four boys in Wellington boots) are described:

> As if in parody of nineteenth-century plantation prints . . . the boys, with sullen, downcast eyes, as though performing an unpleasant duty, were planting out long-stalked tomato seedlings which, as fast as they were set in their dusty little holes, quailed and drooped (pp. 20–1).

The evocation of the print suggests a carefully framed tableau. Indeed Roche comments that 'That's laid on for us' (p. 13). Unusually the boys are working in the heat of the day, as a display for the benefit of their visitors, a show staged with complete disregard for productive economic practices. Jane and Roche collude in Jimmy's drama, allowing his fantasy of growing cash crops to go unchallenged. As Jacqueline Brice-Finch has noted, all three characters are functioning at levels of deception which, while apparent to each other, are accepted as necessary ruses.[10] The scene establishes both the importance of Jane and Roche as audience, confirming Jimmy's fantasy as real, and the degree to which the social text is framed, its limits set, by economic interests. Jimmy's signboard had a partial frame of its own: 'In a strip at the bottom, in letters cut out white on red, was the name of the local firm, Sablich's, who had put the board up' (p. 12). The fantasy of revolution has been set up by Roche's employers, the former slave-owning company, and is equipped only with their cast-off, junked machinery. Jimmy's project can have meaning only as far as Sablich's permits; they establish the real frame of the situation. In reality Jimmy is sponsored – economically and in terms of identity – by neo-colonial commercial interests. He has been bought by Sablich's who are now selling him as part of a public relations exercise. The return to 'origins' is doubly ironic: Jimmy has indeed gone back to an earlier time – he is as good as owned anew by the former slaveholders. More generally, Naipaul ironises Jimmy's project by underlining the lack of an economic base to the island, which appears to have only bauxite to exchange. Naipaul's invented island is a client culture and a satellite economy.[11]

A second foundational plank in Jimmy's political platform is that of Black Power. A poster at the Grange displays him as 'all hair, eyes and moustache, and more negroid than he was' (p. 17). Black Power politics (at least in Jimmy's simplified form) are clearly racially based upon an essentialist notion of the body as corporeal ground. Awkwardly for Jimmy, he does not actually look black. As a Heathcliff returning to claim the

Grange from which he has been excluded, Jimmy sees himself in Brontëan terms. He imagines that after the revolution

> everybody will say then 'This man was born in the back room of a Chinese grocery, but as Catherine said to Heathcliff "Your mother was an Indian princess and your father was the Emperor of China"' (p. 62).

Jimmy seems impervious to the contradiction here; his revolutionary programme exploits the notion of Black Power and makes no reference whatsoever to those inhabitants of the island who are of Indian or Chinese origin. The elitism of the quotation, its reference to royal and imperial roles, is also telling. Jimmy does not live in the communal dormitory with his boys, but separately in the former house of the factory manager. The house has much in common with the Grange as the embodiment of the bourgeois *rentier* class. It is lavishly furnished with imported English carpets and furniture, and contains the 'The Hundred Best Books of the World', an authoritative canon uniformly bound and displayed. In his novel Jimmy imagines a character taking down *Wuthering Heights*, and his narrator commenting:

> 'Ah,' he said, 'you are looking at that great work of the Brontës. What a gifted family, it makes you believe in heredity. Would you like some tea?' (p. 40).

For Jimmy, writing is in the blood, a matter of origins. More English than the English he displays his house as if it were a stage set, an arena of conspicuous consumption. Jimmy's revolution is therefore firmly established as dependent on metropolitan sources – both economic and literary.

A question arises, however, at this point. When Roche asks after Stephens, Jimmy is evasive. Indeed the reader never meets Stephens, whose death is merely reported later in the novel. Where the Eurocentric reader may only have recognised the allusions to the Brontës,[12] the alert Caribbean reader would see quite a different social text as a potential frame to the action: the events described in Naipaul's 'Michael X and the Black Power Killings in Trinidad'. Indeed more than one reader has understood *Guerrillas* as a work of 'faction', grounded, despite its shape-shifting opening, in real events. In his account of the killings in Trinidad (originally a series of articles for the *Sunday Times Magazine* in 1974) Naipaul chronicled the life of Michael de Freitas, also known as Michael Abdul Malik, or Michael X, a figure in the Black Power movement of the 1960s. Malik spent fourteen years in London (1957–71), at first in gangster circles, as pimp, drug-pusher and strong-arm man for racketeers. Jailed in 1967 under the race relations legislation, for an anti-white speech, he later converted to Islam, and transformed himself from gangster to would-be guerrilla, setting up communes, first in Islington, then in a suburban house in his native Trinidad. In 1972 this commune included Gale Benson, a twenty-seven-year-old English woman, and her boyfriend Hakim Jamal, an American adherent to Black Power. On 2 January 1972 Benson was stabbed to death and buried in a pit at the commune, the motive apparently being that it did not 'look good' for a potential Black Power leader to have a white girlfriend. Benson was not immediately missed. Malik gave out that she had simply had a quarrel with them and had left the island. Later, however, the discovery of other bodies led to hers, and Malik was eventually hanged for murder in 1975. The killings did not stop with Benson: other victims included Joseph Skerritt who shares resemblances with Stephens.[13] These are, of course, the essential outlines of the plot of *Guerrillas*, in which Jane is murdered by Jimmy and Bryant, and in which Roche gives out that she has left the island. The reader of *Guerrillas*, familiar with the events of Malik's life, will immediately spot the absence of Stephens and the evasive nature of Jimmy's replies to questions, and may well also see Jane's fate on the horizon. In the case of Stephens, this local knowledge is something of a red herring: Stephens is not one of Jimmy's victims, and the intertextual frame comes close to 'framing' Jimmy in the colloquial, underworld sense. In the case of Jane, however, the absence of local reading proves crucial. Jimmy foreshadows Jane's fate in the novel which he is writing. At one moment she lifts a page – but fails to read on. Had she done so, she might well have avoided the slaughter with which the novel ends (p. 166). The point deserves emphasis – since it foregrounds the operations of reader and writer in the context of quite distinct readerships – the local and the metropolitan audience – and has an intimate link to Malik's activities.

Paradoxically, the story of Michael Abdul Malik, just like Jimmy's, provides in its apparent **facts** a demonstration of textual power – both social and literary. Naipaul comments in the postscript to 'Michael X and the Black Power Killings in Trinidad' that 'This was a literary murder, if ever there was one'.[14] Writing had, in Naipaul's view, led Malik to murder. In London, Malik had picked up the 'jargon' of the Black Power movement, and adopted a fictional identity. We are told that 'It was in London that Malik became a Negro.'[15] (His father was a Portuguese shopkeeper.) Adopted by the English as 'everybody's Negro' and conveniently 'not too Negroid',[16] Naipaul presents Malik as having borrowed every attitude and statement from others – from the conversion to Islam to the adoption of X as surname (following Malcolm X). His autobiography is not, in Naipaul's account, so much the story of a life or the development of a personality as a haphazard collection of groundless roles, an acting out of clichés, rather than a programme for action. Naipaul draws the economic moral:

> Malik's career proves how much of Black Power – away from its
> United States source – is jargon, how much a sentimental hoax. In

a place like Trinidad, racial redemption is as irrelevant for the Negro as for everybody else. It obscures the problems of a small independent country with a lopsided economy.[17]

In Naipaul's analysis, Malik appealed to a metropolitan audience, to 'radical chic' (today's political correctness), to

that section of the middle class that knows only that it is secure; has no views, only reflexes and scattered irritations, and sometimes indulges in play : the people who keep up with 'revolution' **as with the theatre** [my emphasis], the revolutionaries who visit centres of revolution, but with return air-tickets, the people for whom Malik's kind of Black Power was an exotic but safe brothel.[18]

It is a precise description of Jane in *Guerrillas*: a middle-class lady in search of excitement, who toys with revolutionary and apocalyptic slogans, has casual sex with Jimmy, and travels with a return air ticket – though in this case it does not preserve her.

Significantly Malik was also a writer who had left behind him an unfinished novel. Malik's novel provided a curious foreshadowing of later events, particularly in the sudden disappearance of its female narrator. This narrator, an Englishwoman, admires Malik's 'English-looking' house, and compliments him on his reading. She takes down a volume of Flaubert from his shelves (Naipaul makes it *Wuthering Heights*). She is spellbound by him, develops some sort of relationship, becomes afraid of him, and then mysteriously disappears from the story. Naipaul reworks this novel, as Jimmy's, in order to suggest that Jimmy, like Malik, was led by the logic of fantasy to rape and murder.[19] Naipaul's Jimmy is therefore not so much a copy of an 'original' in Malik, as a copy of a copy. Malik himself is portrayed as profoundly imitative, the ultimate mimic man. *Guerrillas* recreates and emends the situation of 'Michael X and the Black Power Killings in Trinidad', in a complicated series of manoeuvres, beginning from Naipaul's articles (1974) and followed by *Guerrillas* in 1975, and 'Michael X and the Black Power Killings in Trinidad' in 1980. In sequence the writings have a rather self-cancelling quality – as if Charlotte Brontë had written both *Jane Eyre* and *Wide Sargasso Sea*. Eve Shelnutt[20] has noted the fashion in which Naipaul repeatedly doubles back, going over the same ground more than once, in fiction and travelogue, for example. Generic hesitation is Naipaul's key strategy in modifying European cultural paradigms, whether in interrogating the relation between what has been called the history of a myth and the myth of a history *(The Loss of El Dorado)* or between masked autobiography and the autobiography of a mask *(The Enigma of Arrival)*.[21] In similar fashion metropolitan cultural norms are called into question by a blurring of the lines between literary forms, and a conscious trespassing across the boundaries of novel, history, essay, cultural critique, travelogue and autobiography. In addition the positions of author/narrator/persona/ character continually criss-cross,[22] so that the reader finds it impossible to 'place' a discourse in terms of origins, and therefore undergoes a process of rethinking events, while going over the ground anew.

*Guerrillas* is often a puzzling novel for the reader, notably in the untold story of Stephens, and in the events of the disturbances at its centre, presented only at second hand. It is even more puzzling for its major characters, all in various ways reader-resistant. At separate points Jimmy (p.16), Jane (p. 14) and the indigenous population (p. 179) are described as 'unreadable'.[23] When the riots occur, Jane and Roche, isolated on the Ridge, know what is happening only through newspaper reports. Jane glances at the front page which contains 'a number of separate and apparently unrelated stories' (p. 178), that a guerrilla has been '*Slain in Dawn Shoot-out*', that a politician has been recalled to government, and that a 'police operation' has been taking place in the city. To a local eye, the stories spell out riots, revolt and repression.[24] Stephens, a criminal reader, is described earlier in the novel as reading the paper in a quite different way. Ignoring the foreign news, he concentrates on police items, able to tell from the casual details of incidents and their locations precisely what all his friends and enemies are up to. 'This was how Stephens read the evening paper, like a private circular' (p. 63). Harry de Tunja also treats the paper in this way. Wary of his home being attacked by looters, he telephones the paper's editor to suggest a story '*Ridge Residents Starve Dogs*', to deter other criminal readers. For Harry, also local, the paper is like a crossword puzzle, full of hints, clues and messages, readable in more than one direction, its current solution deferred to the next day. Jane and Roche, however, as Western readers, are reduced to incomprehension, and have to fall back on the radio news from London:

> Earlier reports of police desertions and the resignation of the government have now been officially denied. Government sources now say that the police have returned in strength to most areas of the capital from which they had previously withdrawn (p. 192).

The disturbances are described, in a fashion which discounts and infantilises them, as protests by radical youth groups against unemployment and foreign domination of the economy. Jane is sardonically relieved: 'I'm glad to know what it's all about' (p. 192). Roche points out that 'That's how it will go down in the books. That's how it will be discussed. That's what you can start believing yourself' (p. 192). Quite obviously, here, the message from London, its version of political 'reality' on the island, dominates the experiences of those who have actually been through the disturbances. Jane might as well have stayed in London for all the 'real' experience she has had. In a sense, as the ending demonstrates, she has never really been there on the island. The situation has been read, defined, and written up elsewhere, authoritatively, for a metropolitan audience.

Importantly, Jane and Roche's position here, as a baffled audience, look-ing down on events from their distant heights, is the culmination of a long process of disconfirmation of their 'frame'. Rather than having a role to play in events they are reduced to spectators. When the last plane takes off, stranding them on the island, their horizon effectively shrinks. Secure in her metropolitan assumptions, Jane cannot contemplate this abandon-ment: 'the place just can't stay like this. It can't just turn into a great ripe cheese' (p. 189). She is, of course, right. The Americans, acting in defence of their bauxite interests, send in helicopters. As they appear on the hori-zon, the frame, both physical and political, reexpands to include the adja-cent neocolonialist power, and the rising is all over, bar the reprisals. As the choppers move in to settle scores, in a scene which draws upon a post-Vietnam iconic representation of reactionary, neocolonialist violence, Jane protests against her relegation to spectatorhood: 'You mean we just have to sit here and watch this happen?' (p. 195). The reader has the same lack of choice and the same disorienting sensation of disconfirmation of iden-tity, of a cancelled reality. As Borges comments, 'If the characters in a story can be readers or spectators, then we, their readers or spectators, can be fictitious.'[25] If the presence of novels-within-the-novel (e.g. Jimmy's) and novels-without-the-novel (the Brontës) have already knocked the ground from under the reader's feet, the action itself, its scenes strongly marked for audience presence, denies the reader any stable position. Third-person narration implies that the reader has no authoritative point of view to attach the story to – unlike *Jane Eyre* ('Reader I married him') or even *Wuthering Heights* (a choice between Lockwood and Nelly as narrators). As a result, Naipaul fosters the impression of writing proceeding from a void. Reading becomes roleplay. Repeatedly the reader reads over the shoulder of a character (Jane reading Jimmy's letter, the newspaper accounts) or is part of an audience already constituted by the fiction (the social gathering at which Jane is frozen out, the radio interview). We are repeatedly coached into the position of readers, only to find the frame shifting, and the position disappearing. Like Jane and Roche the reader is placed off-centre, between competing frames, watching an audience watch events. As a result we become uncertain of the 'ins and outs' of the situ-ation – both in the sense of the tangled interweaving of events, and in the political sense of inclusion and exclusion. By demolishing any univocal frame for events Naipaul thus leaves his readers 'at sea' – an apposite metaphor for a novel about a colonised island – their horizon continually and vertiginously shifting, the base beneath their feet fundamentally inse-cure. It is almost as if he put the colonists back on the boat. The reader's difficulties in reading the novel highlight the politics of postcolonial read-ing. Without a sense of a shared horizon, a shared definition of a situa-tion, Jane and Roche may be in the island, but they are not of it. In Naipaul's writing, distance is not a separate social or aesthetic concept, but coterminous with geographical reality. Jane carries her metropolitan distance, her extended horizon, with her. In her first sexual encounter with Jimmy it is her role distance, her coolly detached manner, which is massively inappropriate to the situation. She seeks Jimmy out again only at the close when, about to depart, she is on the point of putting real distance permanently between them, when her action 'does not count'.

At the close of the novel, when Jimmy and Roche collude to suppress the metropolitan story of the latter-day Jane, Eyre/heir to colonial guilts, they effectively set up their own reality team. Where Rhys restored a hidden silenced story, Naipaul demonstrates how a story can be silenced, when it is unvalidated by social and economic interests. For each of the main characters, a major event in the novel is the loss of an audience to confirm them in a socially constituted identity: Jimmy is rejected as a politician and a writer; Roche in the radio interview is seen playing to an audience which does not exist; Bryant is ignored; Jane finds herself frozen out. Importantly the reason why Jane can be written off as she is, is that she has no official **origin**. No record exists of her date of entry to the island. Her passport was not stamped on arrival; she was waved through customs in the company of two representatives of the bauxite company with whom she had struck up an acquaintance on the plane. Her existence on the island has no proper 'beginning'. On the plane the two company men spend the flight time reading. When Jane stretches out her hand towards the books her neighbour restrains her. They are works of hard-core pornography: *Easy Lay* and *Sucked Dry*. Her story opens, therefore, with the experience of being prevented from reading by the neocolonialist exploiters of the island – criminal readers whose material exploitation goes hand in hand with control of access to the book as physical object. At the close, the absolute erasure of Jane's West Indian existence completes the process by which she has been marginalised and cut out of events. When Jane is told that the pornography is 'unreadable' as far as she is concerned, embargoed under male *diktat*, her female exclusion mirrors that of Jimmy Ahmed, similarly excluded by neocolonialism from any productive future and condemned to groundless performance – 'acting' rather than 'action'. Unable to read the text, it is Jane's fate to act in it, as it is Jimmy's.

The pornography is worth pausing over, precisely because of the way Naipaul uses sex in the novel as an index of exploitation. The rape and murder of Jane has been frequently attacked by critics as an example of a racist scenario (of the 'white woman raped by black man' variety) or of Naipaul's essential anti-feminism – a vision of woman as in some way 'asking for it'. Helen Pyne-Timothy's comment is representative: 'Jane is made so extremely unsympathetic in this work that one can only feel that this woman deserves her end.'[26] The problem is compounded by Naipaul's rewriting of the Malik material in this respect. In *Guerrillas* Jimmy is bisexual – or, at least, he performs sexual acts with both Jane and Bryant, his male follower. Where Malik, apparently heterosexual, lived in his commune with his wife and children, and other men and women, Thrushcross Grange is emphatically masculine. The commune is a collection of so many rescued Heathcliffs, orphans procured for Jimmy by Roche, who live in an all-male dormitory, as if in a dissolute male version of Lowood. Naipaul makes no reference to Jimmy's family, with the exception of a photograph showing his children, but not his wife. Her image has been mutilated, cut out of the frame to remove the woman. This adaptation of sources is, of course, open to charges of deliberate bias, demonising Jimmy by homophobic identification. In the context of Naipaul's critique of origins, and in the light of his attack on corporeal foundationalism in Black Power, it makes more sense to envisage it as a careful strategy to avoid gender as foundation. Arguably Jimmy's bisexuality is designed as a means to destabilise distinctions between natural/artificial, depth/surface, inner/outer, male/female. Goffman had studied 'body idiom' as a conventionalised discourse. In a thesis which extends Goffman's frame analysis of social interaction to the arena of gender, Judith Butler has raised the notion of gender as performative, as a persistent impersonation which passes as the real.[27] Taking as her starting point the notion of drag as dramatising the signifying gestures through which discourse about gender operates, Butler exposes the foundational categories of sex and gender as effects of a specific formation of power. To paraphrase – Butler refuses to look for an inner truth of gender (some original self which repression conceals, a silenced story) and instead investigates the political stakes in designating as origin and cause those identity categories which are actually the **results** of institutions, discourses and practices.

In the light of Butler's argument, the characterisation of Jane begins to make sense. Naipaul shows Jane as a mimic woman, continually performing her gender. Like Jimmy, Jane has felt marginalised from the main centre of events, in her case as a woman rather than a postcolonial subject. She is initially attracted to Roche because 'He seemed to make accessible that remote world, of real events and real action, whose existence she had half divined' (p. 49). She comes to Roche, as to a fictional character, through his book which appears to demonstrate that 'He was a doer; his book and his life proved that' (p. 49). In a world dominated by men, Jane performs to their scripts, allowing them to hold the definitions, to frame her. She is in some respects less a 'real' female subject, than a discursive construct, as the Brontëan echoes suggest. Roche describes her personality as essentially a composite of the attitudes, gestures and catchphrases which she has picked up from her various lovers (p. 25). The point is substantiated for the reader when Jane mouths to Roche, on arrival, the two phrases absorbed from her travelling companions: 'The hard stuff' (pp. 45–6) and 'I need intensive care' (pp. 45–6). The parallel with Jimmy, also a creation of other people's jargon, is made more explicit in Jane's personal history which associates her with the West Indian victim. Jane married young, an innocent schoolgirl. She speaks of the marriage as 'something forced upon her' (p. 96) and blames her mother and an uncle. Like many a Rhys heroine, Jane is thereafter confirmed into a dependent and self-dramatising role. Naipaul described Rhys's heroines as embodying 'dependence as drama'.[28] Roche recalls that Jane describes her love affairs as 'a continuing violation; she spoke, with brutal detail, of the affront of her abortions. She spoke as though she had never exercised choice' (p. 97). With Roche, Jane swiftly establishes the roles which suit her: 'she the violated, he the comforter' (p. 97). Duress also excites her (as indicated in her physical pleasure when slapped by a lover, p. 48). If 'properly gendered' roles are always socially regulated, then violence is in the wings of any sexual encounter, as the punitive sanctions for inapproprate role involvement. Jane first impresses Roche as a performer, 'in her role as executive' (p. 95), staging an angry display on the telephone for his benefit. As a result, 'She became the doer, the seeker; he became her audience' (p. 95). Once out of her London context, however, her radical chic loses its power to convince. At a party on the island, as Jane trots out apocalyptic clichés, an island woman 'refused to acknowledge Jane's presence' (p. 99). The result is predictable. 'Without an audience, then, to give her a familiar idea of herself, she had . . . begun to relapse into her class certainties' (p. 100). If Jane has any foundation it is implicitly economic – her assumption of an absolute class security which guarantees her fundamental inviolability, her belief that 'everything could be undone' (p. 101).

Society, however, permits no such security. Both Jane's politics and her gender are stylisations and when the one falters she is vulnerable also in the other. When the island audience registers its disapproval of Jane, Roche suddenly finds himself detecting in her 'a physical gracelessness' (p. 99). The island woman who freezes Jane out is, in contrast, strongly marked for conformity to a 'feminine' role, neat in a tight-waisted blue dress, carefully made up for the evening party. Critics of Naipaul have, mistakenly, focused on the scenes in which Jane's body is presented in less than enticing fashion as evidence of Naipaul's own essential distaste for female flesh. Jane sweats, smells, develops pimples and (notoriously) is depicted inserting a tampon. Arguably, however, what Naipaul is doing is highlighting the chasm between the body and the various stylisations imposed upon it by the performance of a normative gender role. When Roche surprises Jane, menstruating (p. 127), he is first struck by her size, ('she looked big and tall') and by the 'athletic' speed with which she throws herself backwards, raises her legs, and inserts the tampon, 'shooting' the empty container into a corner with 'a low, level flick of the wrist', and pulling her trousers back on in one swift movement. Jane is quite independent of her audience here. Apart from one glance at Roche as he enters the room, she does not acknowledge him. In terms of a conventional gender performance the sporty body in trousers, 'inserting' and then 'shooting' with effortless mastery, is marked less for female than for male. Sexual innuendo aside, Jane sounds more like a cricketer than a woman who is 'indisposed'. Yet the reason for her performance could hardly be less intractably female. Biological intractability, however, is at odds here with the cultural constructions of gender. Roche comments to himself that 'it was as though she didn't belong to her body' (p. 127).

The backcloth to the scene is also significant. When a performance is not validated by an audience, when it is taken to be deviant, the role generally offered by society is that of lunatic (as Goffman's studies of asylums, or *Wide Sargasso Sea* indicate). Naipaul makes much of an entire background of madness in the novel – street people in particular – to emphasise the social constitution of reality and the group definition of the norm. Religious belief is a similar case in point. (**He** is nuts; **they** are members of a cult; **we** are the true church.) Just before Roche surprises Jane, she and Harry watch a curious performance on the beach, 'a drama taking place' (p. 120). A black-gowned man, up to his waist in the sea, rings a bell, while others launch candles on the waves. A blindfolded group march into the sea, one woman 'like a leader' (p. 121), another man 'like a clown' (p. 121), the chief bellringer 'something of the showman, pleased to draw a crowd' (p. 122). On the beach another woman is shouting 'gibberish':

> She looked down at the beach; she seemed to be addressing some-
> one stretched out there, for whom, from her gestures, she continu-
> ally spread an imaginary rug or sheet. It was a private frenzy. No
> one was listening to her; no one stopped to watch (p. 121).

To the external eye, the uncomprehending audience, the events are performance shading into madness. To a Caribbean resident, the scene is perfectly recognisable as a ceremony of the 'Shouters' religion, a focus for colonial resistance. Melville Herskovits comments in his classic study that the religious persecution of the Shouters symbolised for others the struggle which they all had against economic and social disability.[29] As the scene demonstrates, audience is all. In a society in which spirit possession is validated, there is nothing odd about the woman's behaviour in speaking to an apparently imaginary audience, someone who is 'not there'. Or, at least, it is no odder than a Western telephone call, or a radio broadcast (Jane's playacting call at her publishing office, or Roche's maid, Adela, permanently tuned to religious broadcasting, for example). In the island, the religious and the political are conflated in the repeated slogan 'After Israel, Africa'. Whether the slogan represents delusion or political activism will depend on audience endorsement or disconfirmation.

Jane, however, cannot afford to ignore her audience. In her first sexual encounter with Jimmy he notes her 'masculine' (p. 80) posture, her genitalia 'displayed, as though she were alone' (p. 81), and the contrast between her emotional coolness and the evidence of physical pleasure: 'her body seemed independent of her manner, her words, her attitudes' (p. 81). For Jimmy, Jane has not met her 'female' role obligations. Since he himself, barely tumescent, doesn't quite match the image he propounds of himself as bronze god, Jane is also discomfited. As she departs she finds that 'Words began to go through her head, words addressed to no one in particular' (p. 83). Audience silence, in its turn, silences the performer. Jane acts as if the world were fiction, as if events on the island 'don't count', are reversible. Murder proves her wrong. When she revisits Jimmy he is infuriated by her assumption of security based upon her ability to put real distance between them, and he kills her. Jane declines, from being at centre stage, to losing her audience, to becoming a character in a novel (Jimmy's) and thence to being written out of the story. Over the telephone at the close, Roche tells Jimmy that Jane is 'in', though she is already dead.

Why does Roche collude in this fashion? At the close, visiting the Grange, Roche spots Jane's cigarette lighter and knows that she is dead. He walks away and subsequently tells their friends that she has left the island. When Jimmy phones him he announces 'I'm leaving you alone. I am leaving. I am going away. Jane and I are leaving tomorrow. Jane is in her room packing. We are leaving you here' (p. 253). The children's primer vocabulary and repetitions of simple statements with minor variations, establish Roche's role, coaching and instructing Jimmy in how the situation is to be read. Roche has decided how events are to be recorded; he and Jimmy form the reality team which erases Jane's existence. It is important to note here that Roche is also a discomfited performer, revenging himself in his final actions for a bruising experience at the hands of a local radio presenter and politician, Meredith Herbert, who sets up a radio interview with Roche. Since the interview is prerecorded, there is no audience. The tape will be edited before broadcasting. Roche is therefore ostensibly entirely free in his performance. The only other person present is the black studio manager. Because of his presence, however, Roche is unwilling to complain about the uncomfortable recording conditions and the lack of ventilation. Irritated by the heat and dust, he lets his tongue run away with him, indicting Jimmy and writing off all possibility of successful revolution. Afterwards what had seemed like 'a logical and controlled performance' (p. 215) appals him. When Jane asks why he remained in the room, once Meredith's hostile intentions were clear, he responds: 'there was a third person there. A big black man from the country. He was in the cubicle. That's always fatal: a third person. You start acting for this third person' (p. 218). As Meredith reveals at the close of the interview, however, the man is quite impervious: 'Those people hear nothing. They only hear sound and level. They can read a book or write a letter while they're listening' (p. 214). Playing to an audience betrays Roche. The audience here is actually immersed in other discourses. Roche's interview, a claustrophobic experience in the heat of the studio, takes place behind a hermetically sealed picture window, framing a magnificently expansive view of the city. The juxtaposition of the large framed view with Roche's confinement is telling. Although Roche is apparently at liberty to frame his own role as a public figure, in enlarged terms, he is actually confined by an audience of one. Roche complains in the course of the interview that 'I'm not on display' (p. 204). He wants to act, to be a doer. But the crux of the novel concerns the difficulty of such action, of making a performance count.

In the interview, in which much is made of Roche's sweating, uncomfortable body and of the contrast between his public performance and his private sensations, Meredith focuses on Roche's book, which describes his experience of torture in South Africa. Although his suffering was seen as some sort of guarantee of his political good faith (Roche's body as ground and foundation of his role), Meredith notes that in his book 'there seems to be no framework of political belief . . . . You write as though certain things merely happened to you, were forced upon you' (p. 209). In his view, Roche's activism and subsequent violation is not dissimilar to Jane's: 'It was a gesture' (p. 209). Roche was then, and is now, merely playing at involvement. Even worse, in an accusation sometimes levelled at Naipaul himself, he has allowed himself to be cast as professional conscience, thus setting his audience free to act as they will.

> Don't you think you've allowed yourself to become the conscience of your society? . . . People are perfectly willing for you to be their conscience and to suffer, while they get on with the business of aggressing, and the thugs and psychopaths get on with their work in the torture-chambers (p. 211).

Roche had not displayed anger at being tortured, forced under duress to conform to the norm, merely shame (p. 212). In his writing he was unable to overcome his instinct to 'muffle the personal drama of arrest, torture, imprisonment, and release' (p. 94) and as a result his book is diffuse, unfocused. In 'The Documentary Heresy', Naipaul commented that the documentary artist, the writer who merely records, who fails to impose a vision on the world, abdicates responsibility, and finally accepts his world. He cannot do more than record violence, for example, which remains violence which 'makes no statement beyond that of bodily pain and degradation. It is like the obscene photograph. It deals anonymously with anonymous flesh, quickened only by pleasure or pain.'[30] Roche's book may appear as the reverse of Jimmy's private fantasy, as a 'true' and public record of events, but it will in the end merely accept. He allows the frame to be set for him by his projected audience. His book is styled from without: the publisher has induced him, for example, to include additional material on the Nazi camps. The events of the novel lend credence to Meredith's accusations. When Roche visits Stephens' mother, for example, he becomes aware that her house is under surveillance, and that he is therefore also being watched. In response to his awareness of this invisible, but authoritative audience, Roche thinks 'I mustn't become involved' (p. 115). He is relieved to be greeted by his office watchman (p. 116), carefully rehearses (p. 115) the potential dangers of his drive home, and submits without reaction to a police search. As he admits to Jane, he has always accepted authority (p.54). Naipaul's Roche(ster) is not simply designed for a Western audience which can pick up a literary allusion – he is an exemplification of the coercive force of that audience, its effect on Roche as both a body and as a member of a body politic.

Bryant and Jimmy are similarly confined by audience definitions. Although strategically targeted at feminist practice, Butler's argument can be productively transposed into questions of racial politics. If Jane performs herself as a woman, Jimmy performs himself no less as a black. Where Butler is optimistic, envisaging the proliferation of varying gender performances as potentially subversive of the universal norm, Naipaul, however, strikes a tragic note. To recap: Butler leaves the witness to the performance out of the equation; she does not consider the possibility that performance needs audience, that the witness to a scene has an effect in limiting what an individual can be. The appalling scene of violence at the close of *Guerrillas* is designed to underline the extent to which sexual and racial roles are artificially and meretriciously constructed, and that the result of becoming mired in such roles is dependence for existence upon an audience. Just as Gale Benson was murdered partly as a result of racial rhetoric, so Jane dies as the result of the scripts in accordance with which she, Bryant, Jimmy and Roche are acting. It is important to note that all four are involved in an essentially dramaturgical process. Indictments against Naipaul of anti-feminism or racism are therefore groundless. In this novel 'woman', 'man', 'black' and 'white' are all identity constructions – performances – which are open to deconstruction. Naipaul's aim is precisely to underline the lack of firm foundation to his characters, continually redefined as their frame shifts.

The position is at its clearest in the case of Bryant, whose part in the murder is explicitly connected to Hollywood fantasies. Early in the novel Bryant begs a dollar from Jane which finances a trip to the cinema. En route he pauses to order a punch in a bar, 'banging on the counter as he did so and shouting "*Ai! Ai! Ai!* " for no reason, only to make a little scene' (p. 36). The barman ignores him. Bryant seeks an audience – but merely becomes one. Renouncing the interracial sex films on offer Bryant chooses a Sidney Poitier double bill, two Hollywood movies not noted for the honesty of their representation of blacks. In the first, Poitier is 'a man with a gun' (p. 36). In the second, *For the Love of Ivy*, Hollywood's first bow towards portraying a black love affair, Bryant sees in Poitier a version of himself that nobody will ever know, a self closed off forever by the norms of gender, from bodily performance:

> the man who had died within the body Bryant carried . . . the man Bryant knew to be himself, without the edginess and the anger, and the pretend ugliness, the laughing man, the tender joker. Watching the film he began to grieve for what was denied him: that future in which he became what he truly was, not a man with a gun, a big profession or big talk, but himself, and as himself was loved (pp. 36–7).

Bryant's mourning for a future forever foreclosed on him is carefully distinguished from action-as-violence ('a man with a gun') or action-as-acting. Naipaul has described how in his youth the American ideal in Trinidad crystallised around the gangster movie: 'Trinidadians of all races and classes are remaking themselves in the image of the Hollywood B-man.'[31] The audiences in Port of Spain preferred films which humiliated women, westerns and fight scenes. (*The Spoilers* was widely advertised on the basis that it had the longest-ever fight sequence, between Randolph Scott and John Wayne.) In contrast, Bryant longs for a gentler self which can never find an audience – and the audience of the film sob with him. As Bryant's ugly body (remarked upon at several reprises) suggests, and as Judith Butler underlines, the body is always already the victim of violence against its possibilities, its 'reality' shaped in violent ways by social fictions. The object of Bryant's affections is, of course, Jimmy. When Jimmy replaces Bryant, taking Jane as his sexual partner, Bryant reverts to the roles which have been offered to him of male violence, culminating in murder. Jimmy and Jane 'perform' in an interracial sex scene. Then, quite knowingly, Jimmy hands Jane over to Bryant to be killed, in order to cement their relationship once more. 'Bryant and I are not friends now, Jane', he tells her. 'You'll help to make us friends' (p. 240).

Like Bryant, Jimmy is obscurely caught between fantasies of power and action, and a foreclosed role. Jimmy's novel does not so much **express** his inner desires as rehearse and facilitate their performance. In order to control and dominate Jane, to read the unreadable outsider, Jimmy first has to write her. He therefore creates a fictional identity for Jane in his novel and reacts to that rather than to Jane herself. The novel also allows him to construct an exceptionally flattering self-image, a presentation self. The narrator describes Jimmy as a 'bronze god' (p. 39) with a dark-brown voice, and 'lithe, panther-like body' (p. 64). She marvels at 'the perfection of his form' (p. 39) and notes his Aston Martin with approval (Jimmy transmogrified into James Bond). In addition to seeking an audience by writing a novel for publication, Jimmy constructs an audience for his fictional self within the novel itself, writing a respondent into his pages. Much of its apparent action is focused on audience reaction. The narrator also describes the standing ovation gained by his speech to another fictional audience: 'it seemed there would be no end to the acclamations' (p. 64). The novel contrasts with the frame tale, in which Jimmy finds that his writing fails to satisfy, merely returning him to 'the interior he had so carefully prepared, for an audience that didn't exist' (p. 65).

Jimmy's gender performance is also incoherent. He is as much Catherine as Heathcliff. In his novel, by choosing a female narrator, Jimmy writes as a woman. As a result he slowly associates himself with the female figure in his other compulsive fantasy, a story he had heard as a boy about a white girl raped by a gang at the beach, on a car fender. After the rape one of the rapists had pitied the girl, and brought her water in his cupped hands. Importantly the story (like *Wuthering Heights*) has both a male and a female point of origin. Jimmy had heard it from a boy, but 'in the boy's voice could be detected the accents of the women of the backyard where he lived' (p. 65). Indeed its origins were multiple. The story had been brought to school by several boys 'who told the story as it might have been told by the older women of the backyards' (p. 65). The story appears at several points, both inside and outside Jimmy's novel, circulating and repeating without a clear beginning. When Jimmy repeats the story he takes up both male and female roles. He writes as the girl (p. 64), grateful for water, and yet he describes himself as threatening the narrator, now named Clarissa. The reference to Richardson's heroine[32] suggests that Jimmy acts as both Lovelace and Clarissa, victim and aggressor, male and female. Earlier Jimmy had remembered playing football as a boy in front of the hotel guests: 'The white people would watch us. And we would act up for them' (p. 72). A white girl he had met in England had compared dates with him and established that she had been in that audience. Now he places her fictional counterpart in the position of being watched by unfriendly spectators. After Clarissa has borne witness to Jimmy's ecstatic audience, she herself becomes the object of specular attention. In the next novel extract Clarissa finds everyone looking at her in a hostile fashion, and ends up running from a gang towards the fender of an old Ford.

Outside his personal reality-fiction, however, Jimmy has lost his political following and his London audience. When he writes to a London friend offering a series of articles, the response is a brush-off. There is no market for his brand of analysis; hard news is what the readership prefer. The rejection letter continues with a placatory reference to Jimmy's novel as providing a necessary 'fillip to the form' (p. 165), as if the postcolonial writer's only function was to refresh the metropolitan genre. It is Jimmy's fate to be merely 'literary', to be unable to translate acting into action. In

the variety of roles performed by Jimmy, racial and sexual identities proliferate. Judith Butler has argued that gender is always a practice, a set of
repeated acts within a fairly rigid regulatory frame, congealing over time
into the appearance of naturalness. If, however, the regulatory fictions of
sex and gender are multiply contested sites of meaning, then the very mul-
tiplicity of their construction disrupts univocality. In other words, forms
of repetition may act, not as simple imitation and consolidation of the
law, but as subversion. 'Gay is to straight **not** as copy is to original, but
rather as copy is to copy.'[33] In the arena of gender the repetition of heterosexual constructs within gay sexual cultures brings into relief the constructed status of the so-called heterosexual original. 'The parodic
repetition of "the original" reveals the original to be nothing other than
a parody of the **idea** of the natural and the original.'[34] In literary terms,
*Guerrillas* is to *Wuthering Heights* or 'Michael X and the Black Power
Killings in Trinidad' not as copy to original but as copy to copy. In terms
of race, Naipaul insists on the unavailability of the body as corporeal
ground, and upon the performative nature of identity, by constant reference to audiences, actors and roleplay. In addition Jimmy's bisexuality,
Jane's stylisations, highlight the fictionality of gender. Jimmy laments at
one point that he had thought that 'childhood was just a time of disguise'
(p. 226) but that everything would be all right 'when I became a man'.
But actually all is disguise. Jimmy can never escape from the male role
imposed upon him. As Butler notes, homosexuality is almost always conceived (in the homophobic signifying economy) as both uncivilised and
unnatural, as 'arty' rather than 'primitive' or 'savage'. In this economy it
can never be foundational.

For Naipaul, however, the economy is not merely symbolic. In his tragic
reading of the postcolonial subject, he draws attention to the problem of
audience and economics. Since there is no foundation for the society in
economic terms, its performances are unvalidated. Butler sees repetition
of different bodily stylisations, genders and gestures as subversive – but
this must depend upon who witnesses them, who constitutes the audience
which transforms acting into activism. Without a validating audience for
his subversion, Jimmy is reduced to unsuccessful theatre. By adopting the
politics of race, Jimmy performs his body as a construct, as a fiction of
blackness. When he displays the body of Stephens in an attempt to foment
a revolt, there is a similar failure to mobilise an audience to revolutionary ends: Jimmy discovers that the procession is not, after all, acting as
doing, but acting as impersonation – a mere carnival without consequences. As Butler notes, society punishes those who get their gender
'wrong'; there are often punitive consequences when a performance fails
to convince. Jane has failed to perform a female gender; Jimmy has failed
as a Black Power activist. As a result Jimmy falls back upon a gender identity (machismo) which (if it has nothing else to recommend it) is at least

stable. As a result he becomes complicit with a masculine regulatory fiction in the punishment of Jane.

In 'The Return of Eva Perón', his companion piece to 'Michael X and the Black Power Killings in Trinidad', Naipaul devoted one section (written in May to July 1974 when he was writing *Guerrillas*) to 'The Brothels Behind the Graveyard'. The brothels in question, an entire avenue of them, are situated in Buenos Aires, right behind the Recoleta Cemetery, the burial place of Eva Perón. For Naipaul, Argentina is a colonial mimicry, a society ruled by machismo, in a highly specific local sense of the term. The life of Carlos Monzon, the Argentinian streetfighter turned successful middleweight boxer and filmstar, may be seen as exemplary. Monzon died in prison where he was serving time for murdering his third wife. At his trial, crowds of men cheered for him. Monzon's brief movie career included *El Macho*.[35] In an analysis which has a special relevance to the rape of Jane, Naipaul highlights the key element of machismo as the humiliation of women:

> The act of straight sex, easily bought, is of no great moment to the macho. His conquest of a woman is complete only when he has buggered her . . . . By imposing on her what prostitutes reject . . . the Argentine macho . . . consciously dishonours his victim. So diminished men, turning to machismo, diminish themselves further, replacing even sex by a parody.[36]

In his anal rape of Jane, Jimmy shrinks his own warring selves to one, performing a stock role as macho. In making Jane 'take it like a man' he wipes out her female sexual identity, as if she were merely a substitute for Bryant in the sexual act. He then passes her on to Bryant to be killed. The connection to Argentinian machismo is made explicit by a hallucination which comes at the moment of murder – a hallucination which supplants Jimmy's own proliferating raped girl story with a regulatory fiction. As Jane dies, Jimmy's mind returns to his fantasy of woman as grateful victim – Jane as violated, Jimmy as comforter:

> He saw a day of sun at the beach, sea and sky bright beyond the coconut grove, the girl bleeding on the fender of the motor car, accepting water from his cupped hands, and love coming to her frightened eyes. But the eyes below him were closed. They knew nothing; they acknowledged nothing; they had taken away everything with them. He entered a void (p. 243).

With the disappearance of the girl – Jimmy's imaginary audience and admirer, Clarissa and Jane – the horizon shrinks decisively. In a moment of hallucinatory horror, Jimmy has a vision of claustrophobic enclosure: 'himself, in a stone room, full of incense, with stone coffins on stone shelves, where dead women lay without being dead among white lilies'

(p. 243). In 'The Return of Eva Perón' Naipaul dwelt upon the legend of the miraculously preserved body of Eva Perón, skilfully embalmed to maintain the appearance of life; and of her 'return' (as a corpse) with her huband from his long exile. Eva Perón was a professional performer, an actress, whose skill in performing her gender underpinned her later political career. Her photographs portray her as 'the macho's ideal victim woman',[37] very blonde (she began as a brunette) with extremely pale skin and pronounced red lips, a visual allusion to her reputed skill at fellatio. Eva Perón, in Naipaul's evocation, provides an apparently successful example of playing a culturally standardised role to the hilt, for politically subversive ends:

> by imposing his women on Argentina, first Evita and then Isabelita, one an actress, the other a cabaret dancer, both provincials, by turning women branded as the macho's easy victims into the macho's rulers, he [Perón] did the roughest kind of justice on a society still ruled by a degenerate machismo, which decrees that a woman's place is essentially in the brothel.[38]

After Perón's overthrow in 1955, Evita's enemies, in an attempt to underline her extravagance, put on a public exhibition of her luxurious underclothes. The plan backfired; the public were entranced by the display of fairy-tale wealth in quintessentially 'feminine' form, and the show fuelled the Evita legend. She became an unofficial saint with a cult following. Naipaul visited her tomb, in the Recoleta Cemetery, a mimic town of stone and marble, where devotees tied white lilies to the rail of her vault. In Jimmy's hallucination, however, when the woman moves, it is not as a returning saint:

> A woman sat up in her coffin, the lilies tumbled off . . . . She had the wanton face, the leer, the degraded mouth of a French prostitute he had seen in a pornographic photograph at school (pp. 243–4).

When in Argentina Naipaul had watched a film, *Boquitas Pintadas* (Little Painted Mouths), the tale of the life and death of a tubercular small-town macho. The audience wept for the tragedy of a foreseeable death. Naipaul, however, formed a second audience and a sceptical one:

> To the outsider the tragedy lay elsewhere in the apparent motivelessness of so much of the action . . . it was as though, in the society of machismo, the very knowledge of the possibility of deeper relationships had been lost. After the macho's death one of his women had a dream: in bleached colour and in very slow motion, the macho rose from his grave in his pretty macho clothes, lifted her in his arms, flew with her through a bedroom window and placed her on a bed. On this necrophiliac fantasy the film ended.[39]

In the street afterwards Naipaul had a particularly sharp sense of the alien-
ated mimicry of the city, and of its people's fascination with death, celebrated in the papers with the display of the bodies of murder victims (often
the victims of guerrillas) photographed lying in their coffins. In the final
fantasy of Jimmy's, Naipaul reverses the sexes: the woman, not the man,
rises from the grave. The painted mouth has become the degraded leer.
The macho is the murderer, not the tragic victim. Jimmy recognises that
he cannot 'undo' Jane's death, that she cannot return. Jane is not Eva
Perón. The Gothic quality of this interpolated vision should not surprise
the reader of postcolonial fiction. The Gothic image surfaces as a story –
and a woman – is suppressed, rendered unspeakable by two males in collusion, establishing a secret which is shared but which cannot be acknowledged to be shared. As the woman turns towards Jimmy to ask for a dollar,
he feels that 'he was betrayed, his secret known' (p. 244). Again the sexes
are transposed; in the novel Bryant asks Jane for a dollar. Later Jimmy
tells Jane that he will meet her to refund the dollar, though in fact he
returns it to her only in the context of his novel (pp. 64, 66, 73). When
Jimmy gives Jane to Bryant she has become a mere counter of exchange
between two men. In the circulation of the dollar, which is converted
almost immediately by Jimmy into a fictional exchange, Naipaul highlights
the central process of the exchange of means for meanings in the novel.
Despite Evita's performance as fairy-tale princess for populist ends,
Argentina remained economically at sea, bedevilled by galloping inflation.
('The Return of Eva Perón' begins with several pages of economic analysis.) As a result it is a society 'ruled by the idea of plunder'[40] in which
'money makes the macho', there is widespread amateur prostitution, and
a gigantic brothel industry.[41] Peronism, in short, may have worked as a
faith but had no economic programme.[42] Where economics rules, the roles
supported – however these roles proliferate or are exalted – remain performances of the most exploited type, rather than subversive practices.
The result can only be a vision of the world as brothel, the vision on
which Jimmy's story effectively ends. When Jimmy becomes a macho,
entering a punitive regulatory fiction, he enters a world in which relationships can only be affairs of buying and selling; he converts his world
into the safe brothel invoked by Naipaul as the First World's image of the
Third. *Guerrillas*, therefore, far from being a sexist or racist novel bears
out Naipaul's own conclusion to 'The Return of Eva Perón': 'The politics
of a country can only be an extension of its idea of human relationships.'[43]

In *Guerrillas* Naipaul dissects the stylisations which masquerade as 'natural' or 'essential', foundationalisms which, in a culture which lacks an
economic base, can only be parodic, empty. Only an audience can supply
legitimation to the character's gestures, transforming them into action.
Without it they become not agents but unemployed actors, mired in puerile
male fantasies of toughness, or female dramatisations of dependence.

Naipaul suggests that for action to count it is less important that it have a legitimating origin, than a society to act upon it and act it out. As has often been remarked, absence of action marks *Guerrillas*. Very little happens in the novel until near its close. As readers we are, in a sense, always back at the ranch, never witnesses to the gunfight. Many of us will be tempted to supply the action from other sources. Ironically, the novel brought Naipaul a huge American public who read (misread) it as a denunciation of guerrilla warfare, especially in the Caribbean.[44] Other readers have supplied the action from other sources, identifying the text with its author (Naipaul as anti-feminist or neocolonialist), with a presumed social referent (the murder story), with geographical locations or political events (Trinidad), or with a literary antecedent (the Brontës). Readers need frames. In this connection the current writer is aware of the risks of invoking 'The Return of Eva Perón', though the secondary intertextuality of the chapter title signals its concern with multivocality. In *Guerrillas*, Naipaul's key strategy is to write against his reader's own dependence, to refuse to allow us an 'authority' outside the text, which will frame events and tell us what is going on. Dispassionately, pessimistically, the novel considers the possibilities for action in its imaginary island, and discounts them. The fundamental achievement of the novel remains to maintain the sense of a world entirely at sea, a shifting chaos without form, foundation or future.

# Notes

1  George Lamming, *The Pleasures of Exile* (London, Michael Joseph, 1960), p. 225. See also Edward W. Said, 'Intellectuals in the Post-Colonial World', *Salmagundi*, 70–1 (1986), pp. 44–81.
2  V. S. Naipaul, 'Our Universal Civilization', *New York Review of Books*, 31 January 1991, p. 22.
3  See Stephen R. Clingman, *The Novels of Nadine Gordimer: History from the Inside* (London, Allen and Unwin, 1986) for the origin of this phrase.
4  V. S. Naipaul, *Guerrillas* (London, Penguin, 1976), p. 9, first published by André Deutsch, 1975. Subsequent citations which follow quotations in parentheses are to the Penguin edition.
5  Erving Goffman's major works include *The Presentation of Self in Everyday Life* (London, Allan Lane, 1969), *Encounters* (Indianapolis, Bobbs-Merrill, 1961), *Asylums* (New York, Penguin, 1968), *Behavior in Public Places* (New York, Free Press, 1966), and *Frame Analysis* (Cambridge, Mass., Harvard University Press, 1974). An excellent commentary is provided in Susan Stewart, *Nonsense: Aspects of Intertextuality In Folklore and Literature* (Baltimore, Johns Hopkins University Press, 1979).
6  John Cooke, 'A Vision of the Land: V. S. Naipaul's Later Novels', *Journal of Caribbean Studies*, I (1980), pp. 140–61 notes the frequency with which the placing of the island in a broad frame contrasts with a narrower enclosure.

7   See Stewart, *Nonsense*.
8   Michael Neill, 'Guerrillas and Gangs: Frantz Fanon and V. S. Naipaul', *Ariel*, 13, 2 (1982), p. 40.
9   Frantz Fanon, *The Wretched of the Earth* (London, Penguin, 1967), p. 54.
10  Jacqueline Brice-Finch, 'V. S. Naipaul's Dystopic Vision in *Guerrillas*', *Studies in the Literary Imagination* XXVI, 2 (Fall 1993), pp. 33–43. Other writers who have commented on the importance of audience in the novel include Helen Tiffin, 'Freedom After the Fall: Renaissance and Disillusionment in *Water With Berries* and *Guerrillas*', in Daniel Massa, ed., *Individual and Community in Commonwealth Literature* (Malta, Old University Press, 1979), pp. 90–8; and Richard Johnstone, 'Politics and V. S. Naipaul', *Journal of Commonwealth Literature* XIV, 1 (1979), pp. 100–8.
11  Naipaul goes to some trouble to distinguish the island from Trinidad: e.g. Sablich 'left Trinidad and came over here', p. 72. Naipaul mentions Sablich's history in *The Loss of El Dorado: A History* (London, André Deutsch, 1969), p. 285. There are also obvious links between the novel and the Black Power revolts in Trinidad in 1970 and in Jamaica. Two commentators suggest that in each case Black Power was an American importation without real relevance to the Caribbean. See Ivar Oxaal, *Race and Revolutionary Consciousness: A Documentary Interpretation of the 1970 Black Power Revolt in Trinidad* (Cambridge. Mass., Schenkman, 1971) and Rex M. Nettleford, *Mirror Mirror: Identity, Race and Protest in Jamaica* (Jamaica, William Collins and Sangster, 1990).
12  There are other references. John Thieme, *The Web of Tradition* (London, Hansib, 1987), provides a comprehensive discussion of Naipaul's allusions to the nineteenth-century novel and establishes that Naipaul uses allusion in a highly original way, extending the Western literary tradition to accommodate other fictive worlds. Hana Wirth-Nesher, 'The Curse of Marginality: Colonialism in Naipaul's *Guerrillas*', *Modern Fiction Studies* 30 (1984), pp. 531–47, argues that Naipaul's originality lies in his denial of originality, his insistence on derivation as the essence of a culture born of colonialism.
13  Maria Grazia Lolla, 'V. S. Naipaul's Poetics of Reality: "The Killings in Trinidad" and *Guerrillas*', *Caribana* I (1990), 41–50 gives a full account of the evolution of the story, between articles, novel, and non-fiction book, and draws attention to the parallel between Stephens and Skerritt.
14  V. S. Naipaul, *The Return of Eva Perón with The Killings in Trinidad* (London, Penguin, 1981), p. 76. The murder has become even more literary in the aftermath. Since Naipaul made the remark almost everyone involved with Michael X has written a book about him. See Michael Abdul Malik, *From Michael de Freitas to Michael X* (London, André Deutsch, 1968); Hakim A. Jamal, *From the Dead Level: Malcolm X and Me* (London, André Deutsch, 1971), which is written by Michael X's main associate and Gale Benson's boyfriend; Diana Athill, *Make Believe: A True Story* (London, Sinclair Stevenson, 1993), which primarily concerns Jamal, her friend and lover; Derek Humphrey and David Tindall, *False Messiah* (London, Hart-Davis, MacGibbon, 1977), a factual account; James Sharp, *The Life and Death of Michael X* (Waterford, Uni Books, 1981), a factual account with illustrations including corpses.
15  Naipaul, *Killings*, p. 29.
16  Naipaul, *Killings*, p. 30.
17  Naipaul, *Killings*, p. 73.
18  Naipaul, *Killings*, p. 35.
19  See Patrick Parrinder, 'V. S. Naipaul and the uses of literacy', *Critical Quarterly* 21, 2 (1979), pp. 5–13.

20 See Eve Shelnutt, 'Estimating V. S. Naipaul: An Oblique Approach', *Genre* XXII, I (1989), pp. 69–84, and especially p. 73. Shelnutt remarks on the fashion in which *The Enigma of Arrival* sends the reader back to the politics of reading itself.

21 I have been unable to trace the origin of this ringing phrase, but am grateful to its author. No one else has put it quite so well.

22 Shashi Kamra, *The Novels of V. S. Naipaul: A Study in Theme and Form* (New Delhi, Prestige, 1990) reads Naipaul as a Third World writer, offering an analysis of the function of the polarised narrator and protagonist positions as an index of his commitment. In his view, by emphasising subjective truth, Naipaul deconstructs social authoritarianism.

23 Neil ten Kortenaar, 'Writers and Readers, The Written and the Read: V. S. Naipaul and *Guerrillas*', *Contemporary Literature* XXXI, 3 (1990), pp. 324–34, draws attention to this image in the novel which he reads, illuminatingly, as a struggle between two writers (Naipaul and Jimmy) for control of the story.

24 Diana Brydon and Helen Tiffin, *Decolonising Fictions* (Mundelstrup and Sydney, Dangaroo Press, 1993), pp. 114–15, see Stephens as a subversive local reader, and the novel as a search for him, as representing the absent revolutionary potential.

25 Quoted in Jeanine Parisier Plottel and Hanna Charney, eds., 'Intertextuality: New Perspectives in Criticism', *New York Literary Forum*, 2 (1978), p. 17.

26 Helen Pyne-Timothy, 'Women and Sexuality in the Later Novels of V. S. Naipaul', *World Literature Written in English* 25, 2 (1985), p. 305. See also Consuelo López de Villegas, 'Matriarchs and Man-Eaters: Naipaul's Fictional Women', *Revista/Review Interamericana* 7 (1977–8), pp. 605–14; Robert Hemenway, 'Sex and Politics in V. S. Naipaul', *Studies in the Novel* XIV, 2 (1982), pp. 189–202.

27 Judith Butler, *Gender Trouble: Feminism and the Subversion of Identity* (London, Routledge, 1990). For a helpful critique of Butler see Pam Morris, 'Re-routing Kristeva: from Pessimism to Parody', *Textual Practice* (Spring 1992), pp. 32–3.

28 V. S. Naipaul, ' Without a Dog's Chance', *New York Review of Books*, XVIII, 9 (18 May 1972), p. 31.

29 Melville J. and Frances S. Herskovits, *Trinidad Village* (New York, Alfred A. Knopf, 1947). The Shouters were proscribed from 1917 to 1951 in Trinidad.

30 V. S. Naipaul, 'The Documentary Heresy', *Twentieth Century* 173 (Winter 1964), p. 107.

31 V. S. Naipaul, *The Middle Passage* (London, Penguin, 1969), p. 65.

32 See Thieme, *The Web of Tradition*.

33 Butler, *Gender Trouble*, p. 31

34 Butler, *Gender Trouble*, p. 31.

35 See Monzon's obituary, *The Guardian*, 13 January 1995, p. 21.

36 Naipaul, *The Return of Eva Perón*, p. 150.

37 Naipaul, *The Return of Eva Perón*, p. 106.

38 Naipaul, *The Return of Eva Perón*, p. 143

39 Naipaul, *The Return of Eva Perón*, p. 151.

40 Naipaul, *The Return of Eva Perón*, p. 149.

41 Naipaul, *The Return of Eva Perón*, p. 149.

42 Naipaul, *The Return of Eva Perón*, p. 105.

43 Naipaul, *The Return of Eva Perón*, p. 151.

44 Dolly Zulakha Hassan, *V. S. Naipaul and the West Indies* (New York and Bern, Peter Lang, 1989) gives a full account of the reception of *Guerrillas*.

# 9

# *The madwoman in the motel*
## *Bharati Mukherjee, 'Jasmine' and* Jasmine

For V. S. Naipaul, the situation of the postcolonial subject is at best one of political stasis and steady state economics, at worst one of inexorable decline. In *Guerrillas* the imaginary island is an area in which there is little potential for fruitful change. Richness and possibility are excluded, except in the realm of fantasy. Naipaul closed his essay 'Jasmine' with an account of a visit to an Indian woman in British Guiana:

> Suddenly the tropical daylight was gone, and from the garden came the scent of a flower. I knew the flower from my childhood; yet I had never found out its name. I asked now.

> 'We call it jasmine.'

> Jasmine! So I had known it all those years! To me it had been a word in a book, a word to play with, something removed from the dull vegetation I knew.

> The old lady cut a sprig for me. I stuck it in the top buttonhole of my shirt. I smelled it as I walked back to the hotel. Jasmine, jasmine. But the word and the flower had been separate in my mind for too long. They did not come together. [1]

As Naipaul implictly recognises in the anecdote, there is for him an unbridgeable gap between a dull, unnamed reality and the exotic word. As *Guerrillas* demonstrates, the gap between fantasy fiction and prosaic documentary can be bridged only by violence to the postcolonial subject. In the anecdote Naipaul is careful to specify the age of his hostess, an elderly lady. Had the flower been presented to him by a nubile beauty, the reader would have seen him transposing flower and woman as he exclaimed 'Jasmine, jasmine.' As it stands, however, the incident is carefully de-eroticised. Just as there can be no connection between dull shrub and exotic name, so the separation between flower and woman is maintained. As a result, the dominant feeling here is one of impotence, frustrated desire and a failed connection between childhood and maturity, men and women, word and thing, which is emblematic of Naipaul's position as exile. For Naipaul, that which blooms can only be deracinated, cut off. All connection has been severed between the dull shrub and the developed flower. Naipaul, is of course, notorious for his refusal to see possibility in postcolonial cultures, both in relation to *Guerrillas*, and even more so in *A Bend in the River*, which opens with the words 'The world is what it is; men who are nothing, who allow themselves to become nothing, have no place in it.'[2] Indeed, asked in an interview 'What is the future, in Africa?', Naipaul simply replied, 'Africa has no future.'[3] Selwyn R. Cudjoe comments that 'The theme of *A Bend in the River* is the gradual darkening of African society as it returns to its age-old condition of bush and blood.'[4]

Bharati Mukherjee has more than once acknowledged a connection to Naipaul. Writing in 1977, she expressed straightforward admiration:

> for me, an accidental immigrant, the brave and appropriate model is . . . V. S. Naipaul. In myself I detect a pale and immature reflection of Naipaul; it is he who has written most movingly about the pain and absurdity of art and exile.[5]

Like Naipaul, Mukherjee has left her origins behind to become transnational, emerging as a distinctive literary voice, whether she is claimed by India (and her origins in a Hindu Bengali Brahmin family), Canada (her next nationality) or America (where, sickened by persistent racist harassment in Toronto, she now lives and writes, an American citizen). Whereas Mukherjee's earlier work centred on expatriation and dislocation (in *The Tiger's Daughter* [6] the disappointments of a return visit from America to Calcutta, in *Wife*[7] the loneliness and culture shock of a Bengali in New York), the later fiction extends its scope, exploring a variety of Asian-American encounters, and chronicling not merely the incomer's adaptation to America, but also America's transformation by its immigrants. If many of her stories centre upon 'chiffon saris'[8] – women attempting to live between two worlds, cooking matar panir with pork, or silently suffering David Mamet's Patel jokes in the front row of a New York theatre – others (in her 1988 collection *The Middleman*)[9] feature such protagonists as the eponymous Turkish-Jewish middleman, selling death in Latin America, a Marcos supporter in exile from the Philippines, an Afghan spending Thanksgiving with his girlfriend's Italian-American family, a middle-class war veteran whose Vietnamese daughter returns to haunt him, Ugandan Asians in Flushing, a Tamil refugee in Hamburg and (in a story of quite exceptional emotional power) the relatives of those murdered in the Air India disaster, into which Mukherjee conducted a 'citizen's inquiry'.[10] In Mukherjee's later work, exile is transformed into immigration, cross-fertilisation and transformation.

Interviewing Naipaul in 1981 Mukherjee began to register reservations. For her, *A Bend in the River* was a terrifying novel 'because of the vision which said all politics is silly, and the African people will necessarily revert to the bush'.[11] Naipaul's fiction was a 'dismissal of the passions of people in these far-off places'.[12] By 1988, when Mukherjee herself selected the title 'Jasmine' for a short story, her intentions had hardened into opposition.

> I very deliberately set the story in V. S. Naipaul's birthplace because it was my 'in' joke, challenging, if you like, Naipaul's thesis of tragedy being geographical. Naipaul's fiction seems to suggest that if you are born far from the centre of the universe you are doomed to an incomplete and worthless little life. You are bound to be, if you're born like a Jasmine, an Indian in the Caribbean, a comic character, you can come to nothing. So I wanted to say, 'Hey, look at Jasmine. She's smart, and desirous, and ambitious enough to make something of her life.'[13]

In the short story, Jasmine migrates from Trinidad to Canada, and thence to the Plantations Motel, Detroit, which is 'run by a family of Trinidad Indians who had come from the tuppenny ha'penny country town, Chaguanas'.[14] Predictably, Jasmine removes herself with all possible speed from these 'nobodies' from Naipaul's birthplace, to Ann Arbor and a job as nanny with the liberal Moffitts, succumbing at the close of the tale to Bill Moffitt's advances. Reactions to the story tended to cast Jasmine as a victim, an economically oppressed illegal immigrant who is sexually exploited to boot. Mukherjee, however, disagreed:

> Reviewers . . . saw Jasmine as an exploited young woman, and the white male, her employer, as a sleazy boss who is taking advantage of this poor, innocent, put-upon au-pair girl. Whereas I meant for Jasmine to know exactly what it is she wants and what she is will-ing to trade off in order to get what she wants. She is in charge of the situation there. The man has succumbed to lust and to her sex-uality.[15]

In the story Mukherjee does not underestimate how hard Jasmine has to work and for what paltry rewards. (The character is seen through an ironic lens, slaving over her employer's pure silk shirts while vigorously thanking Jesus for her good luck.) Yet Jasmine has a hardheaded sense of economic values, succinctly expressed in her preference for dull, worn dol-lar bills rather than the prettier Caribbean or Canadian currencies.

> Pretty money is only good for putting on your walls . . . . Back home at work, she used to count out thousands of Trinidad dollars every day, and not even think of them as real. Real money was worn and green, American dollars (p. 128).

For Jasmine exotic prettiness is firmly subordinated to dull economic values. She is, for example, unromantically aware that in order to remain in America the smartest course of action would be 'to put a down payment on a husband' (p. 128). Mukherjee picks up the stereotypical associations of her heroine's name – typically described by one critic as evoking 'the sweetness and exotic qualities of the Orient'[16] – to articulate a direct riposte to Naipaul. At the close of the story Bill propositions Jasmine in terms of cliché. 'You're a blossom, a flower . . . . You smell so good. You're really something, flower of Trinidad' (p. 138). Despite having kept pace erotically with Bill's rapid striptease, Jasmine instantly corrects him: 'Flower of Ann Arbor', she said, 'not Trinidad' (p. 138). For Mukherjee's fragrant heroine her identity is not confined to the role of exotic flower; she blooms, economically and erotically, on an American campus. In transplanting herself Jasmine corrects the stereotypical expectation by the First World of the Third World as exotic Other and firmly refuses victim and exile status. Where Naipaul is unable to connect an exotic bloom with the dull shrub of its original location, Mukherjee asserts the right of the deracinated individual to transplant herself and flourish. In Jasmine's terms to be 'nothing' is synonymous with possibility: 'she was a bright, pretty girl with no visa, no papers, and no birth certificate. No nothing other than what she wanted to invent and tell' (p. 138). No 'nothing' indeed, Jasmine engineers her own de-naturing, seizing upon the divorce between word and thing as an opportunity to be grasped. Where Naipaul envisages the loss of 'organic' connection as a regrettable, but now irremediable unhousing of the postcolonial subject, Mukherjee displays a postmodern valorisation of the transformation of language from mimetic representation of a world of objects to a sign system generating its own significances through a series of relational differences. Just as intertextuality severs the relationship between tale and source, transplanting and reembedding the text in a context far removed from its point of origins, so Jasmine migrates from the West Indies to Canada and America, and then, in a second intertextual trajectory, from the Punjab to Florida and Iowa; from Naipaul's essay to the short story and thence to Mukherjee's 1989 novel, also entitled *Jasmine*. As Mukherjee reflected, 'The character wouldn't die. I am intrigued by that particular kind of survival.'[17]

Crucially, in the novel, Mukherjee abandons the omniscient narration of the short story in favour of restoring her own voice to Jasmine, now an illegal immigrant into America from the Punjab. In the short story the third-person narration tends to function ironically, revealing the limitations of omniscience in representations of resistance to a culture which creates the Third World woman as Other in the very process of 'looking' itself. Jasmine exists in the narrator's sights as object, almost as much as she does in Bill's. By shifting to the first person, Mukherjee avoids reduplicating the male gaze in the scopic constructions of patriarchy, and facilitates the emphasis on self-transformation, in a vision which emanates from a female centre. Mukherjee has stated her belief that:

> instead of seeing my Indianness as a fragile identity to be preserved against obliteration (or worse, a 'visible' disfigurement to be hidden), I see it now as a set of fluid identities to be celebrated.[18]

It is this sense of the existence of alternate realities, of life as a continual emigration from one self to another, which pervades *Jasmine*, in which the heroine, Jyoti (Light), born in a mud hut in Hasnapur, becomes successively Jasmine (renamed by a progressive husband), a split-tongued Kali (murdering her American rapist), Jazzy (an 'undocumented' in Florida), Jyoti again (taking refuge in an enclave of Punjabi-speaking Jats in Flushing), Jase (as the 'day mummy' to the child of liberal Manhattan yuppies), and lastly, though not finally, Jane (as the mistress of Bud Ripplemeyer, an Iowan banker). Bud also undergoes a transformation. Having previously thought of Asia only as a soy-bean market, he now finds himself living with an Indian woman and an adopted Vietnamese son, Du, while the Lutheran (Hmong)[19] Church raises funds for Ethiopia, by selling quilts at a Mennonite fair, in a drought-ridden Iowa stalked by the Aryan Nations. The separation and reembedding of these very different identities in the American context creates the impression of a soup of signs, colliding to create new meanings. Jasmine's previous textual experience of America, limited to *Shane* ('about an American village much like the Punjab')[20] and a film which she vaguely recalls as 'Seven Village Girls Find Seven Boys to Marry', turns out, however, to be rather better preparation than she imagines for a country specialising as much as her own in rapine and murder. Readers of the earlier novels who recall the ambiguous fate of Tara (*The Tiger's Daughter*) or the moment when Dimple Dasgupta (*Wife*) decapitates her husband over his breakfast cereal, will be unsurprised by a succession of violent incidents, from her mother's attempt to strangle the infant Jyoti (a dowry-less bride), to the braining of a rabid dog, a father gored to death by a bull, a beloved teacher shot and a husband blown up by Sikh terrorists, rape, murder, one lover crippled by a gun-toting bankrupt farmer, another (would-be) lover half eaten by his own pigs. Small wonder that Jasmine comments that 'Dullness is a kind of luxury' (p. 6) for her fellow immigrants, longing for lives of total ordinariness, after events beyond description have hurtled them across continents, into a world of transit lounges, furtive night flights from unofficial airfields, and roundabout routes from India to America, via Sudan, Hamburg, Amsterdam and Paramaribo. Paradoxically, however, the overall impression of the novel is of jubilant and affirmative energy, in which the inventiveness of survivors is matched by pullulating linguistic variety and control. Statistically South Asian immigrants are the most successful of any immigrant group moving to the USA.[21] Although Mukherjee con-

templates them without false illusions (many of her characters are unre-
pentant hustlers, forced to become so by their history) she none the less
celebrates their achievements as risk-takers and shape-shifters, with lives
which are sometimes remarkable, often, indeed, heroic. She also recognises the human cost of such transformation, in the realisation that there
are no harmless compassionate ways to remake oneself: 'We murder who
we were so we can rebirth ourselves in the images of dreams' (p. 29).

In India Jasmine had found *Great Expectations* and *Jane Eyre* too difficult to read (p. 41). Part of Mukherjee's stated intention in the novel was
to play with the idea of an updated, American Jane Eyre, as is suggested
by Jasmine's renaming, her various roles as caregiver, her transformation
by fire into an alternative self, her crippled husband-to-be, and the would-
be lover who wants to transport her to foreign parts (in this case Tahiti
not St John Rivers' India, for obvious reasons). It is a conception which
has drawn hostile comment:

> A novel about a peasant woman's life, *Jasmine* is unable to shake
> off a Western-oriented postcolonial consciousness, which most clearly
> manifests itself in literary allusions to English texts: *Jane Eyre, Great
> Expectations,* and *Pygmalion.*[22]

As Mukherjee argues, however, it is Bud who wants to make Jasmine into
a Jane, renaming her as part of a nineteenth-century conception of America
as the all-assimilating melting-pot. 'But Jasmine is a true American in the
sense that she's a romantic: she wants to keep the frontier open, and is
constantly seeing a remaking of herself in the future.'[23] In his adoption of
Du and his new openness to Asia, it is Bud who assimilates to Jasmine.
It is rather as if Rochester adored his madwoman and took up callaloo,
saltfish and ackee. Interviewed in *Bazaar,* Mukherjee rejected any suggestion that Jasmine assimilates:

> Jasmine is helping transform the way the white characters think
> about America: that's not assimilation at all, and it's a very tough
> position for white readers to accept. I'm saying that we haven't come
> to accommodate or to mimic; we have changed ourselves, but we
> have also come to change you.[24]

At the close of the novel, this particular Jane unsentimentally abandons
her crippled Rochester to escape to California with a younger and livelier
lover. An 'Indian Giver' in the American sense, she repossesses her self and
lights out for the West, a survivor with a survivor's guilts and glories.

As this rapid summary indicates, *Jasmine* centres upon rapid change –
and its costs. Bud Ripplemeyer's abandoned first wife sees Jasmine as a
force of nature, not in fragrant form but as a tornado 'leaving a path of
destruction behind you' (p. 205). Critics have also registered reservations
concerning the degree to which Jasmine's rampant individualism damages

all it touches, and reinforces the image of woman as *femme fatale* or exotic
Other. More mundanely, when the novel was serialised by the BBC on
Radio 4's *Woman's Hour* it was censured by the Broadcasting Standards
Council as 'unsuitable and offensive'.[25] In adapting Naipaul's botanical
figure, however, Mukherjee contests the paradigm of the inevitable return
to nature as destructive (the bush in its dullness, woman as a danger to
culture) in favour of the sign as flowering possibility. Jasmine, in her successive incarnations, remains a force of nature in some respects, but with
a remarkable affinity for technology, soldering connections, repairing light
electrical goods, operating the devices necessary for the paralysed Bud.
Even her voice resembles computer-generated telephone voices (p. 13).
What critics have missed in their readings of the novel is that, rather than
remaining in the 'bush' of underdevelopment and exoticism, Jasmine is
actually linked to the most sophisticated forms of technology, and the very
latest scientific advances. Mukherjee repositions Jasmine within a paradigm which abolishes the conventional binary oppositions of male/female,
nature/culture, body/mind: that of chaos theory.

In the novel it is true that violence continually questions the value of
Jasmine's achievements, as the pattern of her life forms, dissolves, re-forms
only to explode again. In her first real act of defiance – avoiding an
arranged marriage – Jasmine is roundly condemned by her grandmother:
'The girl is mad. Her mother is mad. The whole country is mad. Kali Yuga
has already come' (p. 52). Kali Yuga – the age of social decline, of chaos
– is one way of envisaging Jasmine's world, in a fashion consonant with
Naipaul's vision of postcolonial societies reverting to anarchy. Mukherjee's
epigraph, however, suggests a different reading:

> The new geometry mirrors a universe that is rough, not rounded,
> scabrous, not smooth. It is a geometry of the pitted, pocked and bro-
> ken up, the twisted, tangled, and intertwined.

The quotation, from James Gleick's *Chaos*, foregrounds a very different
way of envisaging what appears to be anarchic and chaotic, as constituting instead a form of fruitful order.[26] In the passage, Gleick was himself
paraphrasing Benoit Mandelbrot, the founder of fractal geometry, who
began his investigations from the perception that nature is non-linear, that
clouds are not spheres, mountains not cones, lightning does not travel in
a straight line, and that these odd shapes none the less carry meaning. Pits
and tangles are not blemishes, distorting the classic shapes of Einsteinian
geometry, but the very essence of the thing. Even in the most turbulent
behaviour there is a deep structure of order. A hurricane (Gleick's example) is not just a huge storm but a continuum, from the swirling of litter
in the street to vast cyclonic systems. Throughout *Jasmine,* Mukherjee
employs a set of metaphors and concepts taken from chaos theory to inves-
tigate the possibility that what looks like 'madness', the descent into

confusion, may mask growth and rich future possibilities. In this paradigm nature gives the lead to technology, the migrant and the marginal are the sites of new discovery, and the image of the 'madwoman', uncontrolled, messy, anarchic, takes over from the Plain Jane of patriarchal systems.

Since chaos theory (or dynamical systems theory, or non-linear dynamics) is a relatively new phenomenon in literary criticism, it is as well to pause here to outline its major tenets. Antonio Benítez-Rojo has drawn a link between chaos theory and Caribbean writing:

> for a literary critic who wants to find cultural specificities that might differentiate one region from another, the Chaos perspective offers great advantages; its way of looking right at noise and turbulence to find common dynamics comes up with graphic models that allow us to appreciate that a given region's flight of textual signifiers is neither wholly disorganized nor absolutely unpredictable; rather it responds to the influx of 'strange attractors' in whose codes the dynamics tend to follow determined movements and, therefore, to draw certain regularly repetitive and self-referential figures.[27]

Benítez-Rojo acknowledges the extremely complex nature of the Caribbean cultural spectrum as a supersyncretic referential space, a point which might well be extended to almost all creolised or hybrid postcolonial cultures in which a chain of signifiers is involved. Such a culture, rather than being 'pure' (an impossible proposition) is a discourse always in transformation. In terms of chaos theory such cultures are rich in information, in noisy data, rather than poor in order. (A crucial step in the development of chaos theory was the separation of information from meaning.) Benítez-Rojo's description of the Caribbean also has strong affinities with Naipaul's in *Guerrillas*, as a location which is repetitive and confusing, but opposed to apocalypse:

> The notion of the apocalypse is not important within the culture of the Caribbean. The choices of all or nothing, for or against, honor or blood have little to do with the culture of the Caribbean. These are ideological propositions articulated in Europe.[28]

Like Naipaul, Benítez-Rojo finds the Caribbean chaotic; the difference, however, lies in the fact that his usage of the term 'chaos' is entirely positive. Chaos is not absence of meaning, but presence, a sea of inexhaustible information and an active force in its own right, no mere void:

> The Caribbean is the natural and indispensable realm of marine currents, of waves, of folds and double-folds, of fluidity and sinuosity. It is, in the final analysis, a culture of the meta-archipelago: a chaos that returns, a detour without a purpose, a continual flow of paradoxes; it is a feed-back machine with asymmetrical workings, like

the sea, the wind, the clouds, the uncanny novel, the food chain, the music of Malaya, Gödel's theorem and fractal mathematics.[29]

This description of the Caribbean is almost as packed with references to chaos theory – turbulence, folds, fractal geometry, feedback loops – as is Mukherjee's novel, itself written in a succession of twenty-six 'short takes',[30] fast-moving, varied, and noisy on data. Michiko Kakutani, reviewing the novel for the *New York Times* described it as overwhelming the reader with the sheer amount of its plot.[31] In interview, Mukherjee stated that she had crammed in 'a sense of the entire world' intentionally, as a reaction against the current vague for minimalism in American writing.[32]

> I feel that minimalism disguises a dangerous social agenda. Minimalism is nativist, it speaks in whispers to the initiated . . . as though it were designed to keep out anyone with too much story to tell.[33]

As a result the action had to be very compressed, to avoid mimicking the Dickensian or Thackerian novel. A series of jump-cuts gives the novel an unusual combination of density and irregularity, a sense of abundant – yet broken-up – action. Indeed, Jasmine's trajectory breaks up and reforms precisely in the nature of a fractal. Images of splitting, breaking, spiralling, twisting and scarring pullulate along her path, together with technological referents. Candia McWilliam offers an apt description:

> The temporal form of the book is as intricately logical as electric wiring, moving not serially but in bundled threads between the area of darkness of the East and the often artificial light of America. From the electrical storm of 'high status goods' which hit India thirty years ago, from the floodlighting over hogpens on an Iowan farm, to the hybrid gismos built by Jane's adopted Vietnamese son Du, electricity makes its illuminating, shocking circuit of the book.[34]

As commentators have noted, chaos theory has reshaped the face of the scientific establishment and has also broken down the barriers between scientific and humanist disciplines. N. Katherine Hayles offers the most succinct and intelligent history and analysis for the non-specialist.[35] Hayles situates chaos theory in the change from the early part of the twentieth century, when many disciplines attempted to develop totalising theories and unambiguous connections between theory and observation, articulation and reality, and the second half (after the uncertainty principle, Gödel's theorem and relativity) which has become preoccupied with the phenomenon of orderly disorder, focusing on mechanisms that make unpredictability a fact of life rather than the aberration it appears in Newtonian mechanics. In 1961 Edward Lorenz, trying to predict the world's climate on a computer, accidentally arrived at the conclusion that any non-periodic physical system (i.e. one that never repeats exactly) became unpredictable in the long term since the tiniest error in calculation, or a bit more rain in the 'wrong' place, could make the results vary considerably. Later when Lorenz fed data from other non-periodic systems into 3-d functions in his computer, he was astonished to see a graphic form – a double spiral whose lines circumscribed each other without touching. Benoit Mandelbrot studied fractal forms of this nature and discovered that if indeed they were disordered, they none the less followed certain universal patterns. Research developed on complex systems in physics (non-linear dynamics, fluid mechanics, quantum electrodynamics), maths (fractal geometry), thermodynamics and meteorology, concentrating upon deep structures of order appearing within apparent disorder.

As Hayles points out, very different values are none the less ascribed to the new paradigm of orderly disorder. Theorists divide as to whether the preoccupation with chaos brings chaos within rational compass, or signals the defeat of totalising projects. Analogous theories in literary studies tend to be embraced because they are seen as resisting totalising theories. Hayles argues persuasively that theories of deconstruction stem from the same paradigm shifts which led to the formation of chaos theory. As literary texts have been transformed 'from ordered sets of words to permeable membranes',[36] through which flow the currents of history, language and culture, 'The well-wrought urn, it seemed, was actually a reservoir of chaos.'[37] In political terms the world itself features as a complex system, economically, technologically and environmentally, with the awareness that small fluctuations on the microscale can quickly lead to very large-scale instabilities – the famous 'butterfly effect': 'the notion that a butterfly stirring the air today in Peking can transform storm systems next month in New York'.[38] At its most banal this means that small causes can lead to very large effects (as opposed to the classical paradigm in which small causes have small effects). The local speedily becomes the global. Chaos is not true randomness, because it can be shown to contain deeply encoded structures ('strange attractors'). When mapped into phase space, chaotic systems contract to a limited area and trace complex patterns. These deep structures of order have been traced in relation to measles epidemics, stock market fluctuations, the rise and fall of the Nile river, eye movements in schizophrenics, cloud formation, the rise and fall of cotton prices, marine turbulence, the decrease and increase in animal populations, and the pattern of swirling flow which is the great red spot of Jupiter:

> Almost but not quite repeating themselves, chaotic systems generate patterns of extreme complexity, in which areas of symmetry are intermixed with asymmetry down through all scales of magnification.[39]

Several key features of chaos theory are formally and thematically present in *Jasmine*: a startling incongruity between causes and effects, non-linearity in its various senses, recursive symmetries, extreme sensitivity to initial conditions, fractal ('broken up' or 'irregular') forms,[40] and feedback mechanisms which create loops in which output from the system feeds back into the system as input. More specifically, four contested areas (which emerge as flashpoints in the debate on chaos theory) impact upon the novel: determinism, individualism, woman, and the relationship of local to global.

Chaoticists tend to speculate about determinism and free will, being and becoming, seeing themselves as turning back the trend towards reductionism. As one member of the Dynamical Systems Collective in Santa Cruz, for example, commented, 'On a philosophical level it [chaos] struck me as an operational way to define free will, in a way that allowed you to reconcile free will with determinism. The system is deterministic, but you can't say what it's going to do next.'[41] Nina Hall observes that chaos is attractive because:

> We are all aware of how small events can drastically change the course of history: the assassin's bullet that triggers a revolution, a chance meeting with a stranger at a party. The impulsive decision to catch a plane doomed to crash. Romantic novels are full of such stories. We expect life to be complicated and uncertain, scattered with random events that make the future difficult to predict. For this reason many people find the 'pure' predictability of traditional science unattractive and difficult to relate to their own lives.[42]

Chaos theory, then, seems to link our everyday experiences with laws of nature by revealing subtle relationships between orderliness and randomness. In *Jasmine* determinism, prolepsis and chance interact in a plot which none the less always offers the sense of possibility, the central reality of chaos theory.

In addition, the status of individuality emerges as problematic in the development of chaos theory. Hayles notes that Gleick presents the emergence of chaos as entirely the result of work by a few solitary individuals outside the mainstream of American scientific society. He thus inscribes scientific investigation into narrative patterns that emphasise science as individual enterprise, rather than as socially constructed, in a fashion entirely consonant with the American myth of rugged individualism opening up the new frontier. It is, however, possible to read chaos theory rather differently, less in terms of rampant individualism and more in terms of marginal intellectual spaces. Outside America, much of the work was done by teams of mathematicians and physicists willing to cross their disciplinary boundaries to work together. Even in America the Santa Cruz collective saw themselves as outside the scientific establishment, less as pioneers of free enterprise than as scavengers, picking up their electronic equipment as scrap, and cultivating a tinkering, recombinant mentality. Benoit Mandelbrot was a Polish-Jewish-French refugee who worked at various points at IBM, taught economics at Harvard, engineering at Yale and physiology at the Einstein School of Medicine, a career trajectory which appears fully to justify Thomas S. Kuhn's judgment that scientific revolutions occur in interdisciplinary spaces. Mandelbrot saw himself as a nomad. He added to his *Who's Who* entry the statement: 'The rare scholars who are nomads-by-choice are essential to the intellectual welfare of the settled disciplines.'[43] In *Jasmine* the character of Du, a genius at electronics, takes its cue from Mandelbrot's observation.

A third area of contention concerns the status of women in chaos. There are, Hayles writes, simply no women in Gleick's account. Scientists are shown in solitary or anti-domestic settings, perhaps because for many scientists chaos represents an opening of the self to the messiness of life, to all the unpredictable phenomena which linear science has taught them to screen out. 'Chaotic unpredictability and nonlinear thinking, however, are just the aspects of life that have tended to be culturally encoded as feminine.'[44] In short, in validating chaos as scientific concept, in admitting the 'feminine', Gleick has to excise the actual women. 'In the Western tradition, chaos has played the role of the Other – the unrepresented, the unarticulated, the unformed, the unthought.'[45]

As that final quotation suggests, chaos has a very intimate connection with the politics of postcolonial representation. Hayles herself sets up an implicit opposition between past and present scientific paradigms and their geopolitical equivalents, in analysing the work of Lord Kelvin, the great British thermodynamicist, for whom entropy represented the tendency of the universe to run down, despite the best of British efforts to the contrary. In his prose, 'the rhetoric of imperialism confronts the inevitability of failure'[46] in the universal tendency towards the dissipation of mechanical energy – a kind of scientific return to the bush. In contrast, chaos theory has obvious links with the postcolonial world: 'Through its concern with conditions that made movement from local sites to global systems possible, it exposes presuppositions within older paradigms that made universalization appear axiomatic.'[47] Local knowledge is now highly valorised in postcolonial studies (as elsewhere) in the typical insistence that local conditions should be respected in their own right, rather than swallowed up in global schemas. (One thinks of Lyotard's *petits récits* as opposed to master narratives, or Foucault's view of the totalising theories of the Enlightenment.) Hayles is quick to point out, however, that local knowledge is not always synonymous with liberation: the abolitionist argument that slaves had souls was a great deal more liberatory than the local knowledge of the American South. The conflict goes to the heart of postcolonial debates concerning the relation of the 'centre' to the marginal, whether in terms of the domination of global systems (as in the American rhetoric of Black Power in Naipaul's Caribbean), or their emancipatory force (Marxism in South Africa, for example). Chaos theory, then, offers a fruitful area in which to dispute the Naipaulian perception of marginal territories as areas of lack, disorder and inevitable entropic regression. In chaos theory, apparent disorder is generative; marginality translates as possibility, and transforms the 'larger' world beyond it. As postcolonial individualist woman, abandoning local determinism for global emancipation, Jasmine is the point at which all these threads intertwine.

*Jasmine* exemplifies that sensitivity to initial conditions which looms so large as a causative factor in chaos theory. In its opening scene, the novel immediately invites the reader to consider the oppositions between determinism and free will, nothingness and infinite aspiration. Jasmine, seven years old and already (in conscious reference to the epigraph) 'scabrous-armed' (p. 3), hears the Hindu astrologer prophesy her widowhood and exile. When she disputes the prediction he strikes her, causing visible disfigurement: 'My teeth cut into my tongue. A twig sticking out of the bundle of firewood I'd scavenged punched a star-shaped wound into my forehead . . . . I was nothing, a speck in the solar system' (pp. 3–4). The setting is emblematically Naipaulian – a bend in a river, a place of little motion, stagnation and death. 'I hated that river bend. The water pooled there, sludgy brown and was choked with hyacinths and feces' (p. 4). Jasmine, however, is distinctly unwilling to accept the place allotted to her. Around her, gnarled and stooped trees remind her of the ghosts of old women: 'I always felt the she-ghosts were guarding me. I didn't feel I was nothing' (p. 4). Taking courage from a feminised, if twisted, nature she refuses to accept the pitting of her forehead as mutilation, a deviation from classical smoothness, but celebrates it instead as a source of vision, the legendary 'third eye' of the sage. Breaking free from her sisters she swims 'to where the river was a sun-gold haze' (p. 5). Physical smoothness is not important to a character who intends to see for herself, rather than exist as an object in the sights of others. An image of that sightless object is presented in the dead dog which Jasmine sees in the river, a stinking, eyeless, broken body which splits into two at her touch, and becomes a permanent emblem of the fate to be avoided: 'I'm twenty-four now, I live in Baden, Elsa County, Iowa, but every time I lift a glass of water to my lips, fleetingly I smell it. I know what I don't want to become' (p. 5).

In rejecting a deterministic heavenly geometry in favour of free will, Jasmine opts for fluidity, rather than stagnation, and with fluidity comes both possibility and the risks of turbulence and fracture. The infant Jyoti was born eighteen years after partition and its riots, into a family forcibly transplanted from Lahore to Hasnapur, to their enduring regret. For them chaos has only negative connotations. After seeing their house sacked, their grottoes defiled, their horse sabred, the old definitions hold: ' In our family lore Lahore was magic and Lahore was chaos' (p. 41). Except when it is absolutely necessary to plant or harvest, her father prefers to remain under a flowering jasmine tree all day, listening to radio broadcasts from Lahore, extolling its beauties, an eternal exile who can never put down new roots in the dull reality of the Punjab. 'Lahore visionaries, Lahore women, Lahore music, Lahore ghazals: my father lived in a bunker' (p. 42). Jasmine, however, has never seen Lahore, and reflects that 'that pitcher is broken. It is the same air this side as that' (p. 43). She accepts fracture, change. At her birth her mother's attempt to strangle her had left her with a scar, seen by Jasmine as adornment, a 'ruby-red choker' (p. 40), rather than as injury: 'In surviving I was already Jane, a fighter and adapter' (p. 40). She is contrasted with her friend Vimla. Informed by **her** astrologer that she should delay marriage until her fiancé is twenty, Vimla dutifully follows the traditional prescription with disastrous results:

> When he was twenty-one her husband died of typhoid, and at twenty-two she doused herself with kerosene and flung herself on a stove . . . . The villagers say when a clay pitcher breaks, you see that the air inside is the same as outside. Vimla set herself on fire because she had broken her pitcher; she saw there were no insides and out-sides (p. 15).

Unlike Vimla, Jasmine embraces the fluidity and permeability which emerge from fracture, as a continuity without conventional binary divi-sions. The floral imagery undergoes a fresh evolution as a result. Threatened with an arranged marriage, Jasmine is saved by the interven-tion of her teacher, Masterji, who invokes the proverbial image of the lotus blooming in the middle of filth: 'An educator's duty, sir, is not to burn the flower with the dung' (p. 50). Jasmine comments that in Hasnapur 'the metaphorical and the literal converge' (p. 50). In the background, buffalo dung is being shaped into fuel cakes by the maidservant's pretty daugh-ter, for whom there is very little room for manoeuvre between word and thing. Similarly, for Jasmine's father biology is determinism. 'Nature's design' (p. 51) is for women to bear sons. Jasmine herself, however, is able to see in nature both danger and possibility as the succeeding incident demonstrates. Attacked by a rabid dog, Jasmine provides herself with a weapon, a staff stuck in a wreath of thorns, by crawling into the bush: 'of course thorns bloodied my arms, but the moment my fist closed over the head of the staff, I felt a buzz of power' (p. 54). Scabrous-armed, she crushes the muzzle of the animal with one blow, and consigns it to the river. For all its heroism the incident strikes a warning note. Jasmine may have escaped contamination by the dead dog, and all that it signifies, but has she merely entered the 'bush' as regression to violence, exchanging the identity of victim for that of killer? The staff had been discarded, after use, by one of the Khalsa Lions, Sikh terrorists. Like Indian independence, Jasmine's is not without costs, as subsequent events reveal.

For Jasmine's grandmother her survival means only that 'God doesn't
think that you're ready for salvation. Individual effort counts for nothing'
(p. 57). The same acceptance of fate is restated by a Lahori friend after
Jasmine's father's death: 'The Lord lends us a body, gives us an assignment, and sends us down. When we get the job done, the Lord calls us
home again for the next assignment' (p. 59). Discussing these events in her
new life in Manhattan with her employer Taylor, a sceptical physicist,
Jasmine defends the Indian view in terms of a non-linear vision of causality: 'Enlightenment meant seeing through the third eye and sensing designs
in history's muddles' (p. 60). In the vastness of God's purposes, she argues,
the human assignment may be a very small one, but with unforeseeable
consequences. Perhaps her father's assignment was merely 'to crunch one
small piece of gravel as he jumped out of the bus' (p. 59). The consoling
idea of an assignment from God is, of course, also readable in terms of
chaos theory, with the crunching of gravel as the equivalent of the butterfly effect. The local/global realignment is carried out here against an
appropriate background. From Taylor's standpoint in the world of particle physics, Jasmine's world is chaos in its older sense: 'If rearranging a
particle of dust is as important as discovering relativity, that's a formula
for total anarchy' (p. 61). Taylor is blissfully unaware of the potential relevance of his comment to his own activities. He is currently smarting from
the rejection of a grant application to study the physical properties of a
subatomic particle known only to theory. Taylor is firmly in the mainstream of physics, which has for most of the twentieth century been particle physics, exploring the building blocks of matter at smaller and smaller
scales, to produce extremely theoretical research.

Despite his local background in 'underdeveloped' India, Jasmine's husband, Prakash, a progressive moderniser, represents the newer scientific
paradigm, which is marginalising the supposedly central Taylor. Prakash
declares himself as 'an engineer, not just of electricity, he said, but of all
the machinery in the world, seen and unseen. It all ran by rules, if we just
understood them' (p. 78). Around the young couple the speed of change
is almost visible, as camels lope past satellite dishes, beggars and shacks
coexist with skyscrapers: 'Centuries coalesced as we picnicked' (p. 80).
When Prakash proposes emigration, Jasmine identifies immediately with
the vision of freedom: 'If we could just get away from India, then all fates
would be canceled. We'd start with new fates, new stars. We could say or
be anything we wanted' (p. 85). Swiftly learning how to mend toasters,
calculators and fans, in the new consumerist India, she sees electronics as
a 'frontier' (p. 88). Prakash, however, is too swift to assume that disorder
can be brought into line by the discovery of rules. His identification with
the frontiers of science is juxtaposed with a less affirmative image of
national boundaries. While 'Vijh and Wife' are scavenging electronic parts
to put appliances back together, Sikh secessionists are stealing radios and

stereos to turn them into bombs. Prakash, global in his sympathies, defending a precarious unity against further fragmentation, argues to one fundamentalist, Sukhwinder, that 'India is for everyone' (p. 66), and thus becomes a target. As he celebrates his impending departure for America he is blown to pieces by a terrrorist bomb. Arif Dirlik has made the point that:

> Within the institutional site of the First World academy, fragmentation of earlier metanarratives appears benign . . . for its promise of more democratic, multicultural, and cosmopolitan epistemologies. In the world outside the academy, however, it shows in murderous ethnic conflict, continued inequalities among societies, classes, and genders, and the absence of oppositional possibilities that, always lacking in coherence, are rendered even more impotent than earlier by the fetishization of difference, fragmentation and so on.[48]

As the British master narrative collapses at partition, as its successors in turn fragment, from the Naxalites in Bengal to the agitation over Khalistan and Kashmir, the possibility of chaos as murderous disorder shadows the progressive thrust of Jasmine's career.

As Prakash's death and Jasmine's subsequent departure for America indicate, although she begins by fighting off determinism, the astrologer has been proved right. Like fractal geometry her life describes a pattern which is both irregular, broken, fractured and yet none the less an ordered continuum. Throughout the novel a complex relation between chance and determinism is highlighted in the oddities of causality, and in the repetitive pattern of Jasmine's flightpath. Jasmine goes to Iowa only because her charge as a nanny was born there. 'Duff, conceived in impulse and error, had given her mother a chance to go to college and me the chance to break out of Flushing' (p. 197). She meets Bud, a banker, purely because she looks for work in a hospital on a Wednesday, the only day that his mother visits it. Her neighbour, Gene Lutz, chokes to death on Mexican food because the waiters, all illegal immigrants, go into hiding at the first sign of trouble. (p. 8). Sukhwinder takes up a job as a hotdog seller in America and promptly spots Jasmine. Small causes none the less have large consequences. From this apparent randomness, a pattern emerges. Repeatedly Jasmine encounters a violent form of determinism, resists, flees and is rescued in a new existence by an older figure (Masterji, Lillian Gordon, Professor Vadhera, Mrs Ripplemeyer senior) only to move on, in a spiralling trajectory which is repetitive yet different. The characteristic note is struck in Jasmine's route to America which takes her from India to the Middle East, to the Sudan, Hamburg, Amsterdam, Paramaribo and Florida. For Jasmine non-linearity is the way forward: 'The zigzag route is straightest' (p. 101). Like an animal veering from side to side in an apparently untrackable path to escape predation, Jasmine recognises that 'the longest line between two points is the least detected' (p. 99). Landing on a beach in Florida, her first sight of the promised land is of America in fractal form: 'The first thing I saw were the two cones of a nuclear plant, and smoke spreading from them in complicated but seemingly purposeful patterns' (p. 107). The chaotic pattern of destructive energy is linked to a more banal chaos at Jasmine's feet: she wades into Eden through a mass of swirling litter. America's ambivalent status as order or disorder is continually underlined.

Jasmine's guide into the United States is, like her, scarred. 'Half-Face', a demolitions expert, has lost an eye, ear and most of one cheek in Vietnam. When he explains to his passengers that at the first sign of trouble they must jump overboard, Jasmine feels that 'the dead dog in the river never seemed so close' (p. 106). The new beginning also marks a recursive symmetry with echoes of the novel's opening scene.[49] For Half-Face, Asia is a benighted 'bush' world, entirely free of technological sophistication. Jasmine's account of her husband's electrical business triggers fury.

> He dragged me to the television and pressed my forehead against the screen. Then he brought my head back and slammed it against the set, again and again. 'Don't tell me you even **seen** a television set' (p. 112).

This time, however, Jasmine's forehead remains unscarred; the screen cracks. Earlier Jasmine had planned to reach America only to commit sati (in the form of the rite known as *anoomarana* – burning with an object belonging to the deceased, in this case a suit). Raped by Half-Face, and therefore dishonoured, she is forced to alter her plans and her self-image, from that of faithful wife to goddess of destruction: Kali as chaos. On the shrimper in the Gulf a fellow immigrant had given her a knife, 'You con count on dat at least, when de end of de world come in' (p. 106). In an America which does appear as apocalypse, as Kali Yuga, Jasmine uses it to slice her tongue, filling her mouth with blood, in order to crouch over Half-Face, a perfect Kali, stabbing him to death. 'I wanted that moment when he saw me above him as he had last seen me, naked, but now with my mouth open, pouring blood, my red tongue out' (p. 118). In embracing a devouring image of destruction Jasmine is reborn in a very different self. Slicing her tongue in the bathroom she cannot see herself in the steamed-up bathroom mirror except as a dark shadow. As one wife 'dies' here, incinerated with Prakash's suit in a trash bin, the phoenix who arises from the flames, the madwoman in the motel, gives birth to Jane, who walks out into the American dream. Half-Face had refused to accept the possibility of a developed future in Asia. Jasmine acts out the logic of his position, performing the role of destructive goddess. The regression to the opening scene, here, in references to the bloody tongue, the blow to the forehead, the brown water (Half-Face's whisky), the dead dog, and Half-Face's own eyeless, broken body, is inescapable.

While elegantly displaying a recursive symmetry in her heroine's progress, Mukherjee is none the less careful not to cater to the kind of view of the East as timeless, which is entertained by Half-Face. In her flashback/flashforward structure, Mukherjee immediately follows Jasmine's transformation into a Hindu goddess with a scene which undercuts any essentialist mythologising. It is the first of three episodes designed to highlight the dangers of 'authenticity' as opposed to hybridity. Trinh T. Minh Ha has remarked that authenticity is the scourge of the immigrant. Just as anthropologists want to study 'primitive' (non-state, non-class) societies, so the Third World representative whom the modern sophisticated public ideally seeks is the unspoiled African or Asian, thus remaining preoccupied with the image of the 'real' native, the truly different, rather than with issues of hegemony, racism, feminism and social change. In these contexts authenticity is a product to be marketed, bought and arranged to one's own liking:

> Today, planned authenticity is rife; as a product of hegemony and a remarkable counterpart of universal standardization, it constitutes an efficacious means of silencing the cry of racial oppression. We no longer wish to erase your difference, We demand, on the contrary, that you remember and assert it.[50]

Cunningly Mukherjee satirises the demands of the First World intellectual that the Third World individual functions as an 'otherness machine manufacturing alterity for the postmodern trade in difference'[51] in Jasmine's encounter with a New Age 'channeler' and academic, interested in past lives and out-of-body experiences. Assuming that she is addressing a fellow believer in reincarnation, Mary Webb confides the insights of her guru (a former battered wife from Medicine Hat, Alberta). Predictably, in her time-travelling, she has skipped over intervening existences to revert to a state of origins, a previous life as a cave-dwelling Australian aborigine in the dawn of time. Confronted by Dr Webb's vivid nostalgia for kangaroo meat and almost orgasmic celebration of the boomerang, Jasmine promptly orders a hearty meal of pork chops, much to the dismay of her interlocuteur. Jasmine agrees that she has been reborn many times, but her comment is to some extent ironic. Her other lives are not constructions of a Western vision of the authentic, timeless primitive, but the different experiences of Jyoti of Hasnapur, Jasmine, Jazzy, Jase and Jane. As Gail Low comments:

> The proper naming of Jyoti/Jasmine/Jase marks the essential hybridization and intersection of multiple narratives and histories which structure the post-colonial identity. Mukherjee rereads

Jasmine's mutation as a strategy of hybridization necessary for survival.[52]

Similarly, Jasmine's metaphor for reincarnation technologises the process, in firm opposition to any timeless mystification, calling up the image of the spirals and strange attractors of chaos theory, with the soul envisaged not as a timeless wheel but as 'a giant long-playing record with millions of tracks, each of them a complete circle with only one diamond-sharp microscopic link to the next life' (p. 127). For Jasmine, extraordinary events have jarred the needle, jumped the tracks and deposited a life in a new groove.

Whereas in India, pressure had been put upon Jasmine to modernise, and to embrace the global, in America the movement is all in the other direction, towards cultural authenticity, Otherness and ghettoisation. In Jasmine's American adventures Mukherjee broadens her theme – to target the demands for 'unspoiledness' which also consign people to the metaphoric bush. Those who want the Third World to remain unchanged and to honour its traditions may be just as pernicious as those who lament its decline from imperial days. In the West, the demand for authenticity can only be self-serving or meretricious. In her five-month stay with the Vadheras in Flushing, Jasmine enters one of the 'archipelago of ghettos' (p. 140) which is New York. The Vadheras live entirely in an Indian milieu, watching Hindi videos, Urdu films, wearing Indian dress, using Indian foodstores and reading Punjabi newspapers. They inhabit a block of fifty apartments so specialised as to the inhabitants' language, caste and religion that they need never fraternise with anyone other than educated Punjabi-speaking Hindu Jats. 'They had kept a certain kind of Punjab alive, even if that Punjab no longer existed' (p. 162). As a result their lives are almost entirely enclosed in second-hand fantasy, enjoyed within an alternative reality inside America, which will last only as long as their supply of videos. (Nirmala has already exhausted the stock of Hindi films, is devouring Urdu videos, and faces an awful future of unintelligible Bengali or Karnataka features.) In this cocoon of security and safety, Jasmine feels immured, 'spiraling' (p. 148) into depression. She makes good her escape through a chance incident, an event which reveals the real connections between the Vadheras' 'authentically Indian' life and their host country. Urgently seeking Professor Vadhera (whose father has injured his head) Jasmine discovers his real workplace. Professor Devinder Vadhera (aka Dave O'Hara) is not in fact an educator, but an importer and sorter of human hair, which he sells to scientific instrument makers. He actually makes his living out of the marketing of the unspoiled. Apparently no synthetic material has the human hair's tensile strength, to gauge humidity and to read the weather. Indian women's hair is particularly prized as the purest material, untouched by harsh dyes or detergents. 'A hair from some peasant's head in Hasnapur could travel across oceans and save an American meteorologist's reputation. Nothing was rooted anymore. Everything was in motion' (p. 152). Since Jasmine's hair is unspoiled, it provides her passport to assimilation. She offers it to Vadhera as security for a forged green card. While the Vadheras apparently form a tight-knit local community of the least assimilated kind, their activities are implicitly global in importance. Some of the hair is sold to the US Defense Department. 'It was no exaggeration to say that the security of the free world, in some small way, depended on the hair of Indian village women' (p. 152). The scenario offers a sharply focused example of the intricacies of the relationship between local and global, cause and effect, unspoiled nature and the most sophisticated examples of scientific engineering.

Where the Flushing ghetto represents the choice of non-assimilation, Jasmine's job with Taylor and Wylie Hayes as 'caregiver' to their adopted daughter offers a different form of exploitation – that of licensed Other. Mukherjee makes the point here that it is always necessary to distinguish carefully between an appreciation of hybridity and forms of ethnic tourism – the scopic feast offered in the insensitive museum exhibit. Ostensibly well-meaning, the Hayeses treat Jasmine as one more object of display, a trophy to the winning ways of their liberalism. Their apartment is stocked like a museum with multicultural *objets d'art*, particularly those which represent the Other as victim: slave auction posters for New Orleans in 1850, old colour prints of Indian massacres, a poster of a woman's naked body labelled as cuts of meat. Very different kinds of oppression are seamlessly integrated into a homogenous decor of alterity as victimhood. Wylie even makes her money out of the cult of the victim, as a book editor working for a publisher who specialises in writers whom she christens the 'New Sob Sisters'. 'She explained about the money to be made signing up celebrity interviews, writing about divorces and drug cases, society murders, child abuse, and rape. She made them sound like grave robbers' (p. 169). Unsurprisingly, perhaps, Wylie eventually leaves Taylor for Stuart, an economist with the World Bank, whose walls are so adorned with Indian paintings, and with the collection of spears and masks belonging to his wife, an Africa expert, that his apartment resembles an art gallery. The general ephemerality of the Hayes' life is characterised by one of Taylor's homespun metaphors for a scientific concept: 'Weak gravity is what keeps your dreams inside your head so they don't go flying out' (p. 178). They lack a sense of the 'grave', except in exploitative terms. Jasmine, although a dreamer, is made of sterner stuff: 'America may be fluid and built on flimsy, invisible lines of weak gravity, but I was a dense object' (p. 179). Mukherjee is careful not to suggest that Jasmine's adaptability is necessarily a matter of lightness, ephemerality and insignificance. For Taylor, weak in any real understanding of the postcolonial situation, Jasmine is merely 'an innocent child he'd picked out of the gutter, discovered and made whole' (p. 189), not a terrorist target, and murderer with a complicated history of her own. When Sukhwinder resurfaces in New York, however, Jasmine has to disabuse Taylor of his innocent illusions and flee.

The reader, expecting the next development of the Sukhwinder-as-stalker plot, turns the page to find: 'Harlan Kroener shot Bud on December 23, two years ago' (p. 190). It is as if violence had jumped the tracks instantaneously between the Sikh fundamentalist and the Iowan, via the fatal 'strange attractor' that is Jasmine. Jasmine's next destination – Iowa – provides a final loop in the recursive symmetry of her path. A series of repetitions alerts the reader to the parallels between Iowa and India. The choice of Iowa – almost as drought-ridden as the Punjab – explicitly attacks the notion of the First World as automatically the locus of achievement. Indeed, as a result of set-aside policies, Iowa is itself returning to bush. In the past Bud's family had tilled to black, ploughing their fields twice a year. Now there is a no-till policy and the weeds are growing high. The results are locally productive. Trash in the fields has brought back the pheasants and Jasmine's freezer is full. On a broader scale, however, economic depression shadows the characters, not least Bud, a banker shot down by an angry client. One farmer has beaten his wife with a spade and hanged himself; another backhoes a moat around **his** banker's house. Where the Punjab had the Khalsa Lions, Iowa has the Aryan Nations, an umbrella organisation for various groups of white survivalists with links to the Ku Klux Klan. 'Jews Take Over Our Farmland' (p. 158) is the message of a leaflet presented to Bud. The agricultural depression in itself highlights the fluctuations of weather, interest rates and the global economy. The Iowans, however, are presented as just as inward-looking and 'local' as the Punjabis. The basic German community in Baden considers the Swedes genetically unpredictable ('The inscrutable Swedes. The sneaky Dutch', p. 11). For the local population Jasmine comes from 'Out There', a place of swamps, deserts and jungles (p. 21), whereas America is 'In Here', a place of security. As Mukherjee reveals, however, that jar is broken; there are no insides and outsides any more. Iowa is a microcosm of America itself, a multicultural society. After nearly a day in America, Jasmine comments that she has yet to see an 'American' face (p. 129). Her first encounter in Florida is with Kanjobals (from Guatemala) whose faces vividly recall Hasnapur. All around her she sees the face of a new America – from the Hmong to Drs Kwang, Liu, Jaswani and Patel, her gynaecologists.

Daringly, Mukherjee poses the question in her plot: is immigration a threat? To Iowans in the grip of economic depression it is, of course, tempting to attribute their own decline to the immigrant presence. Jasmine is infuriated by a televised interview with a bystander who had witnessed a raid by INS agents on a factory employing illegal immigrants. The woman interviewed moves immediately from the presence of Mexicans to her husband's unemployment and inability to make the house and car payments, in a classic 'blame the victim' mental manoeuvre. On the other hand, Jasmine herself trails disaster in her wake, as the fates of Bud and Darrel suggest. Bud is drawn to Jasmine as exotic Other: 'Bud courts me because I am alien. I am darkness, mystery, inscrutability. The East plugs me into instant vitality and wisdom. I rejuvenate him simply by being who I am' (p. 200). Yet Bud is almost blown to pieces by a fundamentalist, as Prakash actually was. Jasmine acknowledges the deterministic reading: 'Bud was wounded in the war between my fate and my will. I think sometimes I saved his life by not marrying him' (p. 12). Indeed Bud promptly rechristens her Jane, but as 'Calamity Jane. Jane as in Jane Russell, not Jane as in Plain Jane' (p. 26.). Ironically, as a result of the shooting, Bud can enjoy his 'Maharani' (p. 35) only with considerable technological assistance, and some of the technology is Asian. (Drs Kwang, Liu, Patel and Jaswani assist in the conception of his child, and his sexual needs can be met only via the intervention of mechanical aids.) Jasmine herself feels guilty; Bud's first wife would have recognised the danger signs in Harlan Kroener and known how to read them. Jasmine, uncomprehending, allows him to lead Bud to the slaughter. 'I feel responsible. For Prakash's death, Bud's maiming. I'm a tornado blowing through Baden' (p. 206).

Nor is Bud the only victim. Bud's neighbour, Darrel, also falls for Jasmine and asks her to run off with him. He kills himself because he can't get away to the exotic paradise of Tahiti with his Indian princess at his side. Darrel's death also replays elements of the Indian plot, looping back to the opening scene, and introducing its own technologial twists and short circuits. Like the young Jasmine, Darrel cannot bear to be stuck in a rural backwater. When Jasmine hears screams (Darrel's unfed pigs) she is transported in memory to Hasnapur and the cries of a baby girl thrown down a well. On the road the two halves of Darrel's dog's body lie, blown apart before his master hanged himself 'slowly twisting and twisting from the rafter' (p. 234). Earlier, as Darrel ranted against the Eastern banks, Jasmine had read 'the blown circuitry behind his eyes' (p. 218), reminiscent of the bomb circuitry which blew Prakash apart. Darrel had also been an ambitious moderniser, planning to expand his farm to a 'self-sufficient city for hogs' (p. 24) with an enormous extension, and electric lighting in the hogpen. In the end he uses his electrical extension cord to hang himself.

Like Prakash's, Darrel's death is also linked to the threat of communal division, in this case American. In 1988 Mukherjee reviewed Studs Terkel's *The Great Divide*, a work of oral history which characterises America as a deeply fractured society. One section of interviews centres on the agricultural depression, bankers attacked by farmers, the rise of the Aryan Nations, and even the problems of pig farming. Mukherjee found the book depressing reading, registering an America sundered between those with historical memory (of neighbourhood, civil rights struggles, war, Depression) and an amnesiac TV culture. 'Terkel noted that the important distinction these days is between winners and losers, not oppressors and victims. The poor are wimps. They should be ashamed.'[53] In Baden, Mother Ripplemeyer with her Depression stories (p. 16) and belief in family and community represents the former. Darrel, however, is a casualty of the new state of things. One of Terkel's informants comments that for the young

> the belief in production, book-keeping and expansion is important
> . . . . Self-centredness and selfishness has become the farmer's way of
> life out here, instead of neighbourliness, conservation and families.[54]

In the past, on family farms, she continued, people were out all night in the hog barn during farrowing. Corporate farming, ruled by the profit motive, leaves no room for this. 'A farm woman put it . . .Who is going to stay up with the corporate sow?'[55] Mukherjee, an acid ironist, gives the question a literal answer: Darrel is last seen swinging up above his pigs, his feet bloodied and chewed. He has been partly eaten by the corporate sow.

Up to this point, therefore, it may appear that the consequences of Jasmine's presence in Baden are uniformly disastrous. Her presence, and by implication that of her fellow immigrants, is allied with decline, anarchy and division – Terkel's Great Divide, the racist divisions of a socially fractured community. A corrective perspective is offered, however, in the character of Du Thien, Jasmine's adopted Vietnamese son. Initially Du appears to embody the amnesiac TV culture so deplored by Terkel. When he learned that he was to be adopted, his first question to Jasmine was, 'You have television? You get?' (p. 18). He is certainly interested in winning. Du is introduced to the reader, shouting encouragement to the Slugger in *Monster Truck Madness*. When he and Jasmine watch a televised arrest of illegal immigrants Du merely snickers 'Asshole', without visible sign of caring one way or another. Jasmine realises that she is not sure whether he is referring to the INS or the Mexicans: 'who were the assholes, the cowboys or the Indians' (p. 27). Du sees his adoptive father as an 'asshole' all too literally (Bud can experience sexual pleasure only via the 'big beads' trick administered by Jasmine) and therefore sees him as a loser (p. 224).

The connection between marginality and chaos, in its scientific sense, however, is not limited to Jasmine, but generalised through Du. Like Jasmine, Du's presence in Iowa is the result of maverick causality, in his case supported by technology. Bud had watched a TV special on the boat people and promptly phoned an adoption agency. Since the agency recognise Jasmine only as 'Asian' in the portmanteau sense of the term, and since Du is a hard-to-place orphan, they readily agree to the adoption. 'Fates are so intertwined in the modern world' (p. 15) comments Jasmine. 'Asia had transformed [Bud], made him reckless and emotional' (p. 14). On arrival Du swiftly proves to be a genius in recombinant electronics. The connection between the immigrant's effects on the American people, and technological futures, is emphasised in Du's metaphors. Combining new functions, reshuffling circuits, he boasts that

> I have altered the gene pool of the common American appliance. I have spliced the gene of a Black & Decker paint sprayer onto the gear drive of a repaired Mixmaster. I have created a multi-use super air-blower with a variable speed maindrive (p. 156).

Du learns fast **because** he is an immigrant. Bud notes that a lot of his genius is for 'scavenging, adaptation, appropriate technology' (p. 155), unsurprising in a veteran of the camps who has survived on a diet of worms, crabs and lizards. The connection between immigration and intellectual nomadism is also made explicitly in the unseeing comments of his condescending teachers, surprised how well he is doing, 'considering'. Jasmine is scathing:

> Considering that he has lived through five or six languages, five or six countries, two or three centuries of history; has seen his country, city, and family butchered, bargained with pirates and bureaucrats, eaten filth in order to stay alive; that he has survived every degradation known to this century, **considering all those liabilities**, isn't it amazing that he can read a Condensed and Simplified for Modern Students edition of *A Tale of Two Cities*? ( p. 214).

The intertextual reference is well chosen. Ironically Du, with his experience, is exceptionally well qualified to understand the novel's themes of violent change, revolutionary violence and multiple identity. For his fellows it is merely a 'classic'.

On the surface, therefore, Du appears to have assimilated rapidly to the American Dream, in some of its less pleasant, individualistic forms. His history teacher describes him as 'in a hurry to become all-American' (p. 28), and is dismissive of him as merely 'a quick study' (p. 29), like the street kids he knew in Saigon. With shocking insensitivity to Du's own history, he promptly tries out some street Vietnamese on him. Du, however, is not as amnesiac as the television age thinks. Technology and memory, individuality and community can go hand in hand. At the close of the novel Du moves on, to Los Angeles to help support his only surviving relative, the sister who kept him alive in the camp. Behind him, on his Scrabble board, he leave only two words, 'deliquesce' and 'scabrous': 'They are clues, but to what? Shadowy road signs for a phantom Columbus?' (p. 225). Du may be heading for the furthest frontiers of science, and America, but in so doing he honours his past and his community. 'For every gesture of loyalty there doesn't have to be a betrayal' (p. 225). Jasmine recognises that 'My transformation has been genetic; Du's was hyphenated . . . he's a hybrid, like the fantasy appliances he wants to build' (p. 222). As a shadowy double to Jasmine, a fellow killer (p. 157), with more than one life behind him, Du none the less typifies positive interpretations of hybridity, marginality and chaos.

The novel ends on an ambiguous note. Leaving Bud behind, Jasmine, six months pregnant with his child, lights out for the West, in best American fashion. 'Adventure, risk, transformation: the frontier is pushing indoors through uncaulked windows. Watch me reposition the stars' (p. 240). She steps out into the landscape of chaos, the potholed and rutted driveway, as the Iowa winter acts out the terms of the novel's epigraph. For the Iowans 'Jane Ripplemeyer' will remain 'a tornado, rubble-maker, arising from nowhere and disappearing into a cloud' (p. 241). Earlier she had thought of herself as 'Jane with my very own Mr Rochester' (p. 236). But even as she leaves she has already ceased to think of herself as Jane (p. 240). She and Du, she reflects, are like creatures in a fairy tale: 'we've shrunk and we've swollen, and we've swallowed the cosmos whole' (p. 240). Images of fracture and destruction coexist with images of a contained, fertile order within. The baby is described as 'a whole new universe' (p. 235) floating inside Jasmine. Earlier in the novel, Jasmine had recalled her grandmother's stories of Vishnu the Preserver, 'containing our world inside his potbellied stomach' (p. 224). In *Days and Nights in Calcutta* Mukherjee discussed a temple relief from Deoghar, reproduced in a book on Indian art by Heinrich Zimmer,[56] which shows the god Vishnu asleep on a multiheaded serpent, in an image packed with an enormity of details:

> Nothing had been excluded. As a viewer, I was free to concentrate on a tiny corner of the relief, and read into the shape of a stone eyelid or stone finger human intrigues and emotions. Or I could view the work as a whole, and see it as the story of Divine Creation.[57]

In America Mukherjee had felt herself becoming overconscious of 'ineradicable barriers, of beginnings and endings, of lines and definitions' as opposed to the 'explosion' of images encountered on her return to India.[58] In the noisy data of the temple frieze, in which several time schemes coexist, Vishnu is the chief god, and the serpent supporting him is also Vishnu, given a magical transformation. In her Indian education, Mukherjee notes, with its Macbeth and Othello, Michelangelo and Gilbert and Sullivan, 'multiheaded serpents who were also cosmic oceans and anthropomorphic gods' did not stand much chance of survival. But for Mukherjee the snakes and gods remain, in the 'Hindu instinct for miraculous transformation of the literal'.[59] The frieze expresses a vision of fluidity, connectedness, non-linear aesthetics, sinuosity and transformation, containing the local detail and the global vision, a Third World aesthetic which coincides with a late twentieth-century scientific conception. Mukherjee has described Hinduism as 'a kind of geophysical vision rather than a religion'.[60] For the West it has often been an apparently chaotic vision, as in the famous example of the 'Temple' sequence of E. M. Forster's *A Passage to India* with its dramatisation of India as mystery and muddle, all certainties dissolving in the flooding and chaos of a Hindu religious festival. Mukherjee, however, has acknowledged the influence of Forster in validating her own fictional world:

> The chaos that I had been trained to perceive by the Anglos as a deformity, a weakness of the Indian character, was really the life-renewing muddle and mystery of Forster.[61]

In *Jasmine* she uses fluidity and transformation to argue that the postcolonial is the future. It is as if Forster's 'only connect' was transformed from well-meaning liberalism to an image which conjoins Indian and Western-scientific paradigms in an entirely new synthesis. Jasmine's story eschews closure, not merely in imitation of the American narrative paradigm of 'lighting out', but because beginnings and endings have been resutured in recursive symmetry. As serpent, Vishnu is Ananta, endless.

Like the temple relief, like Forster's 'Temple', *Jasmine* pullulates with different stories, plots and paradigms, seamlessly interacting and dissolving in a series of feedback loops, in which output from one system feeds back continually into the system as input, in the best chaotic terms. The feedback mechanism offers a highly seductive model of intertextuality – as Naipaul's 'Jasmine' feeds Mukherjee's 'Jasmine', is transformed into *Jasmine,* and flows back into Jane Eyre/Ripplemeyer. What Jasmine's story also suggests is that intertextuality is a literary equivalent of chaos. Even the smallest story can have enormous effects. Like the beat of a butterfly's wing, the 'local' story may become a tornado when it hits the West, demolishing paradigms of the 'universal', the linear, the classic. Rather than assimilating to Western norms, *Jasmine* demonstrates how the Third World story may exert its power on First World criticism and writing. In the interconnections between America and India, Mukherjee insists upon the two-way process involved in all readings:

> All around me I see the face of America changing. So do you . . . But where, in fiction, do you **read** of it? Who, in other words, speaks for us; the new Americans from nontraditional immigrant countries? Which is another way of saying, in this altered America, who speaks for **you**?[62]

# Notes

1 V. S. Naipaul, 'Jasmine', in *The Overcrowded Barracoon* (London, Penguin, 1976), pp. 30–1.
2 V. S. Naipaul, *A Bend in the River* (London, André Deutsch, 1979), p. 9.
3 Selwyn R. Cudjoe, *V. S. Naipaul: A Materialist Reading* (Amherst, University of Massachusetts Press, 1988), p. 186.
4 Irving Howe, 'A Dark Vision', *New York Times Book Review*, 13 May 1979, p. 36.
5 Clark Blaise and Bharati Mukherjee, *Days and Nights in Calcutta* (Garden City, New York, Doubleday, 1977), p. 287.
6 Bharati Mukherjee, *The Tiger's Daughter* (New York , Fawcett Crest, 1971).
7 Bharati Mukherjee, *Wife* (New York, Houghton Mifflin, 1975).
8 See Feroza Jussawalla, 'Chiffon Saris: The Plight of South Asian Immigrants in the New World', *Massachusetts Review* 29 (Winter 1988–9), pp. 583–95.
9 Bharati Mukherjee, *The Middleman and Other Stories* (London, Virago, 1990), first published New York, Grove Press, 1988.
10 Clark Blaise and Bharati Mukherjee, *The Sorrow and the Pity: The Haunting Legacy of the Air India Tragedy* (Ontario, Penguin, 1987).
11 Bharati Mukherjee and Robert Boyers, 'A Conversation with V. S. Naipaul', *Salmagundi* 54 (Fall 1981), p. 18.
12 Mukherjee and Boyars, 'A Conversation with V. S. Naipaul', p. 19.
13 Michael Connell, Jessie Grearson and Tom Grimes, 'An Interview with Bharati Mukherjee', *Iowa Review* 20, 3 (1990), pp. 26–7.
14 Bharati Mukherjee, 'Jasmine', in *The Middleman*, p. 128. Page references follow subsequent citations in parentheses.
15 Connell *et al.*, 'An Interview with Bharati Mukherjee', p. 22.
16 Anindyo Roy, 'The Aesthetics of An (Un)Willing Immigrant: Bharati Mukherjee's *Days and Nights in Calcutta* and *Jasmine*', in Emmanuel S. Nelson, ed., *Bharati Mukherjee: Critical Perspectives* (New York, Garland, 1993), p. 138.
17 Sybil Steinberg, 'Bharati Mukherjee', *Publishers Weekly*, 25 August 1988, p. 47.
18 Bharati Mukherjee, *Darkness* (New York, Fawcett Crest, 1985), p. xv.
19 A people from the hills of Northern Laos.
20 Bharati Mukherjee, *Jasmine* (London, Virago, 1990), p. 40. Page references follow subsequent quotations in parentheses. First published New York, Grove Weidenfeld, 1989.
21 See Jussawalla, 'Chiffon Saris', and Robert W. Gardner, Bryant Robey and Peter C. Smith, 'Asian Americans: Growth, Change and Diversity', *Population Bulletin* (Population Reference Bureau), 40, 4 (October 1985).
22 Gurleen Grewal, 'Born Again American: The Immigrant Consciousness in *Jasmine*', in Emmanuel S. Nelson, ed., *Bharati Mukherjee: Critical Perspectives* (New York, Garland, 1993), p. 193.
23 Maya Jaggi, 'When in America', *Bazaar: South Asian Arts Magazine* 13 (n.d.), Special Roots Issue, p. 9.
24 Jaggi, 'When in America', p. 9.
25 Both *Jasmine* and Mukherjee have had a hostile press. Contributors to the first volume of essays to discuss her work (Emmanuel S. Nelson, *Bharati Mukherjee: Critical Perspectives*) have described her heroine as embodying the collusion of the institutionalised forces of postcoloniality and the West, and the immi-

grant author (Anindyo Roy, p. 133), as a domesticated Other (Alpana Sharma Knippling, p. 147), as aquiescing in her own exoticisation, and wiping out Indian history (Debjani Banerjee, pp. 161–80) and as complicitous with the myth of the American dream (Gurleen Grewal, pp. 189–96). Feroza Jussawalla sees Mukherjee as colluding with racist America ('Chifffon Saris', p. 591); Gayatri Chakravorty Spivak *(In Other Worlds*, London, Methuen, 1987, p. 256) argues that Mukherjee's heroines are 'privileged native informants' of liberal feminists. Samir Dayal (Nelson, *Bharati Mukherjee*, pp. 65–88) finds Jasmine too cynical, cauterised by her experiences. He notes the novel's epigraph but reads Du as banalising and repressing his knowledge of entropy, in order to gain control over a life that threatens to turn into chaos. On a more positive note, Carmen Wickramagamage argues that Mukherjee presents *Jasmine* as a creative reworking of emancipatory narratives of self and identity, embedded within Hindu culture: 'Relocation as Positive Act: The Immigrant Experience in Bharati Mukherjee's Novels', *Diaspora* 2, 2 (1992), pp. 171–200. The censure of the BBC serialisation is described in Maya Jaggi, 'A World Apart', *The Guardian*, 5 November 1993, p. 6.

26 James Gleick, *Chaos: Making a New Science* (London, Heinemann, 1988), p. 94.

27 Antonio Benítez-Rojo, *The Repeating Island: The Caribbean and Postmodern Perspective* (Durham, North Carolina, Duke University Press, 1992), p. 269.

28 Benítez-Rojo, *The Repeating Island*, p. 10.

29 Benítez-Rojo, *The Repeating Island*, p. 11.

30 Connell *et al.*, 'A Conversation with Bharati Mukherjee', p. 29.

31 Michiko Kakutani, 'Third World Refugees Rootless in the U.S.', *New York Times*, 19 September 1989, p. A.16.

32 Bharati Mukherjee, 'Immigrant Writing: Give us Your Maximalists', *New York Times Book Review*, 28 August 1988, p. 29.

33 Mukherjee, 'Immigrant Writing: Give us your Maximalists', p. 28.

34 Candia McWilliam, 'Jazzy, Jyoti, Jase and Jane', *London Review of Books*, 10 May 1990, p. 23.

35 N. Katherine Hayles, *Chaos Bound: Orderly Disorder in Contemporary Literature and Science* (Ithaca, Cornell University Press, 1990). In what follows I have drawn upon the works of Hayles, Gleick, Benítez-Rojo and Nina Hall, ed., *The New Scientist Guide to Chaos* (London, Penguin, 1992). In understanding chaos theory one picture is worth a thousand words. I am grateful to Dr Herman Moisl of the University of Newcastle upon Tyne for patient explanation and graphic assistance.

36 Hayles, *Chaos Bound*, p. 2.

37 Hayles, *Chaos Bound*, p. 2.

38 Gleick, *Chaos*, p. 8.

39 Hayles, *Chaos Bound*, p. 10.

40 A fractal, from the Latin for 'broken up', involves shapes that repeat themselves, often in lifelike forms, over and over on smaller and smaller scales. Although broken up or irregular, they are often aesthetically attractive.

41 Gleick, *Chaos*, p. 251.

42 Hall, *New Scientist Guide to Chaos*, p. 7.

43 Gleick, *Chaos*, p. 90.

44 Hayles, *Chaos Bound*, p. 173.

45 Hayles, *Chaos Bound*, p. 173.

46 Hayles, *Chaos Bound*, p. 40.

47 Hayles, *Chaos Bound*, p. 16.

48 Arif Dirlik, 'The Postcolonial Aura: Third World Criticism in the Age of Global

Capitalism', *Critical Inquiry* 20 (Winter 1994), pp. 328–56.

49 Candia McWilliam, 'Jazzy, Jyoti, Jase and Jane, notes the frequency of proleptic and reflexive images.

50 Trinh T. Minh-ha, *Woman, Native, Other: Writing Postcoloniality and Feminism* (Bloomington, Indiana University Press, 1989), p. 89.

51 Gail Ching-Liang Low, 'In a Free State: Post-Colonialism and Postmodernism in Bharati Mukherjee's Fiction', *Women: A Cultural Review* 4, 1 (Spring 1993), p. 17. The phrase 'otherness machine' originates with Sara Suleri.

52 Low, 'In a Free State', p. 12.

53 Bharati Mukherjee, 'Talking Cures', *The Nation* 247 (17), 5 December 1988, p. 622.

54 Studs Terkel, *The Great Divide: Second Thoughts on the American Dream* (London, Hamish Hamilton, 1988), p. 85.

55 Terkel, *The Great Divide*, p. 97.

56 Heinrich Zimmer, *The Art of Indian Asia* (Delhi, Varanasi and Patna , Motilal Banarsidass, 1984), pp. 12–13, plate 286.

57 Clark Blaise and Bharati Mukherjee, *Days and Nights in Calcutta*, p. 171.

58 Clark Blaise and Bharati Mukherjee, *Days and Nights in Calcutta*, p. 171.

59 Clark Blaise and Bharati Mukherjee, *Days and Nights in Calcutta*, p. 171.

60 Connell *et al.*, 'A Conversation with Bharati Mukherjee', p. 18.

61 Judith Scherer Herz and Robert K. Martin, ed., *E. M. Forster: Centenary Revaluations* (London, Macmillan, 1982), p. 292.

62 Mukherjee, 'Immigrant Writing: Give Us Your Maximalists', p. 1.

# |10|

# *Nadine Gordimer and the naked southern ape*

## 'Something Out There'

Up to this point, the present study has been concerned with intertextual phenomena. Yet intertextuality, even at its broadest, is perhaps too limited a term to describe writers working through other textualisations of experience.[1] Interdiscursivity, where collective modes of discourse are drawn upon, may also be a means of restoring the silenced to history, while simultaneously undermining the master narratives of colonial culture. Nadine Gordimer's novella, 'Something Out There' is a classic example of such interdiscursive, oppositionalist writing, which revises a specific cultural discourse linking archaeology, anthropology and ethology, discussing the relation of nature to technological advance in a fashion which offers a strong contrast to Mukherjee's fluid, female-identified chaos. It has, moreover, a special interest theoretically in relation to the degree to which interdiscursive writing can avoid mimicking colonialist norms. In contrast to Naipaul's scathing dissection of the 'mimic men' of colonialism, Homi Bhabha has highlighted the possibility that mimicry may itself become a source of potential menace in the colonial situation, sapping the authority of colonial discourse by its 'partial presence' which effectively articulates the disturbances of difference. Such mimicry may approximate more to the status of embattled camouflage, than to slavish imitation:

the discourse of mimicry is constructed around an ambivalence; in order to be effective, mimicry must continually produce its slippage, its excess, its difference . . . . Mimicry is, thus, the sign of a double articulation; a complex strategy of reform, regulation, and discipline, which 'appropriates' the Other as it visualizes power. Mimicry is also the sign of the inappropriate, however, a difference or recalcitrance which coheres the dominant strategic function of colonial power, intensifies surveillance, and poses an immanent threat to both 'normalized' knowledges and disciplinary powers.[2]

Bhabha therefore sees colonial discourse as the site of a clash between the Western desire for a uniform self and the need to define that self against 'others' who, although produced in the self's likeness, are never quite the same. Mimicry also challenges the authority of colonial representation by redefining the desire of the colonial power to 'fix' its own position, as a form of fixation, an obsession which, manifested in the fetishisation of the Other through the workings of stereotype, and discriminatory classification (Bhabha cites the 'Simian Black' as example), confirms the fear that the supposedly normative values of the coloniser will be displaced by the colonised.[3] In 'Something Out There' Gordimer exposes white South African mimic men to the full irony of their situation, while keeping in reserve an awareness of the positive power of mimicry in the weaponry of their undercover opponents, whether in scribal or material practices.

In the novella two plots are interwoven, in a sequence of alternating scenes – that of a group of four terrorists, planning an attack on a power station, and that concerning another outlaw and fugitive, a mysterious escaped ape who plunders the affluent suburbs of white Johannesburg. Just as the human saboteurs go under assumed names, their identities elusive, so their animal counterpart is variously described as an ape, a chimpanzee, a vervet monkey, a baboon – even a man. The slippage between categories, the deliberate indeterminacy, is reproduced in the structure of the novella. The two plots evolve in tandem, the monkey disappearing from view at the same time as the terrorists, his attack on a white South African juxtaposed with their attack on the power station, his death reported coincidentally with the death of one of the saboteurs. At various points in the novella ape and man, particularly black man, are identified. This potentially patronising parallel represents an extremely risky narrative procedure on Gordimer's part.[4] The suggestion of similarities between ape and black is part of the standard vocabulary of racism. As recently as 3 August 1989 black South African workers went on strike because a white foreman displayed a baboon's head with a trade union leaflet stuck in it.[5] As Salman Rushdie observed, reviewing 'Something Out There', it is also commonplace for the powerful to see the powerless as animals or monsters:

> Great white sharks, killer bees, werewolves, devils, alien horrors bursting from the chests of movie spacemen: the popular culture of our fearful times has provided us with so many variations on the ancient myth of the Beast, the 'something' lurking out there that hunts us and is hunted by us, as to make it one of the defining metaphors of the age.[6]

In interview, however, Gordimer argued against portraying the terrorist as a monster, even at the risk of putting writers 'in a place where they are seen as supporting terrorists by portraying them as human beings.

Terrorism is real, something that happens all the time. Portraying these people as humans is a more delicate and dangerous matter.'[7] Paradoxically, in her attempt to demystify the twentieth-century 'Beast' of the terrorist, Gordimer employs a structural parallel between these so-called monsters and an actual animal – the escaped baboon. It is a strategy deliberately designed to set up a series of questions : Is the terrorist a brute? What is the justification for terrorism? Do terrorists merely decline into the mirror image of their opponents by embracing violence? Will their projected future simply reenact the nightmares of the past? More generally, the novella places the issues of terrorism in a wider context – of the nature of man. Is man essentially only an animal, a naked ape, irremediably violent, beastly and savage? Or is there hope for his future development?

The answers to these questions – even the manner in which they are posed – depend upon an informed awareness on Gordimer's part of a series of debates in ethology – the science of animal behaviour – which have particular reference both to apes and to Africa. Primates, whether ape, monkey or chimpanzee, have been a focus of attention since the 1960s when a spate of books appeared which claimed first to describe man's 'real' or 'natural' behaviour in ethological style, and second to explain how this behaviour evolved. Robert Ardrey's *African Genesis* and *The Territorial Imperative*, Desmond Morris's *The Naked Ape* and *The Human Zoo*, Konrad Lorenz's *On Aggression* were all popular bestsellers; all purport to document the idea that man is an animal, that there is little we can do but accept our instinctive natures, and that we are naturally aggressive creatures. The animals most often used as models for early human behaviour are baboons, which have been exhaustively studied.[8]

Ethological ideas were given special impetus by archaeological discoveries in Africa. Until the 1920s the hunt for early man had focused on Asia. Then in 1924 Raymond Dart discovered the Taung skull in South Africa. Furious controversy broke out when Dart claimed to recognise features in the skull which took it out of the ape class and placed it in that of the Hominidae, the group which includes man and his early ancestors. Dart christened his find *Australopithecus*, the southern ape. Resistance to the idea that all human beings are descended from Africans was strong. When Dart's paper 'The Predatory Transition from Ape to Man' was published, the editor of *The International Anthropological and Linguistic Review* preceded it with the disclaimer that the australopithecines were 'only the ancestors of the modern Bushman and Negro and of nobody else'.[9] Subsequent discoveries in the 1930s in caves near Johannesburg confirmed Dart's thesis, since when hundreds more such remains have been found on South African sites. Dart, who was professor of anatomy at the University of the Witwatersrand, lived to see his theories vindicated, and in 1984, coincidentally the year of publication of 'Something Out There', there was a conference of world anthropologists in Johannesburg, to celebrate the fortieth anniversary of his discovery.[10]

Not all Dart's ideas, however, have proved so acceptable. Until his discovery it had been assumed that our primal ancestors resembled the shy, vegetarian ape of the forest. Observing fossilised baboon remains, with head injuries, however, Dart concluded that his 'southern ape' had killed them with an antelope humerus bone, and that the hominid hunters lived in bands, systematically killing for a living. Essentially, therefore, Dart argued that man had emerged from the anthropoid background for one reason only – because he was a killer. As he learned to stand erect, to run in pursuit of game and to use weapons, he made new demands on the nervous system for the coordination of muscle, touch and sight. The result was first the enlarged brain, and then man. In other words the weapon had fathered man.

It was to be a view taken up enthusiastically by Robert Ardrey in *African Genesis*, a work which popularised the 'killer ape' theory. *African Genesis* begins as melodramatically as a horror film when the 'thing' awakes:

> Not in innocence, and not in Asia, was mankind born. The home of our fathers was that African highland reaching north from the Cape to the Lakes of the Nile. Here we came about – slowly, ever so slowly – on a sky-swept savannah glowing with menace.[11]

Ardrey's final chapter is entitled 'Children of Cain' and in between he paints a dismal picture of man, and an all too familiar one of Africa as 'dark continent'. In accepting that the carnivorous, predatory australopithecines were the unquestioned antecedents of man, Ardrey appeared to accept violence as the source of progress, arguing that man's best cultural efforts were spent, not on the tool or artefact, but in the perfecting of weapons. For Ardrey, the most significant of our inherited traits – territoriality, hierarchy, dominance – came from the killer apes, our forebears. He noted the popularity of Westerns and of television violence as evidence of our primitive instincts, and acclaimed *West Side Story* as a vivid portrait of the natural man. For Ardrey, juvenile delinquency was not the result of social deprivation, but was entirely normal. Untouched by cramping civilisation, the citizen of the streets found his rank and security in the gang, defending his territory and enjoying the blood and loot of the predator.

When Ardrey expanded his views in *The Territorial Imperative*, he argued that each animal society has a system of dominance and an instinct for territory which he related to the animosities of tribes and nations. Thus, if we defend our title to land, he argued, we do so for reasons no different, no less innate than those of the lower animals. For Ardrey territory was a force older and stronger than sex in evolutionary terms. Studying the behaviour of the Ugandan kob on its stamping grounds, he concluded that males competed for 'real estate' rather than females. Ardrey saw the strenuous competition of the 'arena' (the place where male animals compete for territory and females come to mate with them) as speeding up the evolutionary process. Was man also an 'arena' species, with prizes of property and status in the marketplace of male competition? In his view, the territory held by the pair was the prime reinforcement of the pair bond. In other words, it is territory not sex which holds a pair together.

Ardrey also argued that the human territorial instinct could be exploited by governments. Threats of invasion, alarms of war, the creation of 'incidents' were all a means of welding a disparate society together, by appealing to territorial urges. South Africa was a classic example. Ardrey attributed the success of white South Africa to its departure from the Commonwealth, which set in motion all the paranoid paraphernalia of the territorial imperative, as the population reacted to external boycotts, embargoes, threats of war and terrorist attacks. He concluded that 'Had the world conspired to make apartheid a permanent South African institution, it could have done no better job.'[12] The point has special relevance to Gordimer's novella which considers the possibility that terrorist penetration merely adds fuel to government propaganda based on an external threat – a 'something' out there – and in which the 'lovely home' of Mrs Naas Klopper, wife of a real-estate dealer, features prominently. Ardrey also cautioned that however superior the intruder's motives might be, morally, politically or ideologically, and however contemptible the defender, the intruder would have to be capable of enormous sacrifices in order to overcome the proprietor's inherent advantage – the territorial principle. Otherwise intrusion would not only fail, but would probably accomplish only the reverse of its objectives, by reinforcing resistance. Rejecting any romantic or liberal thesis of human behaviour, Ardrey found hope for the future, not in the soul or innate goodness, but in the image of man as a bad-weather animal, designed for storm and change. In support of his ideas, he pointed out that, after man, the greatest evolutionary success among primates was the baboon:

> The student of man . . . may find the baboon the most instructive of species. Among primates his aggressiveness is second only to man's. He is a born bully, a born criminal, a born candidate for the hangman's noose. As compared with the gorilla – that gentle, inoffensive, submissive creature for whom a minimum of tyranny yields a maximum of results – the baboon represents nature's most lasting challenge to the police state.[13]

Ardrey's thesis has, of course, been attacked on good scientific and moral grounds. If his 'territorial imperative' merely revives the old 'instinct of property' in modern dress, his emphases on competition, biological nationhood and violence as the source of progress are all deeply objectionable.[14] Ralph Holloway has described *The Territorial Imperative* as 'an apology and rationalization for Imperialism, Pax Americana, Laissez Faire, Social Darwinism and that greatest of evolutionary developments, Capitalism'.[15] As a result it makes a particularly apt metaphor for Gordimer to employ in the context of South Africa, a place where definitions of territory and of biological nationhood have pullulated to the point of absurdity. South Africa has been 'fractured, Balkanised, scrambled into an omelette of tribal states, casinostans, white cities, black townships, grey areas, Indian reserves and Coloured suburbs'.[16] The difficulties which Gordimer's whites face in classifying the escaped monkey – as ape, man, chimp, baboon, even wildcat – mirror the bizarre racial classifications of South Africans into white, black, coloured, Malay, Indian, Asian, and so on.

In the world at large 'naked apery' remains popular, despite its flaws, perhaps because it offers absolution to its readers, a means of shifting our guilt on to 'natural inheritance' or 'innate aggression'. Naked apery has an exculpatory function; it provides us with 'attractive excuses for our unpleasant behaviour toward each other'.[17] In 'Something Out There' Gordimer proposes a mock ethological study of contemporary South Africa, precisely in order to strip away all such exculpatory fantasies. The novella proceeds, in ethological fashion, by a structural comparison between man and animal, alternating its plots which provide links and parallels between human and simian behaviour. The dominant imagery is territorial[18] and plot events are carefully designed to set up a series of debating points with Ardrey. The central tenets of 'naked apery' are thus parodically enacted, the fantasy mirrored, in order to display its total absurdity.

For Gordimer, 'Books make South Africans, black and white, see themselves as they cannot from inside themselves. They get a kind of mirror image with which to compare their own feelings and motives. I think fiction raises their consciousness in this way.'[19] In 'Something Out There' the language of 'naked apery' is exploited for just such subversive purposes. In this connection, mirrors, reflections, mimicry, and imitation become key processes. 'Apeing' is central to theme, structure and language. Gordimer's white South Africans are types, satirically rendered in precise mimicry of accent, behaviour and mannerism. They themselves are members of an ersatz culture, 'Europe in Africa', copying the lifestyle of the West. Thus when the Kloppers speak English they feel as if they are imitating television dialogue; Mrs Scholtz names her cat 'Dallas'. These copycat lifestyles are contrasted with the purposeful imitation, the disguises and cover stories, of the terrorists. As a result Gordimer may be said to ape and out-ape Ardrey, masking her own subversive purposes by playful imitation – just as the four terrorists imitate the norms and behaviour of white South Africa, in order to attack it from within.

First and foremost Gordimer encourages the analogy between the mysterious marauder and the 'naked ape'. The baboon's progress through the story recapitulates the popular account of human evolution[20] which may be sketched as follows. The early primates live in trees, eating fruit, nuts and berries. Climatic change, and hence a reduction in forests, leads to the descent from the trees to the ground where a carnivorous diet is adopted. On the ground apes become more erect, better runners; their hands are free to grasp weapons. As the hunt increases in complexity, with longer forays abroad, so a home base, a territory, becomes necessary for the dependent young and females. This development from forest ape to ground ape to carnivorous ape to killer ape to territorial ape is teasingly reproduced in 'Something Out There'. The first sighting of the ape is merely as 'reflected between trees' (p. 119)[21] on the surface of a swimming pool. A photograph captures only 'the thrashing together of two tree tops' (p. 118). The apparently arboreal ape is also associated with a throwback to the past. A vet recalls how elephants in the grip of their genetic homing instinct made for their former mating grounds, now flooded beneath 5,000 miles of Lake Kariba. Though their attachment to territory proved fatal, it is not always so: 'nature sometimes came back, forgot time and survived eight-lane freeways, returning to ancestral haunts' (p. 119). This sense of the creature as an ape-man or missing link is expanded in the second sighting. As two golfers search the ground for a missing ball, 'Exactly where the two men were gazing, someone – something that must have been crouching – rose' (p. 126). The arboreal ape has clearly reached the ground. The ensuing argument – was it a man, a monkey, a baboon? – sparks an interest in a journalist, who digs out from the department of anthropology a popular account of the anatomical differences between man, ape and baboon, together with a chart showing 'the evolutionary phases of anthropoid to hominid, with man an identikit compilation of his past and present' (p. 131). Ironically the main anatomical difference in the illustration is that the newspaper blocks out the human genitalia but leaves the anthropoid's exposed. South African evolution moves towards censorship. Later, Dr Fraser-Smith recalls that the animal's posture appeared to mimic his own, that it bent down just as he was doing, and that he recognised 'someone people had been telling one another about for generations' (p. 176). To himself he adds the secret fantasy that he had 'looked back into a consciousness from which part of his own came' (p. 176), 'into the eyes of hominid evolution' (p. 203).

The ape's next appearance reveals details of its diet. Contemplating the remains of a granadilla vine, an unnamed male comments that 'Only a hungry fruit-eating animal would plunder so indiscriminately' (p. 143). As the narrator informs us, however, 'Like the human animal, it is able to adapt its eating habits to changes of environment' (p. 188). The baboon turns carnivorous, raiding man to snatch a haunch of venison. Pet dogs and cats are hunted down, until finally it attacks its near relation, man (in the shape of Mrs Lily Scholtz) and falls to the superior weaponry of the naked ape. Despite adopting all the evolutionary strategies which have in theory favoured man, the baboon fails to survive. 'Something Out There' therefore poses the question: Will the terrorists succeed (at a price) because of a willingness to make sacrifices, to subdue animal instincts in favour of a conscious choice of goals, or will their adoption of the way of aggression as challenge to the police state end in failure, like the baboon?

It is significant that, throughout its brief career, the ape has consistently maintained a territory, in the affluent suburbs: 'the creature never went beyond the bounds of white Johannesburg . . . it was canny about where it was possible somehow to exist off the pickings of plenty' (p. 181). If its precarious survival on the fringes of white South Africa mirrors the marginal existence of many black South Africans, identifying ape and black, it also holds up an ironic mirror to the affluent themselves. One such is Mrs Naas Klopper, who follows the story of the ape with interest in her 'lovely home' (p. 120 and *passim*) as a pleasant relief from news of boundary disputes, boycotts and censures from abroad. As naked apes go, Mrs Klopper represents the territorial imperative gone berserk. Her home pullulates with territorial markers – plants, ornaments, side-tables, pictures and plaques – and is massively over-enclosed. The eye moves to the boxed-in 'en suite' bathrooms, the glassed-in sun porch, the television set hidden behind carved console doors. The entire place is financed by Mr Klopper's real-estate business and it includes a stylised memorial to his hunting skills; the stools around the mini-bar are covered with the skins of impala which Naas himself has shot. Within this arena, Mrs Klopper is able to sense the presence of outsiders instinctively; she 'could always feel at once, even if no sound were made, when the pine aerosol-fresh space of her lovely home was displaced by any body other than her own' (pp. 121–2). The similarity of the house to a defensive laager is suggested however in the design, in which a dark passage recreates 'the enclosing gloom' (p. 121) of Naas's childhood farmhouse. Despite the move from farmer to estate agent, the passage of time seems to have led Naas less far than he thinks from his past. His defences have in fact already been penetrated by the saboteurs, whom Mrs Klopper's instincts signally fail to detect.

The delusionary quality of the Kloppers' security is underlined in relation to the transitory affair of an adulterous couple. Unlike the terrorists (who have rented a safe house from Naas) the lovers have exhausted the possibilities of the local motels for their rendezvous. The man owns a huge house, set 'in a lair of trees' (p. 140) but because (even in the absence of his wife) 'they are always there' (p. 140) – his black servants – he cannot take the woman he loves on to home territory. For him, 'even his room, his own bed, in a house where he paid for everything – nothing is your own, once you are married' (p. 140). Displaced by blacks, their sex subordinate to the territorial pair bond which imposes these restrictions, the couple are condemned to make love in the emblematic locale of the minedumps, the refuse of the prosperity on which their wealth is founded. When a friend lends them an untenanted property they rejoice: 'They were secure in that cottage – for as long as they would need security' (p. 141). This security is manifestly an illusion, however. It is appropriate that the ape at their window registers his presence only with a laugh. Although the lover denies 'that someone had been laughing at them, that they could ever be something to laugh at' (p. 142), the reader registers the sardonic comment on white pretensions to permanent tenure in South Africa. For all their real estate, their riches, their elaborate precautions, whites in South Africa have ultimately no safety and nowhere to go. In the homeless lovers Gordimer offers an ironic notation of the futility of territory, just as in the useless security devices which fail to exclude the ape from suburban gardens.

If the representation of the white South African as territorial ape serves satiric purposes, its extension into the public sphere strikes a darker note. The corollary to Mrs Klopper's 'lovely home' is the police HQ at John Vorster Square. It, too, has been beautified: 'The blue spandrel panels and glimpses of potted plants in the facade it presented to the passing city freeway, could have been those of an apartment block' (p. 154). The cells in which detainees are interrogated are located within the core of the building, out of sight like Naas's dark passage. Here, in a break from 'interrogation' duties, Sergeant Chapman reminisces fondly about his weekend hunting blesbok and shooting jackals on the land which he loves. Chapman's prisoner, a wealthy doctor, also has access to the plenty of South Africa (specifically a cottage at one of the best places for fishing on the coast) but has chosen to express his identity as a South African in community (trade union activities) rather than territory. In interview Gordimer argued that for blacks identity is with the people, as opposed to land:

> Blacks take the land for granted, it's simply there. It's theirs, although they've been conquered; they were always there. They don't have the necessity to say, 'Well I love this land **because** it's beautiful.'[22]

The sinister side to Chapman's lyrical nostalgia is indicated when he takes a break from work, in a Chinese restaurant. The restaurant is nameless, and has few 'ethnic pretensions' (p. 157). Ethically it has even fewer. The studied image of neutrality is belied by the off-duty policemen, seen enjoying a swordfight in a televised historical romance. This atavistic display of outdated weaponry and theatrical violence is an appropriate prelude to a broadcast from the Prime Minister, speaking from behind a prop desk, and with a ceremonial curtain as territorial marker. In South Africa there is no neutral ground. The narrator remarks that 'Convenient to concentration camps there were such quiet couples, minding their own business, selling coffee and schnapps to refresh jackbooted men off duty' (p. 157).

When Sergeant Chapman's territory is invaded and his prey – the venison haunch – is stolen by the baboon the reaction is telling. Far from recognising that not even the security forces enjoy security, his boss suggests that Chapman arm his wife: 'Next time it might be more than a monkey out there in the yard' (p. 160). The recurrence of the title phrase recalls the public exploitation by the South African security forces of the idea of 'prowling subhuman invaders'.[23] The Prime Minister also exploits the rhetoric of territoriality, inveighing against those who threaten 'the security of your homes', those who 'lurk, outside law and order, ready to strike in the dark' (p. 149). In response, the four saboteurs smile, realising that 'those being referred to as monsters are the human beings drinking a glass of water, cutting a hang nail, writing a letter, in the same room; are themselves' (p. 150). Vusi comments that the government, unable to justify its policies, is reduced to scaring its audience with 'spook people' (p. 150) – the well-known South African tactic of 'swartgevaar', black danger, of the barbarian at the gate.[24]

For black South Africans, however, the term 'spook people' takes on a different application. Where Gordimer draws a parallel between ape and black, it is to mirror the exploited condition of the latter. When the baboon is seen leaving a maid's room, in a suburban backyard, the maid blazes out to the other black servants that they are unprotected, exposed: 'Couldn't they see the whites always ran away and hid and left us to be hurt?' (p. 147). She recalls the fate of the cook's brother, a watchman at a block of flats, employed to guard tenants' cars. Attacked and outgunned, he dies 'while the owners of the cars went on sleeping, stacked twelve storeys high over his dead body' (p. 148). For the blacks, the barbarian is already within the gate. They have no need of mythical bogeymen; danger and death are all around them. For them the 'something out there' is also a spook, 'an urban haunter, a factory or kitchen ghost. Powerless like themselves' (p. 148). Industrialisation and urbanisation have shattered any easy continuity with the past. The apparition has 'long migrated from the remotest possibility of being a spirit of the ancestors' (p. 148). Instead of looking back to mystificatory past fantasies they identify the spook with a specific migrant worker, found dead in the area: 'Someone like that had woken up now, without his body, and was trying to find his way back to the hostel where his worker's contract, thumb-print affixed, had long ago run out' (p. 148). The sense of the black, wandering without title to a home, an unrecognised presence in his own country, is reinforced in the white reaction to the ape's perambulations. When a representative of a suburban residents' association demands a sweep of the area in search of the ape, the victims are all black – several illicit liquor sellers and fifteen men in breach of the Pass Laws. The animal itself evades capture: 'Like the contract labourers who had to leave their families to find work where work was, like the unemployed who were endorsed out to where there was no work and somehow kept getting back in through the barbed strands of Influx Control' (p. 181). What the suburban residents want is 'for the animal to be confined in its appropriate place, that's all, zoo or even circus' (p. 181). The reader might substitute the words 'location' or 'township' for 'circus' and 'zoo'. Although a left-wing writer condemns the interest in one homeless animal, when thousands of blacks are being bulldozed out of their homemade shelters, the conservatives argue that the monkey is 'in self-imposed exile. If it had been content to stay chained in a yard or caged in a zoo, its proper station in life, it wouldn't have had to live the life of an outlaw' (p. 189). The argument suggests the appeal to conservatives of the fiction of the 'homeland', by which people born and bred in Johannesburg suddenly found themselves reclassified as citizens of a place which they had never seen before – Bophuthatswana, Transkei or Venda, for example.[25] A circus proprietor warns that it is unlikely that an ape which has learned to fend for itself in a hostile environment will ever again be psychologically amenable to training. Freedom, once gained, is not lightly abandoned. But a zoologist offers a less comforting scenario for the future. In his opinion, apes, baboons and monkeys may survive around Johannesburg in the summer but 'when the Highveld winter comes . . . *Simiadae* suffer from the common cold, die of pneumonia, like people – just like people' (p. 182). Which people?, the reader asks. Which people die of pneumonia in South Africa in winter? Only blacks. Sure enough, when the baboon is found dead it proves to be 'just a native species' (p. 200), its commonplace death eclipsed by the more newsworthy 'spook people', the white saboteurs.

Although the baboon's fate appears to suggest the inevitability of white territorialists maintaining domination, the terrorists offer a fragile image of a better future, in strong contrast to the brutalist image of man. Importantly, the foursome assume the traits of naked apery only in order to overcome the real monstrosity of South Africa. To survive under cover, they are forced to mimic the behaviour of oppressor and oppressed, the whites performing a charade of 'madam' and 'baas', the blacks impersonating construction workers, ostensibly building and gardening, when their real function is to dismantle the power structures of the apartheid state. Ironically, as would-be liberators, their first action has to be the sacking of Kleynhans' old 'boy', who accepts this as no more than the usual fate of black servants at white hands. Beneath the ox-wagon wheel chandelier, they set up a simulacrum of home: 'a containing: a shell, a habitation' (p. 169), in which, however, they plot an end to the Afrikaner territorial domination which the ox-wagon symbolises. Like the farming families around them, Joy and Charles have a 'combi' van, with 'housewifely curtains' (p. 139) at its windows, but in their case the curtains serve to hide the explosives which are being transported. One scene indicates imagistically the revisionary intent of their imitation of the southern naked ape. As Charles draws up beside the Kloppers at a level crossing,

> A train shuttered past like a camera gone berserk, lens opening and closing, with each flying segment of rolling stock, on flashes of the veld behind it. The optical explosion invigorated Charles (p. 139).

The juxtaposition of the real-estate dealer and the mobile home, against a background of a land exploding in flashes and (camera) shots, projects the very different future envisaged beneath the apparently photographic reproduction of white norms.

In similar fashion the apparent identification of the black saboteurs, Eddie and Vusi, with the ape serves subversive purposes. Like the ape they are not long content with the diet of fruit, nuts and grains which vegetarian Joy provides – though Vusi devours a bag of apricots with as much gusto as any fruit-eating animal. Like the ape they too demand fresh meat. Daringly, Gordimer turns the language of racism back upon itself. Eddie and Vusi are associated with the baboon as an endangered species. Eddie jokes that despite his fringed, Red Indian style jacket 'I'm not going to be extinct' (p. 138). When Charles (featuring as man-the-hunter) draws on his experience as a game ranger in Kruger Park to identify jackal excreta, Vusi remembers that he had once infiltrated South Africa by that route, through 'that vast wilderness of protected species; an endangered one on his way to become operational' (p. 167). Less protected than the wild animals, Eddie spent his childhood 'in street-gang rivalries that unknowingly rehearsed, for his generation of blacks, the awful adventure that was coming to them' (p. 151). Paradoxically Eddie's delinquent youth prepares him for a struggle against a brutal system. Vusi's facial expression is described as buried 'deep in the past of himself . . . in the watergleam of his black eyes hidden in the ancient cave of skull . . . in the fine gills of the nostrils' (p. 161). The emphases – on a deep past, an ancient cave, evolutionary gills – suggest an image of Vusi as a primitive specimen – yet it is he who masterminds the entire mission. Eddie and Vusi hold up an ironic mirror to naked apery and concepts of territoriality. Both have been forced off their territory, Eddie fleeing after the Soweto rising, Vusi forcibly relocated. Joy realises that Vusi 'hadn't lived anywhere that could be called "at home" for years, and his "neighbours" had been fellow refugees in camps and military training centres' (p. 135). The terrorists occupy **not** a physical territory, but 'a habitation of resolve' (p. 170). At the end, sheltering in a crude dugout while waiting for their chance to attack the power station, they are quite prepared to decline to a hole in the ground in order to fulfil their purposes. They too can alter their diet – toward abstinence if the situation requires it. (In the dugout they cannot smoke or cook for fear of detection, and exist on fastfood snacks.) In the torpor of a Sunday afternoon, Eddie listens to reggae just like any other labourer, Charles dozes just like Naas Klopper does, ten kilometres away in his split-level lounge. But the resemblances are misleading. Theirs is a conscious mimicry. For a joke, Eddie deliberately imitates a white prosecutor mistranslating a black witness, and the group laugh in the knowledge of 'the events of their world, which moved beneath the events of the world the newspapers reflected' (p. 153).

The objection remains, none the less, that within their parallel world the saboteurs are potential killers, their mission dependent upon sophisticated weaponry. Gordimer, however, goes to some lengths to emphasise that this is essentially a distortion of their humanity. The terrorists are aiming for a 'classic' mission, involving only economic damage, not loss of life. (The example of Koeberg is cited.)[26] The blacks' situation, sharing their bedroom with boxes of ammunition, is presented as entirely abnormal, not the reflection of 'man the killer'. The weapons are described as forming a horizon in which 'the old real, terrible needs of [Vusi's] life . . . were now so strangely realised' (p. 145). 'All these hungers found their shape, distorted, forged as no one could conceive they ever should have to be, in the objects packed around him' (p. 146). Throughout the story Joy has been aware of Vusi tinkering in the back room. Hearing the clink of small tools she assumes that he is working on the weapons. In fact Vusi has been hammering beer can tabs and cartridge cases into a saxophone. **Some** of the weaponry has already been transformed into an artefact. For Charles the saxophone is depressingly reminiscent of the objects made in concentration camps, 'effigies of the beautiful possibilities of a life to be lived' (p. 163). The noise which comes from it is certainly thin and weak, 'the feeble cry of something new-born' (p. 162). Yet although Gordimer does not underestimate the vulnerability of an emergent, indigenous black culture, she does indicate that future possibilities exist, if only embryonically.

The point is made in symbolic terms in the following sequence, in which the baboon appears to a woman who is taking a bath. A reference to 'pan pipes' (p. 164) (actually the woman's toes) links back to the preceding music of the saxophone. An artefact is also introduced, a green ceramic statuette of a sacred monkey, in a local art gallery. It is described as 'carved out of deep water. It lives in a cupboard behind glass' (p. 163). In place of a mirror, the woman's bath has a glass wall, overlooking a courtyard full of greenery, where the baboon appears. The positioning of the glass sets up a parallel between the two figures. Who is on display in a glass-fronted space, ape or woman? Which is the animal, which the embodiment of culture? The imagery suggests that the woman is animalistic. In the distorted mirror of the faucet her face becomes a bulging gourd, her lower torso is foreshortened, so that 'Her legs become gangling and bowed, joined by huge feet at one end and a curved perspective that leads back to a hairy creature, crouched. There is nothing behind this voracious pudenda; it has swallowed the body and head behind it' (p. 164). From this image of the body as mere flesh, dominated by 'animal' drives, the woman's mind moves to sex, to her monstrous stomach rising 'like the Leviathan' (p. 164), and to the fate of her ageing friends, 'being brought down all around her, as a lion moves into a herd, tearing into the flesh of his victims' (p. 164). The image of humanity as a herd of beasts at first appears to be confirmed by the statuette, a Viennese copy of an Indian piece. In India the hanuman monkey is worshipped as the guardian god of settlement.[27] The first duty of the founder of a village is to erect a statue of the monkey god. Significantly the museum, with its monkey culture, apeing Europe, has no example of the African sacred ape, 'of the dog-faced ape of ancient Egyptian mythology, Cynocephalus, often depicted attendant upon the god Thoth' (p. 164). Thoth is, of course, the god of writing, and in ancient Egypt the sacred baboon was considered as the scribe to the gods. When the real baboon appears, it crosses the woman's mind that he is an erotic hallucination – a man – but he is also associated with 'the head of antiquity, the Egyptian basalt rigidity, twice removed – as animal and attribute of a god – from man' (p. 165). The foreign settler ape yields therefore to an African sacred ape, indicating that the comparison of man to ape is suspect, and that man can be a creature of ideals and of culture, rather than a territorial ape. The imagery also reminds the reader that nature always wears a mask of theory – that the naked ape is only one in a succession of fantasy masks placed over the animal world.

Where this scene challenges the Ardrey thesis in symbolic terms, and in principle, emphasising transformative future possibilities, rather than an unchangeable animal nature, there remains the question of the kind of future to be realised in South Africa. When Eddie absconds from the group for a day in Johannesburg, his disappearance coincides with that of the ape. Eddie finds the city 'blacker than he remembered it' with 'no white centre' (p. 174) any more, its streets full of prosperous-looking blacks. The suggestion hovers of an eventual victory for blacks in demographic terms.[28] People will eventually prove a greater force than territory. But it also raises the possibility that, as a Communist-trained revolutionary, Eddie may yet become extinct, as the creation of a black middle class offers liberation by embourgeoisement. Eddie tours a supermarket, with 'arsenals' (p. 172) of tinned fruit on display. He learns that new clothes are coming in all the time, and admires the latest in electronic technology. There can, of course, be no guarantee that free South Africa will not be merely an ape-ing of Western bourgeois forms. Joy points out, however, that the apparent possibilities for blacks are in fact very firmly circumscribed. Black doctors are allowed to practise only in black areas, black lawyers are barred from taking chambers in white areas 'where the courts are'

(p. 179). Territory is still demarcated. When their spending is over, the crowds in the streets 'would have to go back to the places for blacks' (p. 174). In contrast Eddie returns to his 'place' in a group held together by cooperative bonds and a common purpose: 'Vusi could not function without Eddie, Eddie and Vusi without Charles and Joy, Charles and Joy without Eddie and Vusi. The entity reconstituted itself irresistibly' (p. 178). As the foursome celebrate Eddie's return, Vusi appears with the saxophone, his face emerging from the darkness like 'a head from a submerged statue' (p. 180).

As the image implies, recalling the sacred ape, Gordimer cannot go further than indicating possibilities which must, for the moment, remain concealed beneath the surface. Indeed, when Eddie and Vusi move to the temporary shelter of the 'cave' (actually an old mine-working) the suggestion lingers that nothing much has changed. They carry loads of ammunition, just as 'their brothers had for generations carried coal and sacks of potatoes' (p. 191). With his unwashed clothes and earthy smell, Eddie blends in with the rural blacks, only one of the many farm labourers crowding the nearby Indian store. Digging out a pit for weapons, he jokes that he had not expected to end up 'working in the mines' (p. 191). Similarly Joy falls back into the charade of the white 'madam' to see off Kleynhans' 'boy'; Charles finds himself burning books. Yet despite the implications of a reassertion of past patterns, a return to the cave, a reenactment of past evils, the reader is well aware of the story which moves below the events of the surface, beyond the superficial behaviour which an ethologist might observe. Theirs is a conscious choice of strategy, not to repeat the past, but to bring to birth a different future. The point is illustrated in the final image of diminished territoriality. In his own cramped shelter, Eddie finds some lizard eggs 'in a crevice of warm rock' (p. 193). Tiny, but perfect, so small as to 'scarcely contain the pulse of life' (p. 193), the baby lizards none the less slide away 'to begin to live' (p. 193).

At the end of the novella the reader is left with a similarly tenuous and vestigial sense of the terrorists' achievement. Was the effort worthwhile merely to ensure a power cut, even if its symbolic meaning is appreciated? Was the price (Eddie's life) too high? Did the intrusion merely play into the hands of a government which is keen to use 'bogeyman' scare tactics? It certainly works to the advantage of the prime minister. Instead of having to justify his farming policy, he is able to issue a rousing call for support 'to meet the threat from beyond our borders which was always ready to strike at our country' (p. 196). The arms cache makes good photographic propaganda; the attack provides an excuse to round up and interrogate numbers of blacks. Just as nobody ever discovered the origin of the baboon, so at the end the terrorists fade back into anonymity. Names and sketchy descriptions are provided, but 'Nobody really knew what names mark the identity each has accepted within himself' (p. 202).

At the close, however, Gordimer intervenes, to reinsert her characters into history. Dr Fraser-Smith's fantasy of having looked into the eyes of hominid evolution is revealed as just that – a fantasy – more attractive perhaps than the reality, his descent from Maisie McCulloch, the keeper of a Victorian brothel. A rotgut liquor bottle is discovered, from the first distillery in the area, Die Eerste Fabriek, founded to encourage black workers to drink, just as whites were encouraged to take prostitutes, in order to maintain them in the position of wage slaves.[29] The alternatives of real history, in all its complexity, replace the timeless myths of 'naked apery'. Charles may be named, patriotically, after Winston Churchill; he may also resemble a distant ancestor, a missionary, who believed in brotherhood outside the narrow biological nation of colour. Even the statue of the Indian monkey has a history. Ironically it was a gift to South Africa from a European refugee (presumably Jewish) fleeing from racial persecution at home. Gordimer makes the point here that individuals cannot know all the forces of environment, genetic endowment and cultural conditioning which make them what they are, but that they can make conscious choices, not to repeat the evils of the past but to contribute to a different future. The most significant detail is saved until last. The mine-working where Eddie and Vusi hid, assumed to be only a nineteenth-century excavation, is actually much older: 'It goes back further than anything in conventional or alternative history, or even oral tradition, back to the human presences who people anthropology and archaeology' (p. 203). With Eddie and Vusi's reoccupation, history reaffirms itself over myth, for this was 'an ancient mine-working **out there**, and metals precious to men were discovered, dug and smelted, for themselves, by black men' (p. 203, my emphasis).[30] The novella therefore ends with something 'out there' which is no longer a myth, a bogeyman, a monster, but an image of a past black culture, independent, in a territory all its own, which is now being reclaimed.

# Notes

1  Linda Hutcheon, *A Poetics of Postmodernism* (London, Routledge, 1988), Chapter 8.
2  Homi Bhabha, 'Of Mimicry and Man: The Ambivalence of Colonial Discourse', in Philip Rice and Patricia Waugh, *Modern Literary Theory* (London, Edward Arnold, 1989), p. 235. Originally published in *October*, no. 28, Spring 1984.
3  For a succinct account of Bhabha's ideas (paraphrased here) see Graham Huggan, 'Decolonizing the Map: Post-Colonialism, Post-Structuralism and the

Cartographic Connection', *Ariel*, 20, 4 (October 1989), pp. 115–31.

4  Wendy Smith notes the 'risky, potentially condescending parallel between the baboon and black South Africans' in 'A Voice from South Africa', *Wall Street Journal*, 204 (9 July 1984), p. 221.

5  *The Guardian*, 4 August 1989, p. 10.

6  Salman Rushdie, 'No One is Ever Safe', *New York Times Book Review*, 29 July 1984, p. 7.

7  Quoted in the *New York Times Book Review*, 29 July 1984, p. 7.

8  I am using the term 'man' advisedly, rather than more inclusive language, to reflect the view expressed by ethologists of the male as the norm. On baboons see Irven Devore, ed., *Primate Behavior* (New York, Holt, Rinehart and Winston, 1965). On ethology see Robert Ardrey, *African Genesis* (London, Collins, 1961) and *The Territorial Imperative* (New York, Dell, 1966); Desmond Morris, *The Naked Ape* (London, Cape, 1967) and *The Human Zoo* (London: Cape, 1969); Konrad Lorenz, *On Aggression* (London, Methuen, 1966).

9  Ardrey, *African Genesis*, p. 29.

10  See Michael H. Day, 'Dart's Baby', *Guardian*, 25 November, 1988 (obituary of Raymond Dart).

11  Ardrey, *African Genesis*, p. 9.

12  Ardrey, *The Territorial Imperative*, p. 292.

13  Ardrey, *The Territorial Imperative*, p. 227.

14  For a collection of critical views see Ashley Montagu, ed., *Man and Aggression* (Oxford, Oxford University Press, 1972).

15  Montagu, *Man and Aggression*, p. 181.

16  Christopher Hope, *White Boy Running* (London, Abacus, 1988), p. 198.

17  David Pilbeam, in Montagu, *Man and Aggression*, p. 113.

18  J. U. Jacobs notes that all the stories in *Something Out There* concern the idea of living space as a construct, but does not make connections to Ardrey, Morris or ethology. See J. U. Jacobs, 'Living Space and Narrative Space in Nadine Gordimer's *Something Out There*', *English in Africa*, 14, 2 (October 1987), pp. 31–43.

19  'A Voice from a Troubled Land', *Ontario Review*, 26 (Spring–Summer, 1987), p. 14.

20  Morris, *The Naked Ape*.

21  Page references which follow quotations in parentheses refer to Nadine Gordimer, *Something Out There* (London, Cape, 1984).

22  Robert Boyers *et al.*, 'A Conversation with Nadine Gordimer', *Salmagundi*, 62 (Winter 1984), p. 6.

23  John Cooke, *The Novels of Nadine Gordimer: Private Lives/Public Landscapes* (Baton Rouge, Louisiana State University Press, 1985), pp. 123–4.

24  Christopher Hope notes in *White Boy Running* (pp. 62–3) that 'black danger' was a tactic in every election fought by the Nationalists.

25  Gordimer condemns the practice in interview with Robert Boyers *et al.*, 'A Conversation with Nadine Gordimer', p. 26.

26  Koeberg, a nuclear power station twenty miles from Cape Town, became operational in March 1984, though sabotage on 19 December 1982 delayed its completion. Nobody was injured. The ANC claimed responsibility. Gordimer has noted that in a five-year period, bombings by underground movements within South Africa have caused $432 million of damage. See Nadine Gordimer, 'The Idea of Gardening', *New York Review of Books*, 2 February 1984, p. 3.

27  Ramona and Desmond Morris, *Men and Apes* (London, Hutchinson, 1966),

Chapter One.

28  In *White Boy Running* (p. 247) Christopher Hope implicitly supports this view, noting that in 1987 half the black population of South Africa were under fifteen.

29  See Charles van Onselen, *Studies in the Social and Economic History of the Witwatersrand 1886–1914*. Volume I. *New Babylon* (London, Longman, 1982).

30  The earliest mine-workings, discovered in Swaziland, date from *c.* 43,000 years BC, as reported by Greg Lanning with Marti Mueller, *Africa Undermined: Mining Companies and the Underdevelopment of Africa* (London, Penguin, 1979). Vusi is seen reading this book in *Something Out There*, p. 160.

# |11|
# *Conclusion*

Intertextuality is always something of a paper chase – and in this case the loneliness of the long-distance runner is exacerbated by the absence of a clear finishing line. In India Desai historicises Forster's cave, Jhabvala politicises his liberal humanist beliefs, and Upamanyu Chatterjee promptly satirises Jhabvala. In the Caribbean Rhys revises Brontë, Naipaul revises both, Mukherjee revises Naipaul – the chain of signifiers extends to the future rewriter of Mukherjee herself. To add to the complexity, the area covered by paper grows exponentially. Intertextuality expands from literary allusion (Brontë, Defoe, Shaw) to oral 'literature' (nursery rhymes), the literary genre (Gothic), nineteenth-century colonial discourse (sati), dramaturgical analysis, anthropology, ethology and chaos theory. Indeed the intertextual trajectory spirals outwards in a fashion distinctly reminiscent of the latter's fractal patternings, its wide Sargasso Sea no longer an area of paralysis and shipwreck but a fertile generative soup of signs.

Intertextuality, then, is not the province of arid formalism but rather constitutes a recognition of reader empowerment and author responsibility, even when (as in the case of Naipaul) the writer is rewriting himself. As Michel Butor explains it:

> We are part of a complex of evolving cultures within which all sorts of illusions and blunders are made. To rid ourselves of them we must bring references out into the open and put them to the test. To work on quotations is to give prominence to the fact that one is never sole author of a text, that culture is a tissue; self-quotation is one way of considering oneself as another. All this undermines the walls set up by our society between author and reader, singular and plural; it is an awakening and a liberation.[1]

Reader involvement may nevertheless be a project fraught with perils. Intertextuality demands a degree of knowledge on the reader's part – or it is simply non-existent. When George MacDonald Fraser launched his *Flashman* series (the fictional 'memoirs' of the legendary cad and bully from *Tom Brown's Schooldays* and as thoroughgoing a debunking of Victorian ideals as J. G. Farrell's), ten reviewers accepted the first volume as genuine. The American publisher had to issue a statement assuring readers of its fictionality.[2] In the works selected here for discussion the problem has been tackled by the emphasis on well-known texts (*Jane Eyre* and *Robinson Crusoe* are only a step away from mythical status), on popular cultural materials, and upon novels which to some extent at least supply their own intertexts: Jimmy's letters, the intercalated stories of *Heat and Dust*, Desai's nursery rhymes, the magistrate's dreams. No previous knowledge is presumed on the reader's part for such tales within tales. The workings of intertextuality are exposed, transparent, the innovative narrative strategy immediately accessible.

Postcolonial novelists write with the awareness that stories influence events, that 'texts' bring with them moral, social and political questions which must be faced. It will not have escaped the reader that, despite the challenge which postcolonial writing lays down to the temporal paradigm of 'Eng. Lit.', its deliberations keep turning into an argument with history, whether as pseudo-tradition, commodified past, or silenced trauma. Postcolonial writing descends from the ivory tower and refuses to be confined within purely 'literary' bounds – or even within the bounds of discourse itself. In the postcolonial arena Jane Eyre walks with the zombie of horror film, Shaw rubs shoulders with the heirs of Tarzan, killer apes roam the pages of Nadine Gordimer, and imperial Gothic confronts the popular fascination with the serial killer.

To respect the responsibility of the writer it is, of course, imperative to avoid selective quotation. By such means a writer as allusive as Coetzee, for example, may be turned into a Lawrence or a Kafka, a Beckett or a Defoe. To sidestep the problem, the present study employs what Gilbert Ryle called (in an ethnographical context) 'thick description', allowing a text (whether social or literary) to be considered with full respect for its specificity. The procedure also has a second purpose. 'Theory' has become something of a vexed issue for the postcolonial critic, its agenda often set by Euro-American culture, which turns others into 'Others' and assimilates them to a metropolitan problematic. In particular, 'Post-structural refutation of the referent can underscore a theoretical dismissal of some of the basic survival strategies of subordinated and colonised peoples.'[3] For some cultures categories such as truth, meaning and purpose are still empirically urgent.[3] Aijaz Ahmad has commented that poststructuralism has tended greatly to extend the centrality of reading as the appropriate form of politics, producing a proliferation of readings by intertextual, cross-referential procedures.[4] The danger here is that all forms of agency become merely 'readings' – Marxism as a method of reading, feminism as a method of reading – rather than connecting the cultural productions of a society with other kinds of production, other political processes. As Naipaul indicates in *Guerrillas*, the role of human agency may be circumscribed by the emphasis on language and style; real historical agency has to be distinguished from mere myths of origins. In its concern to decentre humanist notions of individuality and of universal and essential selves, postmodernism has also tended to fragment identity, to reveal it as a flux of differently contextualised selves or as the production of a system of differences. Postcolonial subjects, however, have been silenced too often to take lightly to dismantling. While the present study uses the insights of contemporary literary theory (and of anthropological, scientific and psychoanalytical theory) where useful, it proceeds upon the assumption that postcolonial fictions are themselves 'theoretical' in their counter-readings of master narratives, taking its cue from Stephen Slemon and Helen Tiffin's argument that postcolonial works have in themselves the interpretive power which dominant theoretical practice usually grants to the literary critic.[5] Postcolonial fictions are not merely performers in some Eurovision theory contest. Diana Brydon cautions that the discourse of marginality treads an uneasy path between appropriation and a new silencing. 'The new discourse has been so constituted as to continue to ignore the contributions of the colonised. The interest is in how some of us have been silenced (those of us seen as sufficiently exotic) and not in what we have to say.'[6] Because readers are rightly wary of over-tidy theoretical structures which 'explain' complex fictions out of existence, the full complexity of the fictional work needs to be respected. Otherwise the possibility looms of conforming to a theoretical orthodoxy which may be just as restrictive in privileging certain texts as the old canons of 'Eng. Lit.' To rephrase Magritte – this is not a canon.

Which brings us back to the ballistic Bard with which this study began, and one last text. Nadine Gordimer's novels have been characterised as 'cross-border texts' (Lewis Nkosi) constituted by readers who are both within and without, according to the alternation of the metropolitan or the South African frame. Individual novels continually pose the questions: Whose story is it? White or black? Male or female? European or African? by a variety of narrative strategies. Thus Gordimer undermines the notion of a master narrative by establishing a counterpoint between male and female protagonists, white and black interpreters; by employing double plots which readjust the relation between text, context and subtext; and by the reconstruction of the implied reader.[7] While subverting Eurocentric concepts of the novel, Gordimer is also aware of the potential redundancy of the language and conventions within which – and against which – her voice is raised.

Her 1990 novel, *My Son's Story*,[8] returns to the ballistic Bard with a different emphasis. In the novel Will catches his father Sonny, a political activist of mixed race, leaving a cinema with a white mistress. Ironically it is only because the cinema is desegregated that this event can occur, and only because of hard-won reforms that Sonny can pursue his adulterous affair without fear of prosecution. The story draws its ironies as much from the consequences of liberation as from the struggle against repression. In the end Sonny is sidelined and painfully marginalised by the very freedoms he helped to win. After a failed suicide attempt, his daughter, Baby, becomes a political exile, his mistress leaves, his apparently apolitical wife, Aila, is caught hiding terrorist arms. Unsentimentally Gordimer spells out the consequences of incipient national liberation. For the writer, coming out of battledress poses new problems of identity and purpose. Will, who is named after Shakespeare, narrates the novel in such a way as to pose this question of the relation of writing to political activity. Will is very much his father's son. Sonny (the father) was originally a schoolmaster, devoted to Shakespeare, who used literary phrases as passwords, and corrected the spelling of his students' posters during the Soweto rising. In addition the child is very much father to the man, as Will Shakespeare is to Sonny. As Gordimer's teasing reversal of father/son relations indicates, for both men words are power. Aila's habitual silence is seen as a sign of submissiveness, as absence of political intent, rather than being equated with the secrecy of her own purposes. The female silence, however, emerges as finally more powerful than the patriarchal word. Baby, Hannah and Aila all move on, the men remain becalmed. Where the women resist appropriation into patriarchal dialogues, the men remain caught in the habits of 'writing back'. Despite the epigraph 'You had a Father, let your son say so', this is a novel which gives back the story of Sonnet 13, to the Dark Lady. The Shakespearean echoes of the text (Will as Hamlet to Sonny's Claudius and Baby's Ophelia, Sonny as Lear, among others) reveal that words take their meanings only from action. As the title implies, the story may appear to be owned and appropriated by the father, and by literary forefathers, but Will is also the son of a mother who keeps her story to herself for excellent strategic reasons. In the denouement Aila jumps bail in order definitively to silence Will who had intended to testify on her behalf, to **speak for** her at her trial. The Shakespearian is now silenced in his turn. When Will, a would-be writer, ends the novel with the words 'This is my first book which I can never publish', he pays tribute to the strength of female silence.

As that conclusion indicates, Gordimer is clearsighted enough to recognise that the verdict upon the white South African writer may yet be a harsh one, and the fate of being eventually silenced in favour of a black story is that to which her activity must tend. The traffic between European and African culture is none the less two-way. Sonny had read and re-read Shakespeare in the past without ever understanding what his own adultery reveals to him – what it is to almost lose a daughter and to be 'vile esteemed'. It is only in action therefore that Sonny learns the full meaning of the Bard. It is worth recalling that Sonny has a distinguished African predecessor in Julius Nyerere, who followed up his translation of *Julius Caesar* with *Mabepari wa Venisi*, best translated as *The Capitalists of Venice*, a text which both informs – and is informed by – the Arusha Declaration of 1967 setting forth the aims of his own form of African socialism. Intertextuality can be revolutionary. When Gordimer incorporated a historical text into *Burger's Daughter* – a banned pamphlet issued by the Soweto Students Representative Council – her own novel was promptly banned. Gordimer sidesteps the dangers of replacing an activist with a textual culture by emphasising the dynamic connections between story and its effects. Shakespeare may yet enrich Sonny's understanding, as action restores his works to new and immediate significance. What, after all, was the origin of the Soweto rising but the demand for full education, and for English as its medium? It is perhaps a fitting paradigm of the ways in which postcolonial writing – a subject worthy of study in its own right – also has a crucial transformative function, both towards the works of the past and to their potential role in the shaping of the future.

# Notes

1  'Dialogue avec Michel Butor', in André Helbo, *Michel Butor: vers une littérature du signe* (Paris, 1975) p. 12, quoted in Michael Evans, *Claude Simon and the Transgressions of Modern Art* (London, Macmillan, 1988), p. 267.
2  David Leon Higdon, *Shadows of the Past in Contemporary British Fiction* (London, Macmillan, 1984), p. 86.
3  Stephen Slemon and Helen Tiffin, 'Introduction', *Kunapipi*, XI (1989), p. xi.
4  Aijaz Ahmad, *In Theory: Classes, Nations, Literatures* (London, Verso, 1992), pp. 3–6.
5  Slemon and Tiffin, 'Introduction', p. xvii.
6  Diana Brydon, ' Commonwealth or Common Poverty? The New Literatures in English and the New Discourse of Marginality', *Kunapipi*, XI (1989), p. 4.
7  See Judie Newman, *Nadine Gordimer* (New York and London, Routledge, 1988).
8  Nadine Gordimer, *My Son's Story* (London, Bloomsbury, 1990).

# Index